DAVID PEACE

Texts & Contexts

For Joy and Michael Shaw, for everything.

DAVID PEACE

Texts & Contexts

KATY SHAW

sussex
ACADEMIC
PRESS
Brighton • Portland • Toronto

2 4 6 8 10 9 7 5 3

First published in hardcover 2011, reprinted in paperback 2018, by
SUSSEX ACADEMIC PRESS
PO Box 139
Eastbourne BN24 9BP

Distributed in North America by
SUSSEX ACADEMIC PRESS
ISBS Publisher Services
920 NE 58th Ave #300, Portland, OR 97213, USA

British Library Cataloguing in Publication Data
A CIP catalogue record for this book is available from the British Library.

Library of Congress Cataloging-in-Publication Data
Shaw, Katy.
David Peace : texts and contexts / Katy Shaw.
p. cm.
Includes bibliographical references and index.
ISBN 978-1-84519-364-5 (hbk. alk. paper)
ISBN 978-1-84519-940-1 (pbk. alk. paper)
  1. Peace, David—Criticism and interpretation.
I. Title.
PR6066.E116Z87 2010
823'.914—dc22

                                            2010026332

Typeset and designed by Sussex Academic Press, Brighton & Eastbourne.
Printed by TJ International, Padstow, Cornwall.

Contents

Acknowledgements

This book would not have been possible without the support of my colleagues at the University of Brighton. Thanks to Anne Boddington, Jonathan Woodham, Richard Jacobs, Andrew Hammond, Kate Aughterson, Jessica Moriarty, John Wrighton, Gina Whisker, Raf Salkie, Jelena Timotijevic, James Ormrod, Rebecca Bramall, Stuart Laing and Margaret Wallis. I am equally indebted to the advice offered by friends at other universities, including Mike Sanders, Catherine Spooner, Andrew Tate and Lynne Crook. Special thanks to Deborah Philips for reading drafts.

Those who have lived through the writing process warrant special mention. Rachel Revell, Corry Shaw, Helen Runalls, Victoria Notman, Rachael Dobson, Paddy Kane and Alistair McNeal have proved great friends.

The author and publisher gratefully acknowledge the following for permission to reproduce copyrighted material:

From *Occupied City* by David Peace, copyright © 2009 by David Peace. Used by permission of Alfred A. Knopf, a division of Random House, Inc.

From *Tokyo Year Zero* by David Peace, copyright © 2007 by David Peace. Used by permission of Alfred A. Knopf, a division of Random House, Inc.

Serpent's Tail for excerpts from *The Red Riding Quartet: 1974, 1977, 1980* and *1983*.

Faber & Faber for excerpts from *GB84*, *The Damned United*, *Tokyo Year Zero* and *Occupied City*.

The English Agency (Japan) Ltd. for excerpts from *GB84*, *The Damned United*, *Tokyo Year Zero* and *Occupied City*.

The author would like to take this opportunity to thank Anna and Rukhsana at Serpent's Tail, Nicci at Faber & Faber, Hamish at EAJ, Jennifer at Random House and Mr Shunichiro Nagashima at Bungei Shunju for their assistance.

I am also grateful to my editor Tony Grahame at Sussex Academic for his patience and guidance.

Love and thanks to my parents, Joy and Mike, my brother Kristian, and my grandmother, without whom none of this, or indeed anything else, would have been possible.

And last, but by no means least, I am eternally grateful to David Peace, who has supported this project from the beginning and remains, I am very glad to say, a friend to the end.

List of Abbreviations

CND   Campaign for Nuclear Disarmament.
FA   Football Association.
IRA   Irish Republican Army.
NCB   National Coal Board.
NUM   National Union of Miners.
OC   *Occupied City.*
RAA   Recreation and Amusement Association.
SCAP   Supreme Commander of Allied Forces.
SM   *Spectres of Marx.*
TUC   Trade Union Council.
TYZ   *Tokyo Year Zero.*
YRA   Yorkshire Republic Army.

DAVID PEACE

Texts & Contexts

introduction
Peace in Our Time

From Premier League football and police politics to Noh drama and industrial disputes, the novels of David Peace offer 'occult' accounts of twentieth-century history.[1] Published consecutively over a period of four years from 1999 to 2002, the novels of his *Red Riding Quartet* – entitled *1974*, *1977*, *1980* and *1983* – confront the secret past of Yorkshire and the UK during the 1970s and 1980s.[2] Exploring the darker side of humanity and society, the quartet spans the North of England to chronicle an alternative account of the period of the hunt for the Yorkshire Ripper and the political ascendency of Prime Minister Margaret Thatcher.

Peace followed the *Red Riding Quartet* with a chronological step in his 2004 novel *GB84*. Published to coincide with the twentieth anniversary of the 1984–5 UK miners' strike, the novel confronts industrial conflict and political tensions in 1980s Britain. Developing narrative seeds sown in the *Red Riding Quartet*, *GB84* draws attention to the legacy of Thatcherism and its intrinsic role in shaping subsequent decades.

In his next novel, Peace focused on a specific period not only in social, cultural and political history but also in sporting history. The year 2006 saw the publication of *The Damned United*, a fictional reappraisal of football manager Brian Clough's forty-four days in charge of top-flight British football club Leeds United. Defamiliarizing popular understandings of infamous historical characters and events, *The Damned United* sets Clough's failure at Leeds against his former success at Derby in a tale of past glories and present conflicts.

A pervading interest in the problematic relationship between past and present reaches a pinnacle in the *Tokyo Trilogy*, addressing the fall and rise of post-war Japan. The first novel of the trilogy, *Tokyo Year Zero*, was published in 2007; the second, *Occupied City*, in 2009. The trilogy will conclude in 2011 with a final novel, provisionally entitled *Tokyo Regained*. After the *Tokyo Trilogy*, Peace intends to begin work on an inverse post-war trilogy that will incorporate

GB84. This new trilogy will return to the recent history of the UK to explore diverse topics including the odd alliances that brought Thatcher to power (in a novel provisionally entitled *UKDK*), the scandals of Yorkshire cricket and Geoffrey Boycott, and a return to the Ripper (in a final novel provisionally entitled *The Yorkshire Rippers*).[3]

Since the publication of his first novel in 1999, Peace's work has quickly achieved critical acclaim. In 2003 *Granta* magazine named him as one of their 'Best Young Novelists' alongside rising stars of contemporary British literature including Monica Ali, Sarah Waters and Philip Hensher. To date he has won the Awards Cognac Prix du Roman Noir in 2002, the James Tait Black Award in 2004 and the Deutscher Krimi Preis in 2006. In 2007 Peace was named *GQ* 'Writer of the Year', while media broadcaster and literary personality Melvyn Bragg claims that Peace is 'one of the strongest voices in contemporary British fiction'.[4]

In recent years Peace's work has also been translated onto television and film. British broadcaster Channel 4 adapted the *Red Riding Quartet* into a trilogy that aired in March 2009 and went on to achieve a theatrical release in America. In the same year, *The Damned United* was adapted into a film featuring *Frost/Nixon* and *The Queen* star Michael Sheen as troubled football manager Brian Clough. This trend of translation into film and television looks set to continue, with production companies in the UK and Japan expressing interest in adapting *GB84* and the *Tokyo Trilogy* respectively.

Raking over uncomfortable histories, the canon of David Peace deliberately examines controversial people and contentious periods. Operating at the interface of fact and fiction, his texts break the surface of received histories, offering dense, noir-driven analyses of the contemporary world. Addressing the many and contradictory demands of history, of reality, truth and causality, as well as the confusions and debates that mask the power operating beneath overarching historical narratives, Peace's novels bleed fact into fiction as part of a wider move towards an evolving understanding of the past.

Although David Peace claims to 'write novels not history', the past and its relationship to the present underpins his work.[5] Fostering a critical historical consciousness, his novels attempt to highlight the fictional nature of the present and in doing so 'reveal' crucial 'hidden histories'. Through this intersection of past and present, attention is drawn to the great number of historical possibilities and possible histories that lie just below the surface of received accounts. In Peace's novels the past is not comprised of hard facts but a great number of knowable histories, invented, overlooked, destroyed, denied or disregarded. Sourced in a belief that 'fiction can illuminate a time and a place more clearly than fact', the value of Peace's fiction comes from its celebration of plurality and lack of conclusions.[6] In refusing to seal off the past hermeneutically, his novels remind readers of the lack of certainty and limitations in our thinking about history, as well as how people are defined by their perceptions of the past. The past continues to assert itself in Peace's work through a half-presence, a recognized and familiar but also strange and unknown bearing. Contesting the monolithic narratives offered by existing histories, his novels establish alternative relationships between time frames, echoing Lyotard's claim that long-range metanarratives of the past are increasingly rejected in favour of local, individualized accounts.[7]

Peace offers the novel form as a contested site in which images of the past, as Walter Benjamin suggests, merely 'flit by' and refuse to be 'fixed' by the centripetalizing forces of either fact or fiction.[8] In his own fictions, Peace does not turn to the past neutrally or offer history as a consensus. Combating the fallout from a post-historical age, his novels transport the recent past from a commodity to be consumed into a period that is constantly being re-examined by contemporary society. Peace describes his openly partisan approach to re-creating the past as:

> trying to place my own 'memories' against what actually happened according to the papers – and it's not only the news and the politics but every single detail from the weather, to the TV, to the gold mine that you can find in the classified adverts and personal columns. At the same time I am working at the library, I am also reading the 'factual' books on the subject [. . .] Anyway once I have these basic photocopies and notes, I don't leave the room anymore. I just hole myself up in there, submerged in a particular period I have chosen. I also have the music from the period playing and watch the films [. . .] I think that this 'cultural' research helps with the detail and the language, which has changed and continues to change dramatically.[9]

Reflecting on well-documented pasts through heavily researched analysis and personal reflection, Peace's narratives are imbued with a depth of cultural materialism that positions his characters and their beliefs not as radical, but as symptomatic of the worlds presented. Engaging with the many cultural and social forces of these periods, Peace explores transitional times through the blurring of the historical and fictional. His claim that 'everything is political' underscores this approach.[10] Taking unnerving perspectives on familiar events and public figures, his novels do not seek to oppose or transcend existing historical accounts, but to heterodox them with new narratives to offer sometimes contradictory ways of reconfiguring the events in question.

With the exception of the *Tokyo Trilogy* (the context of which is discussed in chapter 7), Peace's fictions concentrate on the history of the UK during the 1970s and 1980s. As seen through the prism of Peace, this period is transformed into a new context in which other pasts can be read. While the 1960s have been popularly regarded as a time of hope and progress in the UK, the 1970s emerge in comparison as a rather depressing period of anticlimax. Twentieth-century historian Christopher Booker argues that the 1970s should nevertheless be considered 'the most important decade of the twentieth century' as a result of the social, political and cultural changes that occurred during these years.[11]

Although Peace engages with these cultural markers, his own fictional representations of the period are far removed from the 'I Love the 1970s' package shows that proliferate across contemporary television schedules. Instead, his novels search for the abiding legacy of 1970s and 1980s Britain, refusing to submit to a wider nostalgia for the period. In the face of the 'Abbafication' of the 1970s and the reframing of the 1980s in popular television series such as *Life on Mars* and *Ashes to Ashes*, Peace's novels ask readers to juxtapose these received representations with his own 'I Hate 1974' version of events.[12] Focusing on Britain at a time of discontent, Peace turns the narrative spotlight on changes in government, right-wing militia groups, growing union powers and social unrest. Presenting readers with a futureless past of unrest and decay, greed and conservatism, business and spite, his work scratches beyond cultural stereotypes to reveal the menace and flawed ideals lying just below the surface of familiar images. Confronting decades that have been subject to a sustained 'correction' in the popular historical consciousness, Peace engages in his own fictional reappraisal to represent a sharply dis-United Kingdom.

Through a series of crises during the 1970s, Britain was pushed to the brink of social disintegration. Social historian Alwyn Turner admits that the 1970s was 'a decade when it sometimes appeared that the nation was on the verge of a nervous breakdown', while Andy Beckett reflects that something 'profound and unsettling did happen to Britain in the Seventies, and Britons have been living with the consequences ever since'.[13] Politically, the 1970s saw major changes in the UK government. Edward Heath came to power with the Conservative Party in 1970 at a time when the British economy was at a low point. Productivity was down, while labour unionization and inflation were both on the rise. With increasing unemployment, the curtailing of trade union powers and an emerging economic recession, unrest among workers grew more frequent.[14] With England and 'Englishness' in crisis, a rise in challenges to social relations initiated by the growth of feminism, alternative religions, sexual liberation and racial diversification, the 1970s emerged as a period of change and tension. Set against this 'simmering disenchantment came a temporary pause in the Silver Jubilee of 1977'.[15] This brief period saw the Queen undertake a three-month tour of the UK with street parties to mark the twenty-fifth anniversary of her accession to the throne. As a celebration in the face of seeming catastrophe, the Jubilee served as a moment of respite from an otherwise chaotic reality.

Margaret Thatcher's election victory in May 1979 could have marked a turning point away from the traumas of the 1970s and towards the 1980s, but social, economic and political unrest continued unabated both at home and abroad. Political tension extended to the Troubles in Northern Ireland and the ongoing issue of nuclear proliferation in the mysterious death of Hilda Murrell, a CND (Campaign for Nuclear Disarmament) campaigner.[16] The 1980s also marked a time at which the external spectre of international Communism from the Cold War and Cuban missile crisis re-emerged and became internalized to the British national psyche in the form of sustained industrial unrest from the new 'enemy within' – the industrial worker.[17] Fuelled by Conservative neo-liberal policies to reduce government spending, destroy union powers and promote economic liberalization and privatization, the governments of the 1970s and 1980s inspired a series of industrial strikes culminating in a government confrontation with the mining industry.

Historically, British miners had enjoyed strong union powers and an enviable position in national wage leagues. Previous disputes concerning pay and conditions had produced outstanding results and at the beginning of the 1984 strike most miners were confident of a quick victory. The success of the 1972 strike was fuelled by extremely favourable economic conditions. Low coal stocks meant that miners enjoyed maximum negotiating potential, while the Middle East's restrictions on oil flow meant that UK power stations could not simply turn to oil to counter their lack of coal. Pickets also halted movements of coal as other TUC (Trade Union Council) workers respected their picket lines. As a result, Prime Minister Edward Heath was forced to declare a state of emergency and a three-day week for industry. Miners went on strike again in 1974 at a point when economic conditions similarly favoured their wage demands.[18] On this occasion an overwhelming demonstration of unity through the ballot box also proved very effective, with 81 percent of miners supporting strike action in a national ballot. The scale of this support prompted Heath to confront the miners' challenge to his government's authority, calling an election to answer the question, 'Who runs the country?' The response of the electorate was decisive and the Heath government was defeated.

The 1984–5 miners' strike began as a dual battle of revenge and replication as both factions, fuelled by memories of their 1972/4 struggles, sought to rectify or revive past results. The ascension to power of the left in the National Union of Miners (NUM) signalled by the election of Arthur Scargill in 1982 changed the rules of the game on the union side. Their new leader attempted to centralize power, to encourage industrial confrontation and to teach his members to view the National Coal Board (NCB) as the agent of a malicious government. The arrival of Ian MacGregor at the NCB impacted on the government's engagement in the dispute, signalling an immediate intention to strengthen the hand of management against the power of the unions. Social and political changes during the 1980s - including high unemployment, anti-trade union legislation, tight right-wing control of the press, Cold War hysteria, the political mobilization of the police and the Labour Party's shift to the right – gave the stark warning that economic Thatcherism was here to stay and would not brook resistance. 'New realists' conspired to compound this idea, arguing that the only option was to submit and accept privatization, anti-union laws and the onslaught of neo-liberalism. These movements encouraged the British population to accept passively the right of the Thatcher government to manage society – an assumption that effectively steamrollered the advances made by the UK's working classes over the previous two centuries. At the end of the year-long 1984–5 miners' strike, the core issue – that of the Conservatives' 'right to manage' their people, industries and country in whatever way, and for whatever purpose, they saw fit – had been settled unequivocally in the government's favour. Written against a late-twentieth and early twenty-first-century context of 'New Labour' and 'Cool Britannia', Peace's novels reappraise the 1970s and 1980s as the period in which the foundations of contemporary Britain were laid.

Written in the context of a growing body of critical responses to the work of David Peace, this book does not claim to be exhaustive. Rather, it aims to provide an introduction to the relationship between his novels and the contemporary contexts they attempt to reframe. Moving from the Ripper and the miners' strike to Leeds United and twentieth-century Tokyo, the following pages offer a critical exploration of his canon to date. Chapter 1, 'A Very Yorkshire Tale', explores how and why Peace's *Red Riding Quartet* represents the North of England as both a place apart from the rest of the UK and the logical representation of its dark underside during the 1970s and 1980s. Landscape is examined by this chapter as an articulating vestige of experience and memory. Re-inscribing fresh meanings on an area historically defined by romantic associations with the Brontës and the Yorkshire moors, the quartet establishes a new 'mythology of the North'. Together, the four novels inhabit an effective no-man's-land, a Yorkshire in dispute. This chapter will ask to what extent the battle to apprehend the Yorkshire Ripper becomes a battle for the ownership of space, a war for possession and control of county and country.

Contextual discourses of gender, religion and temporality form a central focus of chapter 2, 'Words Fail'. Across the *Red Riding Quartet* the fear and confusion of the 1970s and 1980s extends in repetition to an almost 'lyrical tic', foregrounding a claustrophobic masculine world. Tortured both physically and linguistically, Peace's male characters witness the breakdown of language and a dissent into meaninglessness. As the quartet develops, evolving and complex narratives unfold through competitive prose dispersed amongst a variety of male voices. The use of repetition to structure these narratives will be highlighted as a key weapon in Peace's armoury against conventional narratological accounts of the past. The language of religion becomes more significant as the quartet develops. The power of religious doctrine is exploited through literary transfiguration, while the rhythm of phrases is repeatedly reframed and turned over in an almost compulsive mission to unpack and understand. This hypnotic prose conveys a fractured sense of self through a prayer-like quality of appeal to a greater knowledge capable of explaining the otherwise inexplicable realities presented. As well as tackling profound moral, existential and theological problems, the language of faith foregrounds a spiritual void, a God experienced primarily through absence. The character of Reverend Laws will be analysed as a manifestation of this absent faith, while his ideology and manipulation of religious discourse will be examined in relation to the darkness inherent in the world presented. Time and its relationship to space will finally be offered as a central concern of the quartet. The army of police and criminals involved in the orbit of the hunt for the Ripper are obsessed with time and with objects of time – watches, clocks, calendars and dates. These temporal tools will be analysed as symbols of urgency, pushing the narrative forwards while making readers uncomfortably aware of an approaching and inescapable conclusion.

Drawing on Derrida's initial use of the term in *Spectres of Marx*, chapter 3, 'Towards a Hauntology of the North', argues that the *Red Riding Quartet* is a work of hauntological literature. Derrida explores the loss of the spirit of revolution in the wake of the fall of the Berlin Wall and the 'end of history', suggesting that in this context the spirit of social and political revolution becomes a ghost which 'haunts' the present. In his *Red Riding Quartet* Peace privileges absences – of people, ideas and emotions – to establish a present that is saturated with the past. The self-conscious disjunctures of his narratives allow spectres to disrupt the closure of the present, opening up new possibilities and realities. Employing the language of spectrality to highlight a movement between time frames, the four novels offer multi-temporalities that are never co-present. Working amongst the ruins of history, Peace represents a retrospective culture, one obsessed with fragments of the past and their incorporation into mainstream life. The Ripper's victims are given voice and re-animated through 'transmissions' that preface each section of *1983*, creating a dialogic meeting of the spiritual and the actual. This chapter will examine how and why Peace transforms these frequently intervening oral hallucinations into strands of theological and narratological enquiry.

David Peace is an author who writes about crime but, significantly, does not consider himself to be a crime writer. His novels may concern crime, but provide more than a Yorkshire version of the James Ellroy series. Chapter 4, 'Yorkshire Noir', suggests that the *Red Riding Quartet* offers contemporary readers a socially conscious form of crime fiction. Peace mobilizes the framework, tropes and conventions of genre fiction to articulate an alternative perspective through a recognized form. Offering the quartet as an example of a new kind of crime fiction, its controversial and explicit content is analysed as an anti-sanitization approach to shifting definitions of crime in contemporary society. The issue of how and why Peace foregrounds the shared humanity of hunter and hunted, the Ripper and police, is explored through representations of human redemption and salvation. The chapter argues that despite a pronounced desire to emphasize their difference, the similarities at the heart of these representations of criminal and victim, accused and accuser, enforcer and deviant, blur and challenge singular notions of good and evil.

From fiction and drama to poetry and autobiography, the literary history of the 1984–5 miners' strike is one of contestation, claim and counterclaim. Yet within this extensive range of published material, a factional account by a professional author with little direct experience of either the mining industry or the 1984–5 coal dispute has triumphed. Chapter 5, 'From the Picket Line to the Page', suggests that *GB84* revisits the strike period in an attempt to offer a speculative history. Fabricating a 'factional' effect in which novelistic dialogue appears to be polyphonic and multi-sourced, the novel reanimates forms and voices from the strike period by manipulating literary and linguistic systems. This chapter considers how and why Peace turns to the novel form to propose alternative accounts of the most significant post-war industrial dispute in British history.

Tackling male competitiveness and masculinity, psychological trauma and the political machinations operating behind the polished veneer of the 'beautiful' game, chapter 6, 'The Life of Brian', argues that *The Damned United* is much more than a novel about football. Exploring universal themes of love, jealousy and ambition, Peace interrogates an already well-documented series of events, adding new perspectives to an increasingly contentious picture of the past. Through the controversial figure of Brian Clough, Peace challenges notions of heroism, questioning the significance of his fall and our need for heroes in contemporary society.

In the *Tokyo Trilogy*, a series of texts concerning the defeat and occupation of post-war Japan, Peace explores tensions between a need to forget the past and a fear of confronting the future. Exploring oppositions between the interior and exterior, the psyche and the social, these novels articulate a growing awareness of the dangers of dislocation from former times. Interrogating a cyclical incantation of language and translation, chapter 7, 'Occupation and Defeat in the *Tokyo Trilogy*', explores the role of the past in shaping the future of twentieth-century Japan and its dialogical relationship to the rest of the world.

This book concludes with a brief analysis of the various screen versions of Peace's novels and the critical debates initiated by their adaptation. The decision to transform the *Red Riding Quartet* into a trilogy (through the omission of *1977*) and the need to put a more optimistic 'spin' on the grim realities of Brian Clough's time at Leeds will be offered as key examples of attempts to edit or censor the very explicit representations foregrounded in Peace's work. Ongoing debates concerning the benefit of these extensions to screen and film are considered in the light of a growing critical response to David Peace as a rising star of contemporary British literature.

chapter one

A Very Yorkshire Tale

'The North is both our glory and our problem.'
[Martin Wainwright, 2009]

Rape and Rhubarb

There is something distinctly nightmarish, but hauntingly recognizable, about the North of England as represented through the eyes of David Peace. His fictional terrains expose readers to a strong sense of a place that defines itself through an innate difference from the rest of the country. This oppositional spatialization posits the North of England as a counterbalance to the more 'civilized' South. In the *Red Riding Quartet*, the North is presented in an obstinate state of marginality, bound closely to issues of power and identity. Peace's North is 'as much a state of mind as a place', a space 'in England but never quite of it'.[1] Re-creating the bleak backdrop of an increasingly post-industrial UK, the four novels unite to present the North of England as a place of perpetually underlying anarchy, anxiety and sadism during the 1970s and 1980s. In stark opposition to the South, the North is described as a place of 'DEATH –
All the gods of the North are dead now, moribund –' [*1980*, 126]. Peace depicts the North of England as a place where there is simply *'no law'* [*1980*, 10]. As the West Yorkshire Police openly warn Eddie Dunford in *1974*, 'THIS IS THE NORTH, WE DO WHAT WE WANT' [*1974*, 265].

Since each novel offers a phase rather than a final ending, the UK is never whole or finalized in Peace's work. Instead, it is broken into named counties that draw on oppositional relations to define one another. Peace does not offer a topographic map of the UK's regions, but a fractured peremptory of them as conflicted and conflicting spaces. All counties have their own individual histories, associations and images, but each also has an unspoken history, unseen images and illicit associations. Across the *Red Riding Quartet* regionalism is foregrounded in opposition to nationalism and counties confront one another as a means of reconfiguring psychic, social and cultural geographies.

The regional landscapes of the *Red Riding Quartet* are especially chilling because they are drawn at least in part from memories of the author's own childhood. Peace was born and raised in Ossett, West Yorkshire and his novels can be viewed as a literary homecoming to this place. Peace has identified a 'homesickness in the *Red Riding Quartet*', an acknowledgement that 'the single biggest influence upon me was growing up when and where I did', even though it was 'not particularly fashionable to write about the North [. . .] then or now'.[2] In many ways his quartet evidences the claim that 'you can take the man out of Yorkshire but not [. . .] Yorkshire out of the man!'[3] Peace recalls the Yorkshire of his youth as:

> a dark and dangerous and threatening place. It's in the very architecture and landscape of the place. This is at the ass end of industrialization. There was massive recession. It was a very bleak, ailing place. And then you had the contrast, as you went further North, and got out of the city, and then it got very very bleak. That's the scene of the Moors Murders. Everything seemed to be charged with some element of threat or danger [. . .] it was more enclosed, and people were stressed.[4]

Throughout his work, Peace breaks down the doors of historically limited spaces and contentious times, employing landscape to make connections between socio-economic and geo-political conditions. Peace remains adamant that 'crime happens in specific times and places for specific reasons [. . .] These things don't happen by chance. It wasn't the Cornwall Ripper, it was the Yorkshire Ripper; it happened here for a variety of very specific reasons that we don't want to look at any more.'[5] Turning back to the landscape of his youth, Peace uses the Northern English county of Yorkshire as a cultural and geographic site as well as a microcosm for the dark underside of the UK during the late twentieth century.[6]

As the largest county in the UK, Yorkshire stretches over 6,000 square miles of moorland, towns and cities. Commonly known for its strong sense of regionalism and faith to 'county before country', for much of the twentieth century it was divided into three Ridings (meaning 'divisions of a county'), North, South and West.

Representing 1970s and 1980s Yorkshire as an area steeped in evil and corruption, Peace offers a mythologizing portrait of place. At the core of the *Red Riding Quartet* lies

> Yorkshire, bloody Yorkshire –
> Primitive Yorkshire, Medieval Yorkshire, Industrial Yorkshire –
> Three ages, three Dark Ages –
> Local Dark Ages,
> Local decay, industrial decay –
> Local murder, industrial murder –
> Local hell, industrial hell –
> Dead hells, dead ages –
> Dead moors, dead mills –
> Dead cities –
> Crows, the rain, and their Ripper –
> The Yorkshire Ripper –
> > Yorkshire bloody Ripper. [*1980*, 305–6]

Created by more than simply topographical factors, the county of Yorkshire exists in a climate of fear that is described as specifically Northern.[7] Peace's vision of his home county circles around shared traumas and times, listing a monotonous history of destruction and death. Challenging popular representations of Yorkshire as 'God's own county', the quartet instead presents a secluded community characterized by parochialism and defiance. In Peace's home county, it is 1970 going on the Dark Ages, his 'poisoned pastoral' reflecting the fallout created by social and political unrest.[8] A right-wing agenda, industrial collapse, religious and racial conflicts, misogyny and economic recession manifest themselves in a Yorkshire struggling to cope with the unwanted effects of change. From this chaos, the Yorkshire Ripper emerges as an image of disorder. Peter Sutcliffe, dubbed by the UK media the 'Yorkshire Ripper', killed thirteen women from 1975 to 1980, casting a shadow over the county for nearly a decade before his arrest in 1981. Revisiting these crimes and their times as a shadowy expression of the social, political and economic ills of the 1970s and 1980s, Peace uses Yorkshire and the Ripper as a lens through which to re-examine the period.

During a twentieth century of industrial decline, Yorkshire turned 'from the avatar of modernisation into a byword for backwardness'.[9] Eddie Dunford is not 'North of England Crime Correspondent'

[*1974*, 3] but 'Edward Dunford, Provincial Journalist' [*1974*, 13], his return to Yorkshire marking a conscious, if reluctant, break away from dreams of 'a Chelsea flat with a beautiful Southern girl called Sophie or Anna' [*1974*, 13]. To Eddie, the North represents not only a different place but a different time, a period 'behind' the South: 'July 1969 . . . Me in Brighton, two thousand light years from home' [*1974*, 16]. A combination of de-industrialization and suburbanization during the 1970s and 1980s produced a power vacuum in Yorkshire leading to urban decay and abandoned spaces inhabited by marginalized people. Peace focuses on the ways in which this moral and spiritual decline extends outwards through the built environment. The gradual erasure of heavy industry is evidenced in the disappearance of structures from the skyline. There are 'black slags where fields have been' [*1977*, 330] and several characters note 'the landscape empty' [*1980*, 9]. Although the economy began a post-industrial shift during the 1970s and 1980s, Peace's Yorkshire refuses to move forwards and continues to lag behind the rest of the UK. Through his historical inflections, Peace raises the ghosts of Britain's former industrial glory against the ubiquity of modern developments to offer alienated voices of despair and loss. The bleakness of a county reliant on dying industries creates a tangible sense of the 1970s and 1980s as a period of 'winters and hate. Darkness and fear.'[10]

The social engineering of 'urban regeneration' programmes that seek to replace these old landscapes is arguably the real crime at the heart of the quartet, as underhand coppers and developers adopt the coy euphemisms of 'business opportunities' and 'agreements' to justify their underground operations. Like many organizations in the *Red Riding Quartet*, the construction industry is shown to be highly localized and extremely corrupt. Its logical development is represented in conspiratorial plans to finance and erect a new Ridings Shopping Centre using the dual resources of building know-how and police vice funds. 'The Swan Centre' [*1983*, 228] at the Hunslet and Beeston exit of the M1, the artery to the rest of the UK, is set to be 'the biggest of its kind in England, or in Europe' [*1983*, 228]. Evidencing a desire for status, power and independence inherent in Peace's Yorkshire, this temple to capitalism and consumption is founded upon corruption. By means of social critique, glimpses are provided of the effects the new centre will have on the established space of the local community, granting the reader an additional dimension of decline. We are asked to note that:

'Across the road was another empty shop, just a name and a big weather beaten sign declaring that the property was to be redeveloped by Foster's Construction, builders of the new Ridings Shopping Centre, Wakefield:

Shopping centres –' [*1983*, 38]. Even solicitor John Piggott comments that 'you wonder what the fuck will happen to this place when they finish the Ridings' [*1983*, 45].

The suburbs of Yorkshire may initially appear more ordered than the chaos and despair of its urban centres, but their sedate fascia is ultimately shown to conceal a dark underside. While questioning suspects in the suburbs, Maurice observes a 'little brown bungalow with its little green garden, next to all the other little brown bungalows with their little green gardens' [*1983*, 105]. In their sinister uniformity the suburbs conceal the horrors of the past beneath the 'beautiful new carpets' of new housing developments. These horrors reach a pinnacle in the modernist construction of Shangrila. In its open-plan design, imposing position and local interest, Shangrila is marked out as an expression of power and control. Over the course of the quartet Shangrila morphs from '*a sleeping swan*' [*1974*, 84] to a Gothic site of encounter and intrigue, an 'enormous bungalow lain bare on a wet black hill' [*1983*, 257]. As a fictional Eden, the building represents an impossible goal driving the corrupt ideals of the county. Named in honour of the 1933 James Hilton novel *Lost Horizon* and traditionally associated with mystical and harmonious isolation from the rest of the world, Shangrila is designed by John Dawson, 'the *Prince of Architecture*', as a present to his wife for their silver wedding anniversary. Manipulating traditional associations of love and fidelity, Peace mobilizes the mythology of the swan to establish haunting connections between this building and an underworld realm of the missing. Shangrila comes to resemble their '*stark white bones rising out of the* ground' [*1983*, 348], an association repeated throughout the quartet until an alignment with the Moors Murders has been unequivocally established.[11]

Focusing on what lies beneath, Peace draws attention to the historical, cultural and social processes through which the environment is shaped. Visualizing a landscape in transition, his quartet sets architectural space against natural space, encouraging readers to observe 'overlooked' elements of Yorkshire life. Characters move 'Over the Moors, across the Moors, under the Moors' [*1977*, 149] to highlight revealed and concealed worlds. Through these subterranean sites Peace explores meditative spaces that illuminate gaps between physical experience and visual perception. In a dark, alternative world of still life, underground spaces position Yorkshire as a 'field of rape and rhubarb' [*1983*, 220], a site of production and consumption, pleasure and pain.

The concept of the subterranean connects the many hidden histories of Yorkshire to highlight covert truths operating under the surface of the public gaze. Clare Kemplay's post-mortem suggests that 'particles taken from the victim's skin and nails revealed a strong presence of coal dust' [*1974*, 51], while the 'Belly' and its cells echo the underground world of George Marsh. Officially an interrogation room, the Belly is actually a 'huge fucking hole of a cell right down in the gut, all strip lights and wash-down floors' [*1977*, 77], inside which normal rules of police procedure do not apply. This underground space is neither safe nor accessible, its profound stillness paradoxically creating an intense energy. By the end of the quartet, Detective Chief Superintendent Maurice Jobson is finally able to look past the 'Great Yorkshire Show' to see this 'underground kingdom' [*1983*, 136]. Juxtaposing what lies above with what lies below, an alternative world operating just below the surface draws attention to the corrupt foundations upon which Yorkshire and the UK were built. Through this underground dimension, Peace encourages a new appreciation of space and time, building a mythological grid of counter-narratives and meanings.

In the *Red Riding Quartet*, Yorkshire is presented as a potent hybrid of surface and subterranea, urban and rural, staunchly barren in both climate and physical composition. Re-inscribing the meaning of a well-known landscape, Peace's *'Moors of Hell'* [*1977*, 340] form the grounds upon which narrative events unfold. Historically, the Yorkshire Moors have enjoyed a mythology of space, authenticity and strength. The *Red Riding Quartet* underscores their savage power, but also offers the Moors as a site of subhuman actions. Historian Hayden White argues that 'in the past, when men were uncertain as to the precise quality of their sensed humanity, they appealed to the concept of wildness to designate an area of sub-humanity that was characterized by everything they hoped they were not'.[12] In *1980*, the actions of Assistant Chief Constable Peter Hunter echo this statement as he recalls through flashback his time spent as a young officer hunting for the victims of the Moors murderers. Traversing the same space in the hunt for the Ripper several years later, Hunter is plagued by memories of travelling 'Over the Moors –

Cold lost bones:
It stank then and it stinks now, that same old smell –
Bloody Yorkshire'. [*1980*, 47]

The symbolic backdrop of the Yorkshire Moors is confronted through a natural world that is resoundingly brown, burnt out and barren. Peace seems to struggle for language adequate to represent this space. Any associations with the Brontës and windswept heather are quickly brushed aside by his novels. This is 'Bloody Yorkshire' [*1980*, 19], and its '*damned Moors*' [*1980*, 20] are a curse not a blessing. They appear 'stained with snow' [*1980*, 257], their weather 'stark and grey, the landscape empty but for telegraph poles' [*1980*, 3]. Peace's depiction of the Moors evidences a kind of anti-Romanticism, a refusal to celebrate landscape. The beauty of nature cannot thrive in this environment, cannot co-exist with a Thatcherite society. Confronting historical constructions of Yorkshire and its Moors and undermining established mythic associations, Peace's aesthetic sensibility does not allow for meaningful experiences with nature. Instead, his vision of Yorkshire is of a deeply foreboding, shadowy world that betrays the wider corruptions of the county and country.

As well as providing the means by which characters move between North and South, East and West, roads discipline the untamed landscape of Yorkshire. Peace's odology provides the reader with a new awareness of site and movement as playing vital psychological and cultural functions. In his quartet, public transport is the home of those on the run, the dispossessed and easily disposed of. Bus stations are for blow jobs and coaches, motels for schemes and sleep, while much of the action takes place in yet 'another lonely car park' [*1977*, 142]. These desolate spaces are connected by a web of roads and railway lines which criss-cross the county. In *1977* Jack endures 'another slow train through hell, hell:

Hell' [*1977*, 264], the rhythmic movement of the train as it strains through reluctant scenery echoing his own journey into a dark and complicated past.

Movement across roads is repetitive and tedious, imaged in the circling and searching of police investigations around 'Netherton/Wood Street/Netherton/Wood Street/Netherton/Wood Street –' [*1983*, 298]. In *1974* Eddie is dumped by the side of the road by the West Yorkshire Police after his warning beating, a polite reminder that he should think about leaving the area, while one of Peter Hunter's earliest and most pertinent assertions about the Ripper is that 'He's mobile, has his own vehicle' [*1980*, 83]. Providing a recognized metaphor for personal and psychological journeys, roads allow communication and access to otherwise solitary locations as an effective 'open door' to the closed shop of Yorkshire.

Roads and railway lines slice across a regional landscape firmly framed by 'the hills and the mills' [*1977*, 219]. The menace of this landscape is felt most profoundly by Mancunian Peter Hunter who considers the county to be the epitome of Northern grimness and dissent, noting in both urban and rural Yorkshire, 'The clouds black above us, the hills darker still –

Hills of hard houses, bleak times –

Warehouse eyes, mill stares' [*1980*, 363]. The weather forms an extension of this hostile landscape. It is always raining in Peace's Yorkshire, hard, loud and vicious; the weather rejects a place in the backdrop in favour of a centre-stage, intruding presence. Across the four novels the climate of Yorkshire is biblically desperate. *1977* is 'the year the world drowned' [*1977*, 264], while Bob Fraser complains about 'the rain outside, it's loud, deafening, like the lorry doors as they slam shut, one after another, in the car park, endlessly' [*1977*, 276].

For Peter Hunter, the weather becomes a logical extension of the dark heart of Yorkshire, 'the looming night and the constant rain into sleet into snow into rain into sleet into snow that seems to be haunting me, plaguing me, cursing me' [*1980*, 237–8]. His repeated note, 'it's still raining', is reiterated throughout *1980*, until it becomes totalizing, falling indiscriminately upon the 'ruined grandeur, ill-gotten, squandered and damned' [*1980*, 235] of the county. In his sweep of this hostile and imposing environment, Hunter sees a history of scars written across the surface of the Moors. On the rare occasions when characters experience any kind of peace and contentment in this landscape – like Bob Fraser's family experience of 'A Yorkshire Summer's Day' – these moments are deliberately undermined by portents of doom [*1977*, 199]. Peace is at pains to emphasize that these are

'Darker times –

No darker day' [*1983*, 273]. As space and time fall victim to the encroaching and seemingly eternal 'dark Yorkshire night' [*1983*, 354], characters attempt to block its approach, keeping 'curtains drawn against the rain, against the afternoon, against the Yorkshire life' [*1977*, 288].

Dead City

A rainswept vision of Yorkshire reaches its zenith in Leeds.[13] Peace's fictional Leeds is a dark, violent and masculine place, described in taut, lyrical prose as the backdrop to much of his work. In Leeds readers witness the iconography of landscape through architecture, an exterior surface of history set against an interior of meaning and experience. Peace recalls that as a child 'Leeds itself seemed to me to be very dark and very depressing (and where they filmed the exteriors for *A Clockwork Orange*). I never felt at ease there and the buildings seemed almost "haunted" – the Dark Arches, the Griffin Hotel, the Millgarth Police Station, the various shopping centres, and Elland Road.'[14] Signs of decay and serious economic damage are visually inflicted on the landscape of his fictional Leeds. The Griffin Hotel is a useful example: dead central yet remote and threatening, the hotel's oppressive interiors, dim lighting and high-backed chairs reflect a darkness that tinges every corner of a building that looks 'like an old church in need of repair' [*1977*, 105]. Buildings and bodies litter the landscape of Peace's Leeds, charting a series of interlocking crises, the disintegration of the city and society and the consequences of the defeat of socialism, modernism and ideas of progress.

Throughout the *Red Riding Quartet* readers are encouraged to question:

> *How can this ancient English shitty city be here! The well-known grey chimney of its oldest mill? How can that be here? There is no spike of rusty iron in the air, between the eye and it, from any point of the real prospect. What is the spike that intervenes, and who has set it up? Maybe it is set up by the Queen's orders for the impaling of a hoarde of Commonwealth robbers, one by one. It is so, for the cymbals clash, and the Queen goes by to her palace in long procession. Ten thousand swords flash in the sunlight, and thrice ten thousand dancing girls strew flowers. Then follow white elephants caparisoned in red, white and blue, infinite in number and attendants. Still, the chimney rises in the background, where it cannot be, and still no writhing figure is on the grim spike. Stay! Is the chimney so low a thing as the rusty spike on the top post of an old bedstead that has*

tumbled all awry. Stay! I am twenty-five years and more, the bells chime in jubilation. Stay. [1977, 23]

Ceaselessly questioning the past and present via familiar vistas, Peace interrogates the city's history of medieval torture and punishment, empire and power, industry and revolution. Subject to constant struggles for power, the chiming bells of jubilation transport the reader back to a present of monarchic 'celebration' [*1977*, 164]. However, these celebrations do not extend to the characters of *Red Riding*. Instead, Peace focuses on 'the morning after the night before, the bunting tattered, the Union Jacks down' [*1977*, 171]. The only light comes from primal flames of discontent as 'Leeds 7 bonfires are going up, and not fucking Jubilee Beacons' [*1977*, 14]. Providing an alternative regional perspective on popular images of the national Jubilee party, Bob Fraser's Jubilee mug, broken on the drainer, is not only suggestive of his own shattered domestic situation [*1977*, 92], but also underscores the lack of impact the Jubilee celebrations enjoyed in the North of England.

Offering tortured visions of a place and the ghosts that inhabit it, Peace's built and imagined environments interact with one another via established historical associations to offer inner-city Leeds as 'Intensive Hell' [*1977*, 75]. Through a Dickensian 'collision of the worst of times, the worst of hells – The Medieval, the Victorian and the Concrete', Peace constructs a Transylvanian Leeds, 'a bloody castle rising out of the bleeding rain, a tear on the landscape' [*1980*, 26]. The quartet draws upon this architectural uncanny to form a haunto-topography. Mapping a landscape of spectral sites, frequent injections into the narratives of street names and addresses encourage the reader to form a geographical awareness of this space. Working from models of reality, fantasy and memory, Peace knits fact and fiction into an expression of time and place to produce landscapes that are more than a reproduction of the obvious or familiar.

In a city marred by destruction, atrophy and decay, a stultifying atmosphere combines with emotionally charged spaces to speak to the depths of characters' minds. As they gradually become overwhelmed by the pressure of events, Peace's Leeds becomes part of their suffering. Prowling the Ripper's territory, the aptly named Peter 'Hunter' carries a *'Leeds and Bradford A to Z'* [*1980*, 33] in an attempt to navigate his way through a maze of back streets and secrets to find the 'ghost bloodied old city of Leodis' [*1983*, 193]. He grows to pray that 'Leeds is just a dream –

A terrible dream –

Like the Ripper, their Ripper' [*1980*, 50], but is ultimately unable to escape the moral and physical darkness of the city. As Hunter notes, 'It's gone noon but already night outside' [*1980*, 64]. His experiences of the area convince him that the Ripper is 'from round here because he hates it, hates it enough to kill it – so he has to have been around here long enough to hate it, to want to kill it' [*1980*, 83].Tortured by 'the unpleasant night and her ugly rain, the haunted station and the silence' [*1980*, 95], Hunter comes to see Leeds as the symbol of a wider '*UK Decay*' [*1983*, 366], a marker scrawled both literally and metaphorically across the city's walls.[15]

Ripper Country

As a multicultural site of conflict, Peace uses Yorkshire to explore tensions produced by social, political and economic change. These tensions manifest themselves in '*Local, local hates*' [*1983*, 151], deeply rooted in a specific place and time. Race is a pervading issue in the quartet, with racial prejudice seen to extend across the county, country and even to the upper echelons of law enforcement. As an early sign of intolerance, *1974* opens with the burning of Hunslet Carr gypsy camp.This episode provides a shocking introduction to the brutality and lawlessness of race relations, as officers approach the camp '*Zulu*,Yorkshire style' [*1974*, 46]. Police officers frequently refer to the white population of Yorkshire as 'Natives' [*1974*, 175], while the quartet as a whole is set against the period of the Chapeltown race riots.[16] Returning to his home county in *1974*, Eddie Dunford reflects that Yorkshire has become

'Paki Town, the only colour left.

Black bricks and saris, brown boys playing cricket in the cold.

The Mosque and the Mill, make it Yorkshire 1974:

The Curry and the Cap' [*1974*, 179]. These changes breed fear and contempt in locals and even policeman Bob Fraser draws Conradian alignments to a 'small gang of West Indians, black shadows dancing and whooping, thinking about finishing off what they've started, sticking the boot in' [*1977*, 15].

As part of a battle for the perceived racial 'purity' of the region, Yorkshire is increasingly subject to racial zoning. In *1977* Jack Whitehead reports driving through 'Durkar, another Ossett, another Sandal:

Another piece of White Yorkshire' [*1977*, 283], later moving on to 'Batley, another Bradford, another Delhi:

Another piece of Black Yorkshire' [*1977*, 284]. Walls are daubed with racially and politically motivated discourse – '*Wogs Out, Fuck The Provos*' [*1974*, 189] – directed not only at the 'Fucking niggers' [*1977*, 15] but also at the 'Bloody jocks, worse than the Micks' [*1977*, 22]. Discrimination even intrudes into the hunt for the Ripper when the investigation of Ka Su Peng's attempted murder is undermined by her race:

"'you know what they say about a Chinky"

"What?"

"An hour later and you could murder another"' [*1977*, 288]. At the end of the quartet racial hatred has not dissipated, but mutates into a more general sense of hatred against any 'Other': 'You read the walls as you go:

Wogs Out, Leeds, NF, Kill A Paki, Leeds.' [*1983*, 313]

Racial conflicts within Yorkshire echo larger, national conflicts and soon 'everyone' is 'talking Northern bloody Ireland' [*1983*, 177]. The external presence of a concerted movement for independence in the form of the IRA is mirrored within the confines of Peace's Yorkshire by the YRA (Yorkshire Republican Army) [*1983*, 49] and the sustained demonization of regional rivals Lancashire.[17] Divisions between the white rose county of Yorkshire and the red rose county of Lancashire are accentuated by local police – 'Frankie hanging around, talking up the Lancs/Yorks rivalry' [*1977*, 52] – and press – '*Police on both sides of the Pennines*' [*1977*, 143] – until Lancashire becomes 'the wrong side of the hills' [*1977*, 150], a place remote in terms of culture, if not in geography:

"'Brought your bloody phrase book?"

"Phrasebook?" No bastard speaks over there."

"Bloody heathens" nods Murphy' [*1980*, 19].[18] For the North West division, Yorkshire likewise represents the edge of civilization where they can expect to receive nothing more than 'good old-fashioned Yorkshire bloody hospitality' [*1980*, 27]. Lancashire police openly mock the 'Yaarkshire' force as comically inept, chauvinist, homophobic and racist. Although both bodies could stand accused of these charges in Peace's novels, the West Yorkshire Police are particularly overcompetitive and confrontational. Their intimidatory tactics extend to the community, as houses are indiscriminately raided and whole streets governed by symbolic gestures of control [*1977*, 77].

Peace rakes over the said but also the necessarily 'unsaid' horror of these regional divisions to offer a culturally determined psychology of Northern England as a place of confrontation. Peace's Yorkshire is comprised of rival sites that do not share a sense of harmony or accord. Old leaders and fresh elites clash to produce a new psycho-geographical atlas of the county, charting ongoing battles for hierarchies and control. Yorkshire is itself presented as a space in which power is unevenly distributed and subject to constant redistribution. Throughout the quartet, a territorial battle rages between competing social, political and economic groups seeking control of the county. These conflicting forces form the basis of a new *'English Civil War'* [*1980*, 47]; by the time third novel *1980* opens, there is 'Nothing Short Of A Total War' [*1980*, Part Two].

As a place of absolutism, Peace's Yorkshire is characterized by hard, fast intolerance. As one caller to *The John Shark Show* on Radio Leeds reminds the host, '*It was a Yorkshireman who invented the guillotine, John, Everyone knows that*' [*1977*, 282]. These revolutionary tendencies and primal systems of governance are celebrated as a source of logic and pride. Chief Constable Angus boasts to Peter Hunter that 'Yorkshire is always the last bastion of common sense. Like the bloody resistance, we are' [*1980*, 29]. To its natives, Peace's Yorkshire is an independent state with its own rules and rulers. Fiercely defensive of their region, its history and people, characters use the county as a hunting ground and attempt to lay claim to a terrain in turmoil. Across the quartet, Yorkshiremen call on regional and, at times, quasi-tribal loyalties to reiterate and reinforce their relatively independent status, charting an ongoing battle for ownership and control of the region at large.

In *1974* the battle for Yorkshire opens with Eddie and Jack, two competing crime correspondents engaged in a battle for control over the county as 'their' land or territory. New boy Eddie is repeatedly made aware of the influence of his predecessor – 'thinking this is Jack's country not mine' [*1974*, 102] – while Jack's knowledge and movement through Yorkshire is described in terms of possession, 'my road' [*1977*, 192]. As the quartet develops, this battle for control extends from reporters and police to the Ripper himself. Early in the investigation Jack's headline for the *Yorkshire Post* implicitly connects the killer to the region, 'Yesterday's news, tomorrow's headline:

The Yorkshire Ripper' [*1977*, 71]. This is underlined by Peter Hunter, who firmly aligns ownership of Yorkshire to 'their killer'

[*1980*, 26], while George Oldman warns during a press conference that all women are at risk in '*Ripper Country*' [*1980*, 192]. Once implicitly connected to a specific place, 'The Yorkshire Ripper' becomes a highly charged moniker.[19] By this point Yorkshire is firmly and frighteningly '*His*' [*1980*, 19], a region clearly under the control of a killer. Peace has argued that '*Red Riding* is about the defeat of Yorkshire, that was the effect this killer had on that place, and the police's failure to catch him'.[20] As a symbol of freedom and absolute action, the Ripper poses a significant threat to the precarious governance of the county during the 1970s and 1980s. The male characters who pursue him are symbols of authority and power and his continued attacks are perceived as an affront to their control. As a result of this struggle, Yorkshire becomes a power vacuum, an effective 'no-man's-land' in a wider war of possession.

Peace's North is a museum of time and place, a space invested with human meaning and codified history. As a grim site of regional devotion, it offers a distinct counter-narrative on an alternative, yet insistent, past. Throughout the quartet, landscape is employed as an articulating vestige of experience, representing 'many interwoven layers of power [. . .] race, gender, class and local identity politics'.[21] Brannigan argues that the 'representation of landscape in literary texts [. . .] is related to and embedded in social and political structures'.[22] While many spaces become charged with meanings over time, the *Red Riding Quartet* takes pains to show how social, economic and cultural deterioration can shape the image of a region. From the new Ridings shopping centre and Shangrila, Millgarth and Stanley Royd, the *Red Riding Quartet* is suggestive of the ways in which landscape can both reflect and articulate social periphery and geographic marginality.

In an environment of threat and neglect scarred by fragmentation both physical and metaphoric, Peace grants symbolic dimensions to space. However, his vision is not one of provincialism. In his quartet, Yorkshire and the North of England are presented as diffuse and decentralized, but specific in terms of environment and socio-cultural anxieties about relationalism. Vistas emerge from the anxieties of the characters and the people of the regions as sites of atrocity and places of memory. Re-mapping the psycho-geography of the UK during the 1970s and 1980s, Peace reconfigures previous assumptions as well as inscribing new meanings to well-known places and spaces. Re-visioning familiar landscapes as a means of accessing a psychological inscape of suffering, psychosis and trauma, Peace uses space as an extension or manifestation of his characters' doubts and fears. Illuminating memories carved into the built and natural environment, his novels offer the Yorkshire of the 1970s and 1980s as a dynamic site of memory and meaning.

Collectively, the *Red Riding Quartet* not only offers a political representation of landscape, but landscape as a political form of representation. Localizing his representations of 1970s and 1980s Britain, Peace documents a geography of the imagination, but also of the recognizable physical world. Through his fictional landscapes, Peace enters into a wider debate concerning trauma, the uncertainty of the present and a legacy of displacement and fracture. His desolate tableau layers terrors and dream images, accentuating troubled and traumatic narratives. Excavating and altering familiar landscapes, his novels question the origins of these places and in doing so establish new formal and thematic relationships. Provoking unease and revelation, Yorkshire and the North of England are represented in unexpected new lights to create disturbing juxtapositions. Setting Leeds against the Moors and Yorkshire against a wider (dis)United Kingdom, the quartet interrogates physical and psychological relationships to suggest that while literary landscapes can be knowable places, they remain impossible to 'locate' definitively.

chapter two

Words Fail

'In prose, the worst thing one can do with words is surrender to them.'
[George Orwell, 1950]

NO WOMAN SAFE

Throughout the *Red Riding Quartet,* dialogic relations between individual narrative voices combine with disparate and contradictory rhetorical genres, jarring in a 'tension-filled environment' to create a dynamic and evolving war of words.[1] In Peace's work power is implicitly aligned to a mastery of language, asserted in competitive exchange and contested between dominant and marginal groups. This chapter suggests that his quartet mobilizes socio-ideological discourses of gender, religion and temporality to interrogate heteroglossic exchange as a key site of contemporary social, political and cultural conflict.

Language does not exist in a social vacuum and as a result the *Red Riding Quartet* is very much a reflection of both the discourses operating in 1970s and 1980s Britain and the capacity of its literary form. Russian linguist Mikhail Bakhtin argues that the novel should exhibit a sense of 'the historical and social concreteness of living discourse [. . .] a feeling for its participation in historical becoming and in social struggle'.[2] Peace mobilizes graphic and unrelenting male voices to dominate the blank prose of the quartet through an extremity of language and subject matter. His narratives regularly alternate between a range of named narrators to explore a series of exclusively male voices. As each character constructs their position narratively, they seek to impose order on inherently disorderly events, using a language that is 'shot through with intentions and accents'.[3] There are no neutral words in Peace's work. Deeply flavoured by the intentions of the speaker and sourced in the very specific knowledge and experience of the period, the competing narratives of the *Red Riding Quartet* intersect to produce a world represented solely through the eyes of men.

A tight focus on male experience is accentuated through the employment of narrative modes that function to draw us closer to male characters, initially Eddie Dunford in *1974*, then Bob Fraser in *1977*, Peter Hunter in *1980* and finally John Piggott in *1983*. Often events are so horrific that these men are reduced to documenting what is happening in the present tense as a means of coping. Their narratives are dominated by the use of 'I', personal verbs creating an immediate, colloquial and dramatic effect. As journalist Eddie Dunford approaches the Strafford Pub in *1974*, his actions are broken down into a first-person step-by-step account:

> I parked outside a shoe shop.
> I opened the boot.
> I took the shotgun out of the black bin-bag.
> I loaded the gun in the boot of the car.
> I put some more shells in my pocket.
> I took the shotgun out of the boot.
> I closed the boot of the car.
> I walked across the Bullring. [*1974*, 293]

Eddie's tightly personal voice is offered as an apparent primary source of information, lived experience enabling the personified narrator to become a distinct character. Providing a systematic level of detail, the first-person mode implicates the reader in his crime and its moral and legal consequences.

Peace writes about a time in which men enjoy dominance and preference. The press are addressed as 'gentlemen' [*1974*, 6] or 'Paper Lads' [*1974*, 26], despite the presence of female journalists, and gradually become animalized as 'The Pack' [*1974*, 28]. Eddie experiences the thrill of their chase, hearing 'The blood of one hundred men pumping hard and fast, hounds the lot of us, the stink of the hunt like bloody marks upon our brows' [*1977*, 8]. The spaces of the press conference, the crime scene and the investigation room are charged with testosterone, dominated by groups of men 'copying, checking, re-checking, like a gang of fucking monks hunched over some holy book' [*1977*, 54]. Competitive in their actions as well as their verbal exchanges, Peace's male characters engage with language in an attempt to define their own masculinity. Men do not just drink alcohol but devour it – 'Barry took a big bite out of his pint' [*1974*, 58] – gaining perverse pleasure from pain and endurance: 'It tasted fucking shit, so fucking shit I found another cup of cold coffee on another desk and had another bloody one' [*1974*, 100]. Hooked on work, drink or food, male characters utilize metaphors of reason and speak in terms of hyper-individualism. These are, in the words of Mrs Dawson, 'reckless men' [*1974*, 145], occupying a space constructed on the basis of their personal power. Derek Box's early assertion that 'Power's like glue. It sticks men like us together, keeps everything in place' [*1974*, 212] establishes an early understanding of the relations underpinning the many male voices of the quartet.

In an apparently wilful abolition of soft language, performative acts of masculinity position men and male experience as the exclusive focus of these novels. There is little room for romance in the quartet – Peace's prose is concerned with illness and injury, violence and vomiting, the collapse of physical and public bodies, dissatisfaction and dirt. Eddie reports his own sickness in terms of competitive consumption, reflecting that 'It hurt and it burned as it all came up, but I didn't want it to ever stop. And, when it finally did, I stared a long time at the whisky and the ham, at the bits in the bog and the bits on the floor' [*1974*, 21]. By *1983*, the practice of vomiting has become systematic as solicitor John Piggott documents another morning of suffering with jaded predictability: 'She leaves. You puke. You dress. You puke again. You clean your teeth. You lock the door. You retch. You go downstairs. You heave. You run back up the stairs. You puke in your hands. You open the door. You puke on the floor. You spew. You start all over again' [*1983*, 106]. Across the quartet, vomiting occurs with alarming regularity, a need for physical expulsion that is symptomatic of a wider social sickness.

Conjuring up the vocabulary of 1970s and 1980s Yorkshire, Peace constructs an emotive soundtrack to his masculine world. Dominated by 'the liver and the onions, the dartboard and the bar' [*1977*, 65], the panic of the personal to the diegetic 'click of pool balls from behind the glass doors' [*1974*, 229], suspense is articulated through male experience to break narrative tension or reveal internal terrors. This can take the form of onomatopoeic resonance in the 'CRACK!

SMASH!' [*1983*, 107] of physical damage, or the heightened state of terror revealed by characters' frantic reactions: 'Outside in the night, a car door slammed.

I jumped up, out of my skin, screaming' [*1974*, 170]. Language functions to provide emphasis and accent to male emotion, a low rhythmic quality rendering these urgent and doom-laden tones an appropriate baseline to the quartet. The physical construction and reiteration of words suggests a very immediate form of fear – 'scrrrrrrrrrrrrrrrrrrrrrrreaming' [*1977*, 323]; '*Fuck, fuck, fuck, fuck, fuck, fuck, fuck, fuck, fuck,* fuck' [*1983*, 17] – as panic slowly penetrates the narrative. In a world where everyone seems on edge and nervous, it is unsurprising that Eddie's mantra quickly becomes his heart 'beating ninety miles an hour' [*1974*, 197], an insistent claim that creates a pounding rhythm of fear and frustration.

Words frequently fail men, forcing them to struggle for a language to represent the horrors they encounter. Even the usually verbose Derek Box admits that sometimes 'There aren't words' [*1974*, 183]. Eddie turns to the written word in times of trouble, but finds that it fails to deliver the catharsis he desperately desires. He recalls searching 'for my pen, as though writing something, anything, might make it all seem a bit better than it was, or a little less real [. . .] it didn't help at all' [*1974*, 48]. Incapable of mobilizing words adequate to capture the horror of the evolving Ripper murders, fellow journalist Jack Whitehead finds himself able to form 'Just a pile of rusty little words, all linked up to make a chain of horror' [*1977*, 33]. Breaking his own reportage into recycled units of representation, Jack highlights the limitations of language during times of profound crisis. Unable to control his own representation of events, Jack's power over language wanes as he, like Eddie, comes to realize that 'the words wouldn't obey me' [*1977*, 35].

Signalling a broader sense of impotence, personal and professional struggles with language draw attention to silence as an operative form of power, as an absence of words is slowly connected to the dark forces of police cover-ups and business censorship. George Oldman demands that Eddie breathe 'Not a bloody word' [*1974*, 26], limiting communication under the tight, unspoken regulations of the West Yorkshire Police, while imposed silences extend across the media in the form of sanctioned 'Reporting restrictions' [*1974*, 176]. Jack becomes consumed by the guilt of his own silence, of the 'things I should've written and the things I had' [*1977*, 34].[4] In an attempt to regain power over language he scrawls across his editor's copy sheet, '*It's not him*' [*1977*, 134]. Authored in the margins of an existing text, Jack's counter-narrative contests the power of the written word to provide a definitive account of events. As the Ripper case develops, Jack grows increasingly conscious of his own journalism, noting the voyeuristic and sensationalist nature of its language: 'Butchered. I never used *savage* and *brutally* so many times, did I?' [*1977*, 207]. Focusing on the power of the single letter or composite word, Peace draws us into an investigation founded on a particular kind of language, from the highly charged 'Ripper' to the 'Brains Trust' and 'Super Squad' [*1980*, 217] who pursue him.[5]

While the male characters of the *Red Riding Quartet* are associated with reason, determination and detection, its female characters are aligned with nature, the home and mysticism and denied a narrative voice. Peace's Yorkshire is populated by a disturbing array of physically and morally repugnant women. From George Oldman's secretaries Julie [*1974*, 23] and Fat Steph to the 'crazy fucking bitch' [*1974*, 126] Mandy Wymer, women are consistently consigned to professionally marginal roles. Others like Marjorie Dawson and Clare Strachan, who 'used to stare out the window and bark at the trains' [*1977*, 45], are disempowered through male accusations of mental illness and sidelined from society [*1974*, 142]. Journalist Kathryn Taylor functions as a more positive representation of women in these texts and has risen to Chief Reporter by *1983*. However, she is also subject to male prejudice – 'I'm not your bloody secretary. I'm a fucking journalist too' [*1974*, 43] – and is punished for her sexual relationship with Eddie through having to undergo an abortion.

Consistently presented at the mercy of words, women are constructed by, and forced to navigate, a language that marks out male characters in an authoritative, intensive and effective form of control. Women's language cannot penetrate the interiority of Peace's masculine world and as a result female characters are regularly subject to semantic derogations and asymmetrical representations. Positioned firmly outside the tightly masculine structure of Yorkshire, women's lives remain largely unexplored. Where male characters choose to facilitate the telling of women's narratives, these are transcribed as 'reports' that do not privilege the teller's experience but rather call it into question. Newspapers are quick to point out that while the Ripper is at large there is 'NO WOMAN SAFE' [*1977*, 190], colluding to construct a disabling image of 'millions of women trapped inside their homes, dependent on lifts from fathers and brothers, husbands and sons, any one of whom might be the Yorkshire Ripper himself' [*1980*, 218]. Subject to systems of oppression that are accepted or validated by the patriarchal groupings around them, female characters are left in a vulnerable position, caught between the Ripper, their husbands and male relatives, subject to a profound form of paternalism with all its well-intended regulations, degrees of care and implied compassion.

The language used by male characters to refer to and communicate with women reveals their anxieties, fears and prejudices about the opposite sex. Female kinship terms such as 'wife' and 'aunt' are subject to overt derogation as motherhood is relegated to the sidelines of the action.[6] Women are regularly cast as victims, losing their children, husbands and even their own lives at the hands of men. By *1980* Peter Hunter has become obsessed with a growing list of 'Motherless children, childless mothers' [*1980*, 12] who fall victim to predatory, aggressive males. Justified as part of a wider search for 'answers', violence against women is seen to operate at every level of society. In *1974* Eddie forces access to Mrs Ashworth's home, 'knocking past her into one of her saggy tits' [*1974*, 206], a scene later mirrored by the police's assault on his own mother. Bob Fraser regularly abuses his power as a police officer to invade women's homes, manipulating their fears of rape to gain access. He reflects that his victim is 'too busy thinking about hiding, thinking she's going to get raped, which is what I want her to think so she'll stay in the room' [*1977*, 76]. Physical expressions of anger against women become more frequent as the novel develops, culminating in the anal rape of a local prostitute [*1977*, 139]. As a 'working girl' Janice Ryan is only acceptable to Fraser as '*my own private whore*' [*1977*, 88], a sense of ownership and exclusivity fuelling his desire to bring this woman off the streets and into his bed.

Male characters eagerly take advantage of female sexuality, using and abusing women as objects of desire and domination. Framing beauty in terms of exploitation rather than celebration, men demonstrate power through their domination of the female body. In a world saturated with sex, readers are encouraged to look 'at the cocks and balls, at the hands and the tongues, the spit and the spunk' [*1974*, 186]. The sexualized female is frequently subject to the murderous thoughts of the male gaze or undermined by perceived flaws and faults. Even a stripper is notable only for 'her arse fat with spots' [*1977*, 87]. In Peace's periodicized construction of sexuality, older women are particularly desexualized and demonized. 'The Widow Sheard' is defined by 'her memories and her lies' [*1974*, 62], dwelling in 'her cold black hole of a room' [*1974*, 63], while Mrs Marsh is a 'hard-faced bitch' with a 'pinched little fucking smile' [*1974*, 277]. The discovery of her husband's underground interests elicits 'laughing and screaming, her whole body shaking, one hand flailing through the plastic sacks upon the floor, the other squeezing her skirt up into her cunt' [*1974*, 279], a response used by Eddie to justify assaulting her. One caller to *The John Shark Show* even moans,

'*Women eh? Can't live with them, can't kill 'em.*

'*Cept round Chapeltown*' [*1977*, 2]. This reference to the evolving Ripper case offers an early indication of the approach adopted by the West Yorkshire Police in subsequent novels. The female victim is nothing more than a 'Silly slag' [*1977*, 5], attention falling on female beauty rather than on the responsibility of the killer:

"'Come both times, though I don't know how he fucking did it. State of her."

"Ugly?"

"Doesn't begin to describe it'" [*1977*, 40]. This perspective only changes when the Ripper claims his first 'innocent' victim, a woman who 'wasn't a slag, she was a good girl' [*1977*, 183].[7]

Women remain severely lacking in agency throughout Peace's work. Police investigations draw upon an existing dossier concerning '*Murder and Assaults Upon Women in the North of England*' [*1977*, 67], positioning the Ripper as part of a wider problem, sourced in the language and culture of the period.[8] Restricting opportunities for women to gather and communicate, acts of male violence ensure their firm and forceful relegation to the sphere of the domestic.[9] That women appear at all in this breakneck masculine world is quite amazing. Consigned to the home, murdered or marginalized, women's interests and interactions are sidelined. The *Red Riding Quartet* does not amplify women's memories, documenting narratives of survival rather than expression. Male language dismembers women as men dominate their conversations and communications. Exercising control over how women view themselves and their lives, the masculine prosaic of Peace's Yorkshire is both a vehicle of power and a prison in which female characters must operate. Employing words burning with the passions and hostilities of intra- and inter-gendered conflict, Peace's highly competitive prose forms part of a sustained interrogation of speech and rhetoric, language and subjectivity across the quartet.

No *Revelation*

Although Yorkshire is popularly known as 'God's Own County', God is regularly questioned in the *Red Riding Quartet* as part of a wider existential debate. Across the quartet, religious language is presented as a form of twisted prayer, motivated and directed against competing claims on reality. Incanted in moments of fear, confusion or doubt, prayers are born from marginality and transience. Eddie Dunford's desperation initially leads him to offer up 'another prayer from the steering wheel' [*1974*, 13], but later charts a growing recognition of the loving power of prayer as he notes: 'for the first time my prayers were not for me but for everyone else [. . .] that the dead were alive and the lost were found [. . .] then I prayed for my mother and sister, for my uncles and aunts, for the friends I'd had, both good and bad, and last for my father wherever he was, Amen' [*1974*, 240]. Encouraging reflection and compassion, prayers offer a form of comforting dialogue during periods of abject isolation and can even evolve into proposed deals with the divine. Uttering 'My new deal, my new prayer' [*1980*, 223], Assistant Chief Constable Peter Hunter prays for a child with his wife and suggests that he would be prepared to 'make that deal again:

I catch him, stop him murdering mothers, orphaning children, then you give us one, just one' [*1980*, 12–13].[10] As much an act as a language, Hunter's prayer negotiates a sequence of words in conflict with a variety of alternative entreaties. His plea transforms the language of prayer into a form of capitalist exchange, transporting a divine request for answers into a trade-off between action and response.

Utilizing the performative power of prayer, characters turn to biblical doctrine in an attempt to comprehend the strangeness of their immediate situation. One anonymous caller to *The John Shark Show* takes particular pride in regularly reading his Bible, quoting to the host 'And the rest of the men which were not killed by these plagues yet repented not of the words of their hands, that they should not worship devils and idols of gold, and silver, and brass, and stone, and of wood, which neither can see, nor hear, nor walk [. . .] Neither repented they of their murders, nor of their sorceries, nor of their fornication, nor of their thefts' [*1977*, 334]. This extract from Revelation 9:20 offers an early warning of internal corruption, disavowing the worship of capitalism over a spiritual God. Many crimes in the quartet are motivated by greed, a desire to exercise control and achieve power. While religion is sometimes challenged, and on occasion rejected, in favour of money and business, characters nevertheless continue to raise religious language as an attempt to find moral guidance or wider meaning.

The child murders that cast a long shadow over *1974* evoke a stark morality in characters – 'Evil they were, just plain bloody evil' [*1974*, 12] – but the series as a whole suggests that demarcations of good and evil are not always simple. The Voltaire claim raised by Part Five of *1983* – '*Every man is guilty of all the good he did not do*' [*1983*, 364] – implies that moral culpability lies as much with those who turn the other way as with those who put into action these terrible deeds. Encouraging awareness of the responsibility of the individual to others as well as to the self, choice and morality are pivotal to future plot developments. As the biblical preface to *1977* warns:

> *When a righteous man*
> *turneth away from his righteousness,*
> *and committeth iniquity, and dieth in them;*
> *for his iniquity that he hath done*
> *shall he die.*
> *Again, when the wicked man*
> *turneth away from his wickedness*
> *that he hath committed, and doeth that*
> *which is lawful and right,*
> *he shall save his soul.*
> Ezekiel 18:26–27 [*1977*, Preface]

The true penitent is a true believer in this doctrine; the pardoning quality of mercy is tied closely to themes of redemption and forgiveness. Underscoring the agency of the individual, this is an entirely appropriate preface to *1977*, a novel in which policeman Bob Fraser and journalist Jack Whitehead are forced to confront weighty moral choices. Providing an early indication of the vividly symbolic language in operation throughout the quartet, the Preface of *1977* offers a promise of God's strengthening power, but also questions the moral choices of the individuals whose actions shape this fictional world, suggesting that the answers they seek may already be known to them.

Possible answers are suggested by the malignant presence of an old woman and young boy who biblically haunt journalist Jack

Whitehead, Assistant Chief Constable Peter Hunter and solicitor John Piggott. Jack takes a copy of the Bible from the pair at Leeds Cathedral and finds it open on Psalm 88. The psalm's appeal by a man whose '*soul is full of troubles*' [*1977*, 132] outlines the torment of one who finds himself the victim of God's wrath despite his own moral behaviour. The man asks, '*O Lord, why do you cast me off* in a time when '*your dread assaults destroy me.*

They surround me like a flood all day long;
from all sides they close in on me' [*1977*, 133].

The deeply despondent nature of Psalm 88 suggests that the author is a fellow sufferer who, like Jack, is drowning without a single hope or expectation of light. In deep despair, abandoned by friends and apparently forsaken by God, his lamentation does not end with hopes of joy to come. Communicating the sorrows of one saint to another, its fragmentatory appeal requests mercy, deliverance and an explanation of the incoherence of grief. The psalm suggests that to those who live in sin, God remains the only salvation. Jack is unable to comprehend this 'answer', running 'from the Cathedral' [*1977*, 134] back to the Griffin Hotel. Returning to Leeds Cathedral later in the novel, Jack takes another Bible from the old lady and child to read, '*During that time these men will seek death, but they will not find it; They will long to die, but death will elude them*' [*1977*, 310]. This extract from Revelation 9:6 suggests that his pain will become a matter of endurance. Death is a much longed-for but absent element in Jack's life, his engagement with the language of religious doctrine encouraging the confrontation of past trauma.

When John Piggott enters St Anne's Church in *1983* he is also approached by a 'familiar' old woman and young boy who hand him a Bible open at Job 30:26–31. Chronicling one man's trials at the hands of God, the book of Job explores the nature of suffering, the problem of evil and the co-existence of God. Piggott's extract claims that the writer is '*a brother to dragons,*

And a companion to owls' [*1983*, 214]. Evoking images associated with a range of the quartet's darkest characters, Job highlights the inter-related nature of good and evil as well as the thin line separating hunter and hunted. The book of Job suggests that a sense of pain and loss is valid, appealing to Piggott as an acknowledgement that his own suffering has meaning and fuelling his quest for 'answers'.

In a world of questions well suited to a mystery narrative, religion is perceived as a means of guiding characters, but the answers it offers are not always convincing. In *1980* Peter Hunter literally 'hunts' the Bible, specifically seeking out the book of Revelation. Flicking through the book, he finds '*Revelation,* gone

No *Revelation* –

Not tonight' [*1980,* 325]. Although Hunter is unable to locate the book of Revelation, the true 'revelations' of the quartet do not come from a holy book but from a series of unassuming, forbidden documents. Having exhausted religious doctrine, characters turn to alternative forms of wisdom in the form of *Spunk* magazines and copies of grainy black-and-white photographs. These items become crucial documents warranting close study of the kind usually only afforded to biblical texts. As a sign of this shift, Hunter sees the word 'Exegesis' [*1980,* 142] etched on his chest, an outward mark of his internal drive to discover the 'answers' concealed by these documents.

Futile searches for 'revelation' lead some characters to engage with the languages of 'magick' and astrology as an attempt to make sense of the chaos around them. The Voltaire quote that prefaces chapter 23 of *1983* – '*The Christian Church has always condemned magick, but she has always believed in it. She did not excommunicate sorcerers as madmen who were mistaken, but as men who were really in communion with the Devil*' [*1983,* 160] – suggests that religious language is only one of all possible languages, of which magick is another.[11] Widely understood to relate to acts undertaken through a personal need to initiate change, magick penetrates the *Red Riding Quartet* to highlight tensions between competing claims to truth.[12] John Piggott turns to astrology to forecast his own ascendency, charting 'The scales falling, the Pig rising' [*1983,* 69], while the West Yorkshire Police experiment with the spiritualism of Mystic Mandy in an attempt to discover the whereabouts of missing children.

Magick extends to the influence of numerology through mystical connections to the number seven. Biblically associated with creation, sins and sacraments, this powerfully magic number is historically related to the spiritual as well to the division of time and the ordering of human life. Taken from the book of Revelation and brought to bear on Peace's narrative, the 'two sevens' [*1977,* 14] connect in the Jubilee celebrations of *1977* as a warning of mystic culmination and confrontation.[13] In Room 77 of the Griffin Hotel – the space Peter Hunter later occupies during the Ripper investigation – Jack witnesses 'the two sevens clash' [*1977,* 338], while John

Piggott notes that Michael Myshkin appears '*As if by magick*' [*1983*, 10].[14]

As the quartet develops, the language of magick is extended in the form of a 'hex', a malevolent curse used to bewitch. Chanted as a bearer of bad luck or a wish for misfortune, the hex is commonly associated with a form of witchcraft worked by amateurs. Connected to the world of black magic and the deployment of charms or talismans, it can be used to rid oneself of unwanted influences or to break a curse. In the *Red Riding Quartet* the word is chanted by characters as a way of signalling misfortune or personal harm. Initially associated with the curse of Jack's memories of his ex-wife Carol, the hex extends to Peter Hunter whose home becomes personally 'hex'd' [*1980*, 148], consonance revealing the rhythmic operation of the incantation on the cursed individual.

Competing languages of magick, superstition and faith reach a pinnacle in the character of Reverend Laws. Martin Laws is an ever-growing presence, from the shadows of the Marshes' home in *1974* to the forefront of the quartet's dramatic conclusion in *1983*. Presented as a person worthy of respect, his role in the local community involves the abuse of religious discourse through the conditioning of residents to his own perverted brand of 'faith'. Laws is quite simply a law unto himself, condemned by bishops and set against the rationality and reason of the police. Manipulating religious vocabulary and syntax and echoing the Quaker use of 'thee', he appeals directly to those suffering with a promise of relief, claiming that he 'can make it go away' [*1977*, 105]. Preaching an acceptance of the status quo and a reliance on his own wisdom and guidance, Laws encourages a profoundly fatalistic approach to personal and social trauma. His advice is simply that 'if the Bible teaches us nothing else, it teaches us that this is the way things are, the way things have always been, and will always be until the end' [*1977*, 291].[15]

Peace draws a close alignment between Laws and the 1973 film *The Exorcist. The Exorcist* explores evil and the mystery of faith and, like the Laws case, was purportedly based on real events.[16] The practice of evicting evil spirits or demons from a host body is usually executed by a member of the church with special skills. This person may use prayers, gestures, symbols and icons to rid the presence, evoking god or angels to drive out evil forces. In the *Red Riding Quartet* the practice of exorcism is related to the murder of Jack's ex-wife Carol and his memories of what the local press termed 'The

Exorcist Killing'.[17] As a result of this incident Jack endures a strained and complicated relationship with Laws, defiant of his piety, reliant on his guidance and vulnerable to his authority in times of doubt.

When the pair meet again in *1977*, Jack notes that Laws is 'still wearing that hat and coat, despite the weather, to spite the weather, still carrying that case, just like the last time' [*1977*, 102–3]. His bitter assessment of Laws as a 'hypocritical cunt, sat there all pompous and papal in your dirty old raincoat with your hat on your cock and your little bag of secrets, your cross and your prayers, your hammer and your nails, blessing the fucking wogs, turning the tea into wine' [*1977*, 104] suggests an intense personal awareness of this man's strengths and limitations. Challenging his piety as an extension of self-interest, greed and will-to-power, Jack sees through Laws's quasi-religious facade to the abuser beneath.

Hiding behind a mask of religious authority and moral obligation, this *'Father of Fear'* [*1983*, 193] lies at the heart of a web of sexual and political abuse. As the 'Northern Son', BJ finally slays his 'Black Angel' [*1983*, 193] in an ultimate act of revenge, destroying Laws with a passion and conviction that can only come from a relationship built on exploitation. BJ's final monologue sets personal suffering against a country in spiritual, political, economic and social decline, claiming the life of Laws 'for every little lad you ever fucked and all their dads who liked to watch, with their cameras in their hands and their cocks in my arse, your tongue in my mouth and your lies in my ear, loving you loving me, his nails in my hands and yours in my head [. . .] Goodbye Dragon' [*1983*, 400]. This farewell effectively implicates Laws in the underground kingdom of George Marsh, bringing the reader back to the opening horrors of *1974* and the many unseen victims of Laws's abandoned church.

Throughout the *Red Riding Quartet* religious language is raised to lay claims to truth as well as to question notions of good and evil. The novels demonstrate that the 'language of religion, like the language of imaginative literature, is a rich and complex fabric, a separate, though not clearly separable, type of discourse'.[18] Peace has outlined the significance of religion to the quartet, claiming that 'I don't distinguish between religion and politics; just as everything is political, so it is religious. For me politics is the asking of questions, religion the receiving of answers.'[19] The world of *Red Riding* is not Godless, but situated explicitly in 'The Year of Our Lord'. The darkness of the quartet is finally rationalized as a form of eclipse from which 'the sun will shine again' [*1983*, 403]. *1983* accordingly ends with a motif of repentance, leading Detective Chief Superintendent Maurice Jobson to salvation through a vision of Clare Kemplay's ghost. This final image offers a form of atonement to the horrors that precede it, the mobilization of religious discourse illuminating relations between two forms of knowledge and spheres of reality. Peace argues that 'faced with the terrible brutality in these books [. . .] I strongly think you have to believe in God, that there's something better within us all and something worth saving that will triumph in the face of whatever you're put through'.[20] Concerned with the initiation of revelations, the exploration of a theology of falsification and the regulation of characters' lives, religious language aids personal searches for the transcendent, for something above all this, offering hope and meaning which enter into dialogic exchange with contesting systems of control and representation. Interlocking languages in bleak, feverish exchange, the *Red Riding Quartet* positions religious discourse in close competition with other languages offering similarly invocative and value-laden 'answers' during the period.

It was happening all over again

Charting split times, perceptions and memories, the *Red Riding Quartet* moves through the 1970s and 1980s with accelerating speed. Rethinking the diverse ways in which time is experienced, each novel is underpinned by a sense of time running out, temporal flow fracturing as recognized markers of time are destroyed or discarded. The past has not gone away in this work, but shifts to articulate itself in new ways. Characters quickly lose grasp of time and begin to doubt their sense of temporality. As Jack muses in *1977*, '*Time?* I didn't even know what fucking year it was' [*1977*, 25]. The progress of the Ripper investigation seems to confound the forward drive of time, taking '*Two steps forward, six steps back*' [*1977*, 39], sinking its participants into 'Circles and secrets, secrets and circles' [*1977*, 277]. In a perpetual state of motion, Peace's novels are rarely synchronized beyond the date of their titles, shifting parameters of space and time demanding a constant readjustment of awareness.

The structure imposed on the quartet is based on thematic divisions in which contrast, repetition and framing form central narrative tools. Articulating the disparate nature of experience as well as the disconnected nature of the contemporary world, each novel is framed by repetition, opening with an evolving series of begs ('Beg', 'Beg again', 'Beg, beg, beg' and finally 'The last beg'), demanding further revelation and relief from the unfolding horrors of the quartet. Used to access alternative perspectives, the reiteration of language illuminates connections between otherwise incongruent events. Combining journalistic dictation with the framing of his own narrative, journalist Eddie Dunford repeats facts as part of a wider attempt to achieve closure:

> Barry's story: 3 rich men: John Dawson, Donald Foster, and a third who Barry couldn't or wouldn't name.
> My story: 3 dead girls: Jeanette, Susan and Clare.
> My story, his story – two stories: Same times, same places, different names, different faces.
> Mystery, History:
> One Link? [*1974*, 110]

The repetition of facts becomes a regular feature of subsequent novels as characters create lists to impose order and coherence on a growing quantity of conflicting information:

> Lists of names.
> Lists of dates.
> Lists of places.
> Lists of girls.
> Lists of boys.
> Lists of the corrupt, the corrupted, and the corruptible.
> Lists of the police.
> Lists of the witnesses.
> Lists of the families.
> Lists of the missing.
> Lists of the accused.
> Lists of the dead.
> I was drowning in lists, drowning in information. [*1974*, 201]

Setting the centrifugal force of the police investigation against competing centripetalizing narratives, language becomes subject to a drive for coherence, centralizing opportunities for variance. As the investigation into the Ripper develops, lists become increasingly specific and emotive, documenting a growing collection of victims, weapons and crime scene measurements:

Jobson.
Bird.
Campbell.
Strachan.
Richards.
Peng.
Watts.
Clark.
Johnson.
On every wall, words:
Screwdriver.
Abdomen.
Boots.
Chest.
Hammer.
Skull.
Bottle.
Rectum.
Knife.
On every wall, numbers:
1.3"
1974.
32.
1975.
239+584.
1976.
X3.
1977.
3.5. [*1977*, 179]

Physically disassociated from one another, words and numbers highlight the dehumanizing effect of a police investigation centred on language. Each seemingly innocent unit interacts with those around it to create an increasingly complicated and sprawling network of information and intrigue.

The language of narrative time shifts to shape this gradual piecing together of words and numbers, incidents and evidence. *1974* begins in a broadly chronological fashion, documenting the breakdown of Eddie Dunford in the face of the corruption of the West Yorkshire Police, the events leading up to the Strafford shootings and the arrest of Michael Myshkin. The systematic approach of Peter Hunter and the structured nature of his investigation are initially reflected in the narrative ordering of *1980*. As this structure becomes punctuated by past events, memories and letters, it charts a progressive breakdown in confidence and clarity. Dates and numbers take on an even greater significance in the final novel, *1983*, as its strictly alternating chapters jump freely and unapologetically from 1969 to 1983 and back again. The suggestion in *1977* that we should:

'Start at the finish.

Begin at the end' [*1977*, 150] is suggestive of this cyclical approach to the past.

The nature of the return is initially explored through the act of homecoming. Eddie Dunford and John Piggott bookend the quartet with individual homecomings to the North of England. Each man returns to Yorkshire because he recognizes a *genius loci*, a sense of place that comes from the memories it holds. The influence of place extends to the act of ritual and Part One of *1974* is accordingly entitled 'Yorkshire Wants Me', an elemental call from the homeland to Brighton-exiled Eddie Dunford. In coming back to the North, Eddie and John share not only the same landscape but also similar memories. Their returns signal a submission to the lure of the local, the familiar now made uncanny through death and destruction. These known spaces prove far from redemptive, a return to the landscapes of their childhoods marking a point at which the lives of both men begin to go horribly wrong.

The ritual of return also extends to crime and deviancy. Jack attempts to re-enact Ka Sun Peng's attack [*1977*, 163], while the Ripper murders evidence a desire for re-enactment, bearing 'some obvious similarities' [*1977*, 29] to one another. Flavoured by repetition and return, these deviant acts encourage new perspectives on 'known' spaces. Peace increasingly draws attention to covert uses of space in time, to 'the playing field [. . .] where the children played their games and their fathers murdered their mothers' [*1977*, 164], or the 'ordinary street in the ordinary suburb where a man took a hammer and a knife to Laureen Bell, an ordinary girl' [*1980*, 75].

The world of *Red Riding* is frighteningly small and characters frequently visit the same spaces, circling locations in quick succession. Each visit offers new perspectives, encouraging the re-reading of material in light of new evidence. The quasi-musical refrain '*it's happening all over again*' echoes across the quartet as characters trace and retrace one another's steps. Occupying the same flat as the recently deceased Mystic Mandy, John Piggott reminds us that 'we all live in dead people's houses' [*1983*, 90], while Room 27 of the Redbeck Cafe and Motel is ritually transferred from Eddie Dunford to Bob Fraser and finally to John Piggott as a secret space of knowledge and detection. Piggott identifies the room as '*the place, the time*' [*1983*, 236], a tangled, circled site of space/time intersection defined by the ritual of return. As a self-confessed 'space invader' [*1983*, 34], BJ is perhaps the ultimate example of this movement through time and space.

In novels that offer déjà vu as a structuring principle, time is frequently repeated, returned to or doubted; in Peace's Yorkshire, relativity itself is brought into question. A futile strain against the forces of time extends to the pervading problem of the Ripper. As victim Anita Bird claims of her attack, 'Sometimes it seems like a lifetime ago, other times like it was just yesterday' [*1977*, 99]. By *1980*, the monotony of the hunt for the Ripper has become a time-consuming nightmare, 'Year after year, month after month, week after week, day after day, hour after hour, minute in, minute out, second in, second out, for –

Five years' [*1980*, 45]. Assistant Chief Constable Peter Hunter describes the investigation as simply,

'*Process –*

Repetitive, tedious process' [*1980*, 45]. The futility of this repetition reaches a zenith in *1983* as solicitor John Piggott drives

all night; drive in circles;
Disintegrating –
Disappearing –
Decreasing –
Declining –
Decaying –
Dying –
Dead –
Circles; circles of hell; local hells. [*1983*, 85]

The Voltaire quote used as an epigraph to Part One of *1983* warns the reader, '*History does not repeat itself, only man*' [*1983*, 2]. Retreading the steps of others', characters become paranoid that they have '*been here before*' [*1983*, 284]. It is almost impossible to escape this sense of 'Déjà bloody vu' [*1983*, 25] as the concept of temporally finite episodes is confronted and confounded. Journalist Jack Whitehead quickly realizes that it is '*Eddie, Eddie, Eddie*, always back to Eddie' [*1977*, 283] as events conspire to draw us back to where we began in *1974*. Peace's cyclical revisiting of scenes and events not only sends his readers back to the beginning but also casts light on future events, illuminating understanding as part of an ongoing project of narrative disclosure.

As a result of these cyclical experiences, characters become fascinated with time and objects of time, charting progress through 'Anniversary checks' [*1983*, 19] and obsessing about reconstructions. Anticipation of future events leads some characters to incant countdowns, most notably in the ghost warnings that appear on John Piggott's bathroom mirror ['D-26',*1983*, 14]. These countdowns chronicle a desperate need for conclusion in a seemingly 'Never ending' [*1983*, 74] chain of events. Constantly aware of 'The clock ticking' [*1983*, 164], victims and those who seek them, or seek justice for them, are '*Trapped in the claws of Time*' [*1983*, 271], unable to move forwards or achieve closure.

Peace utilizes the symbolic meaning of timepieces to offer a mediation on this problem.[21] In the *Red Riding Quartet* the language of time comes to symbolize an elemental aspect of control, a means of making reason and contextualizing events. The constant checking of watches acts as a reminder of the pressures of time and the weight of heritage and history. As doomed policeman Bob Fraser's narrative breaks down into a punctuation-free stream of consciousness at the end of *1977*, he comments, 'I look at my watch and realize how much I've lost track of the time, much I've lost track of the minutes, I've lost track of the hours, lost track of the days, track of the weeks, of the months, the years, decades' [*1977*, 293]. In times of uncertainty and threat, the watch becomes a necessary reminder of the wider world, detaching characters momentarily from the interiority and intensity of the hunt for the Ripper.

When watches are lost, destroyed or cease to function, the reader can expect sinister events to follow. These incidents are significant because, as well as functioning as temporal tools, watches are also memory objects. In *1974*, prior to his confrontation with the West Yorkshire Police, Eddie 'looked at my father's watch. It was fucking gone' [*1974*, 248], while in *1977* Jack's frequently freezing timepiece anticipates unease: 'I looked at my watch. It had stopped' [*1977*, 25].

Like Eddie Dunford, Peter Hunter's watch is an heirloom from his father and a symbol of ties to older values of honesty and justice. When he receives a digital watch from his wife for Christmas, Hunter submits to a ritual exchange: 'I take off my father's old watch and put it on' [*1980*, 264]. His new digital watch signals a growing desire for modernity and technological progress, marking a transition in the narrative from the 1970s to the 1980s. However, Hunter's movement into the digital age is not wholly successful. He appears uncomfortable with his new watch, constantly repeating, 'I keep looking at my watch, my new digital watch' [*1980*, 290], as if to convince himself of its reality. The intricate accuracy of digital measurement proves equally destructive for the increasingly obsessed detective, encouraging him to break time into ever smaller and more urgent fragments. When Hunter's house is destroyed by fire, the missing watch becomes a reminder of his deteriorating grasp of reality and from this point events in his narrative are often measured in digital form ['13:54:45', *1980*, 272]. As a symbol of familial relations as well as the precariously finite nature of past and present, the art of timekeeping foregrounds the language of temporality – and the quality of narrative time in particular – heightening awareness of an approaching apocalyptic conclusion.

In a Yorkshire and UK decaying both literally and morally, the apocalypse is projected as a form of logical finale to the horrors of the quartet. Arriving through characteristic means – dreams and visions, mystical symbolism and local history – it is used to reveal the future or aspects of the previously unrealized. An end to time and space is coupled with the contextual presence of a nationally pervading nuclear anxiety. Policeman Bob Fraser sways helplessly between visions of present-day reality and a man-made future apocalypse:

> *The trees black.*
> *The sky blood.*
> *The shops gone.*
> *The people dead.*
> And we're back:
> Millgarth, Leeds. [*1977*, 118]

Local fear is extended to an international platform by callers to *The John Shark Show* who collectively predict that the only certainly in *1977* will be 'the end of the bloody world [. . .] The end of the bloody world' [*1977*, 204]. These apocalyptic visions extend to occasions of sensory suspension as a form of respite from reality in moments when there is

'No-one; no cars, no lorries, nothing:

Deserted spaces, these overground places.

The world gone in the flash of a bomb' [*1977*, 149]. In Peace's absolute landscape the only conceivable conclusion is all-or-nothing, the total wipeout of humanity and a return to the primeval North. As early as *1977* Jack hears 'those bells ringing in the end of the world' [*1977*, 263], while Peter Hunter frequently dreams of 'Murder and lies, war:

The North after the bomb, machines the only survivors' [*1980*, 19]. This apocalyptic scene echoes the decimation of Northern manu-facturing industries in the late twentieth century, suggesting the ensuing social fallout that produced these alien landscapes. Orwellian associations of 'Big Brother' accentuate a sense of ghostly governance over regions struggling for autonomy and authority. Yorkshire as a site of conflict builds throughout the quartet into a ghettoized space, a rural and urban wound-scape prophesized as the ultimate end to time. BJ's movements towards confrontation as 'The Last Yorkshire Son' [*1983*, 334] are a doom-laden but necessary part of this apocalyptic vision, while Maurice Jobson eventually realizes that he is 'The Last Man In Yorkshire' [*1983*, 85], an open allusion to Shelley's infamous apocalyptic text mobilizing the language of an 'end of earth' fictional literary heritage of narrative closure. By *1983* there is '*No hope for Britain*' [*1983*, 404], just a continued struggle for ownership and control of the language shaping the space and time of past, present and future.

The close and complex concerns of contemporary history are not suited to tidy or closed narratives and Peace is responsive to this. Continuous history is an unrealizable ideal in his novels. Instead, the *Red Riding Quartet* suggests the impossibility of relating our most recent past in a sequential, uni-directorial manner. Reading the quartet in sequence does not offer a safe, familiar framework or parallel chronology of events. The language of time cannot adequately articulate the complexities of historical memories and strives in competition with alternative discourses. In a self-conscious move away from linear narrative dynamics, Peace highlights the intensity, urgency and agency of heteroglossia as a messy amalgam of disagreements and dead ends.

The language of the quartet is necessarily in formation, reflecting its unfolding mysteries as well as the wider 'semantic open-ended-ness' of the novel form. Through a 'living contact with [. . .] unfinished, still evolving contemporary reality', characters do not surrender to, but engage with, competing discourses of the period. Peace fuses these discourses in a conflict of blank terror and explic-itly base prose, of 'everything bad, everything sad, everything dead' [*1980*, 63]. Struggle occurs when a range of intertextual discourses of gender, religion and time enter into competitive exchange to illu-minate meaning and enhance social and historical context. Moving through layered languages, the quartet initiates readers into a battle between words in persistent and profound competition to control and define 1970s and 1980s Britain.

chapter three

Towards a Hauntology
of the North

'To study social life one must confront the ghostly aspects of it.'
[Avery F. Gordon, 2008]

Haunting Absences

Populated by spectres of a recent and disputed past, the *Red Riding Quartet* mobilizes memories to highlight the intrinsically haunted nature of the contemporary world. Visualizing invisibility and identifying alternity, a spectral imperative functions to highlight the potential for further scrutiny of past horrors. Concerned with concealment and revelation, spectrality interrupts the linearity of the past to foreground the agency of formerly marginal narratives. Set against a diegetic backdrop of sonic hauntology, a chorus of un/dead voices unites to examine the agency of a volatile past in the present.

Hauntology has been described as 'a science of ghosts, a science of what returns'.[1] This return is implicitly connected to time. In his *Spectres of Marx*, Derrida associates the concept with that of trauma, emphasizing the dislocation inherent in all hauntology. The act of haunting necessitates a spatial and temporal disjunction, the jarring of past time and present space. This state of disadjustment is relayed through the possession of Hamlet's words 'the time is out of joint'. The logic of the haunt implies that by calling on these spectres in his writings, Marx admitted that there could be temporal disjunctures of the sort Hamlet observes. The ghost makes apparent the 'dislocated time of the present' through its 'joining of a radically disjointed time' [*SM*, 17]. Derrida speculates that 'the more the period is in crisis, the more it is "out of joint", the more one has to convoke the old, "borrow" from it' [*SM*, 109]. It follows that the more unstable a period, the more doubtful, conflicting and jarring, the more ghosts will haunt it.

In the *Red Riding Quartet* a 'troubling effect of déjà vu' [*SM*, 14] highlights the nature of the return, the revisiting of the past to the present. This return is significant, since 'a ghost never dies, it remains always to come and come-back' [*SM*, 99]. In its birth the ghost '*begins by coming back*' [*SM*, 11] and this initial return is closely followed by a pattern of apparitions, a 'rhythm' of 'waves, cycles and periods' [*SM*, 107]. Throughout Peace's quartet vacant spaces are frequently peopled with felt presences. Social interaction continues to take place but with an absent presence, an anima, geist or spectre. The spectre is recognized when interaction is attempted with that which is no longer there. Characters answer doors to no one, pick up ringing phones to silence and find in these absences traces of a powerful presence.

As characters pass through the landscapes of *Red Riding* they note an everyday world inhabited by ghosts, visions or manifest presences. The Yorkshire of these novels is a land densely populated by the ghosts of victims who will not be laid to rest. The agency of their resurgence dislocates temporal boundaries, as ghosts of the past re-emerge to haunt characters of the present. Derrida notes that the ghost may return to highlight 'the crime of the other. A misdeed whose event and reality, whose truth can never present themselves in flesh and blood, but can only allow themselves to be presumed, reconstructed, fanaticised' [*SM*, 21]. Although we might attempt to 'conjure away' [*SM*, 96] the influence of the past, its inheritance lives on in spectral form.

Peace concentrates on the 'nature' and function of spectres as well as the attention they draw to notions of debt, loss and the historical past. He has argued: 'The honesty of the situation is, anyone who has suffered from a crime, and the loss of a friend or loved one, for whatever reason, they know that it doesn't ever go away.'[2] In his own novels, the haunt demonstrates feelings of loss, the noting of absence and the influence of the spectre over the living. Spirits of the past return because the characters of the present owe them something; they come back for vindication. Predominantly, ghosts appear 'in the name of *justice*; Of justice where it is not yet' [*SM*, xix]. In the *Red Riding Quartet* justice is waiting to be realized and ghosts will not be put to rest until justice is done. As journalist Eddie Dunford wakes in *1974*, he sees 'Each time, Clare Kemplay smiling down from the dark ceiling' [*1974*, 22]. Detective Chief Superintendent Maurice Jobson feels Clare's ghost pressing her hand into his as she waves goodbye during the reconstruction of

Hazel Atkins' disappearance [*1983*, 44], while Hazel herself appears purposefully to haunt solicitor John Piggott. Piggott is finally guided by spectres who attempt to aid his quest for justice:

> Haunted, you drive –
> *She is dripping wet and skinny as a rake;*
> Haunted –
> *Silently she points.* [*1983*, 360]

Through these spectral events Piggott realizes the unreal through a hallucinatory suspension of time. Highlighting the disturbance of the dead, he is driven by a need to reveal the cause and alleviate the suffering of this presence. Emphasizing through repetition his intensely haunted state, Hazel's actions cut through Piggott's fear, communicating across a temporal divide. Haunted by old ghosts and new [*1983*, 237], Piggott grows consumed and motivated to repay a debt to these absented victims whose spectres populate his sensory world.

Across the quartet, the haunt forms a powerful trope as ghosts return to invade the safety of interior space as well as the hustle and bustle of the contemporary world. The intrusion of these disrupting presences serves to draw attention to the haunted heritage that produced them. Policeman Bob Fraser sees an apparition of his recently deceased lover, prostitute Janice Ryan, who:

> *lay down beside me on the floor of Room 27 and I felt grey, finished.*
> I close my eyes and she's under them, waiting.
> *She stood before me, her cracked skull and punctured lungs, pregnant, suffocated.* [*1977*, 272]

These nightmare visions of the dead in all their deceased glory haunt those left behind in both unconscious sleep and waking reality. In *1980* Detective Inspector Peter Hunter revisits files on Ripper victims, 'Thinking, *is this how the dead live*' [*1980*, 192]. Bringing the dead back to life through memory, his investigation revives spirits in order that they might be finally laid to rest. After discussing the cases and returning the incident room files, Hunter notes 'the ghosts scattering, scuttling back' [*1980*, 72]. His overall investigation reveals nothing but '*Ghosts, more ghosts*' [*1980*, 78], both literal and metaphoric.

Peace's characters are 'followed' by ghosts in an exhausting pursuit, 'always' tormented by their presence, 'persecuted perhaps' [*SM*, 10]. Ghosts interrupt the quartet, asking us to rethink 'the meaning of past verities' [*SM*, viii]. They act as evidence that the 'witnesses of history fear and hope for a return' [*SM*, 11], a chance to illuminate unseen aspects of the past. Spectres attempt to guide characters, help them to cope with the reality of the present and contextualize its seeming hopelessness from beyond the grave. What is haunting is not the spectres themselves, but the unrealized resolutions and spectral issues they represent. In some cases the living desire communication, invite it and initiate it. Journalist Eddie Dunford is 'desperate to raise the dead for just one second, desperate to raise the dead for just one word' [*1974*, 290]. He hungers for contact to explain away absence, to rationalize it and draw on knowledge of the dead to alleviate the pain of the living. Elsewhere, psychic contact is motivated by a need for explanation, a drive to impose a narrative structure on otherwise unrelatable events. Local psychic Mystic Mandy communicates with the dead for the sake of the living, while Paula Garland hears her missing daughter speak to her 'every day, asking me why?' [*1974*, 161].

The nature of the ghost is bound up in the act of return which is itself an essentially communicative gesture. Ghosts can demand interaction and insist that a dialogic relationship is formed. As Derrida argues, 'It is necessary to speak *of the* ghost, indeed *to the* ghost and *with* it' [*SM*, xix]. However, this can sometimes develop into a more sustained and unwanted dialogue. Jack Whitehead is the most haunted character in the quartet, psychologically stalked by six angels and the ghost of his ex-wife Carol. Jack's experience of ghosts is far more direct than those of other characters. His intimate relationship with Carol and his presence at the moment of her passing may go some way in explaining the vivid nature of his encounters with her spirit. Carol returns in *1977*, but does not come back alone. Jack describes waking 'to see them perched on the furniture, six white angels, holes in their feet, holes in their hands, holes in their heads, stroking their hair and wings' [*1977*, 61]. These angels are obsessed with his collection of Jack the Ripper books and regularly 'rip' him back into the past to witness these historical crimes first hand: 'back into that room, the same room, always the same room [. . .] 1888' [*1977*, 68–9]. Abducting Jack into the living nightmare of the past, Carol and the angels take a pronounced interest in his reporting, hovering over him as he first coins the label 'The Yorkshire Ripper' [*1977*, 71].

The spirits that haunt Jack are aggressive and unrelenting. Carol's ghost can abuse Jack, arouse him, hurt him and be an actual as well as an emotional presence. Jack reports that 'Carol flew across the room, teeth barred and nails out; out for my eyes, out for my ears, out for my tongue, wrenching me out from my chair to the floor' [*1977*, 109]. His pleas are met with an unforgiving realism and honest assessment of her own purgatory: 'Let me be, let me be? And who will let us be, Jack?' [*1977*, 109]. Carol and her angels persist, remain and loiter to cause trouble and anxiety. They frequent Jack to vex and plague him, besetting him with memories of the past. As a site of mourning, Jack's house becomes the locale of these ghosts. In their regularity they turn his space into their own 'haunt', a regular dwelling and site of consciousness. 'Whirling and wailing in murderous cacophony' [*1977*, 137], the ghosts force Jack to pray for peace. He reads from the Bible in an attempt to comfort himself and regularly incants specific lines as a form of protection and explanation: '*your young men shall see visions*' [*1977*, 110].

Through the appropriation of her earthly form, Carol offers herself as a relation of what Derrida terms 'a structure of reproduction', a replica of a past presence with new emphasis and vision in its altered and paradoxical form.[3] Her ghost does not provide the gentle or pleading reminders of the angels, but agitates, agonizes and appals the haunted Jack, harassing him with harrowing and personal vendettas. Permeating and pervading the most personal of his spaces to pester him into action and response, Carol and the angels rise from the dead to weigh on and worry the mind of a man they feel could help put the wronged to rest.

In conjuring these spectral manifestations, Peace is able to 'bring forth with the voice' [*SM*, 41] a physical and psychic reminder of the past in the present. The horror of Jack's reactions and attempts to rid himself of his tormentors aims, as Derrida suggests, to understand the problem that 'one who has disappeared appears still to be *there*' [*SM*, 97]. Making old words heard again, Carol ensures that Jack cannot 'give up the ghost' and move on. Her ghost has not been laid to rest and comes back to disrupt the current state. She and her angel sisters call on us to acknowledge that the inheritance represented by these spectres re-establishes a connection between past and present, that they carry something which resonates.

Intertextual Haunts

The intense intertextuality of the *Red Riding Quartet* constitutes one of its defining features. In each novel meaning is not isolated, but produced through dialogue between a series of intertextual 'haunts' that encourage readers to understand Peace's novels in relation to other sources. Drawing on italicized intercepted communications, the lyrics of contemporary popular music and intentional allusions to familiar fairy-tale narratives, these regular intertextual interplays demand a reorientation of memories of the recent past.

Fairy tales provide a focalizing lens through which the horrors of the quartet can be framed. As well as punning on the topography of Yorkshire, the title of the collection draws on a well-known story of seduction and death. The red cloak was a common symbol of prostitution in seventeenth-century France and consequently the classic children's tale 'Little Red Riding Hood' has been widely interpreted as a warning against the dangers of becoming a 'working girl'. In Peace's quartet intertextual references to Little Red Riding Hood draw together dual investigations into missing children and murdered prostitutes. Jeanette Garland's 'little red coat' [*1974*, 161] quickly aligns the missing schoolgirl to her fairy-tale counterpart. When Hazel Atkins disappears, she is also wearing a 'red quilted sleeveless jacket' [*1983*, 41]. A later reconstruction of her disappearance allows the media to realize the physical journey of Little Red Riding Hood along the path and into the lair of the wolf. Hazel's story is further parabolized as 'the Little Girl Who Never Came Home' [*1983*, 83], transforming a human event into a quasi-fictionalized tale of moral warning. In *1980* 'transmission ten' outlines the fate of Ripper victim Joanne Clare Thornton as a retelling of the 'Little Red Riding Hood' tale [*1980*, 278]. In this encounter, the Ripper stops Joanne and asks her the time. He comments on 'what good eyes you have', finds out where she is going – 'to see her grandmother' – and then drags 'her from the path' [*1980*, 278]. Fairy-tale intertextuality finally develops into open allusion in the epigraph to *1983*:

> *Oh, this is the way to the fairy wood,*
> *Where the wolf ate Little Red Riding Hood;*
> *But this is the riddle that you must tell –*
> *How is it, if it so befell,*
> *That he ate her up in that horrid way,*
> *In these pretty pages she lives today?* – Traditional

Peace's novels establish a desire for a happy ending to this fairy tale, even an expectation of one. Stylistically creating the alternative positioning of a familiar narrative, an intertextual relationship draws on strategies of interpenetration, harnessing recognized representations to underscore a spectrum of victims who fall victim to a 'wolf'.

'The Wolf' is actualized through veiled references to a bestial and ruthless killer. Michael Myshkin maintains that 'The Wolf' is to blame for the missing children [*1983*, 13], while both Detective Chief Superintendent Maurice Jobson and solicitor John Piggott notice the Wolf's presence as:

> Dogs barking –
> Getting near.
> *Wolves*. [*1983*, 14]

'The Wolf' is presented as inherently 'Other', he is marginal, he is monster. Much like the werewolf in traditional tales, 'The Wolf' is an outsider, one who lives on the edges but with an ability to penetrate the very core of the communities he torments. In a pre-animated state, 'The Wolf' inspires fear because he closely resembles the self; he is one of us, but he is also 'Other'. Society wishes to repress this uncanny, the familiar made unfamiliar, but it is the sameness at the heart of that which has been so systematically 'Othered' which brings true horror. History's uncanny habit of repeating itself is made manifest through the reccurring attacks of this predator, a creature that belongs to '*Underground kingdoms, forgotten kingdoms of badgers and angels, worms and insect cities; mute swans upon black lakes*' [*1983*, 21]. Mystic Mandy sees his underground kingdom in her psychic session with Jack, Maurice and the police team. Populated by 'dead dogs and monsters and rats with little wings' [*1974*, 223], this world is ruled by the Rat Man and King, whose swan's wings connect the corrupt characters of the quartet. As well as mirroring the darker dealings of the crime ring underpinning Yorkshire (Michael John Myshkin's MJM comics echoing the MJM publishing of *Spunk* magazine), the discovery of the possibility of the alternative underscores the spectres of a lost future. The underground kingdoms and voices conjured in the mind of Michael Myshkin, the psyche of Mystic Mandy and the activities of George Marsh not only arouse associations of a mythical era, but echo the underground reverberations of an unofficial past erupting in the wasted margins of the present. This haunting intertextuality highlights issues of inclusion and exclusion central to the politics of the quartet. Peace's novels are not product but process, much like the competing versions of the past they offer. Anchoring through association, intertextual connections produce an extensive textual matrix, a web of recall and allusion which readers must navigate in their attempts to negotiate the problematic past presented.

Hauntological music offers another strong index of meaning and power across the quartet. Peace has admitted that 'as I write I only listen to music from the particular time and place about which I am writing. I suppose I use the music as a way back to those times and places. In turn, the music and lyrics then permeate the text.'[4] Memory and cultural artefact are intimately bound up in musical refrain in Peace's work and his novels frequently sample music from the 1970s and 1980s as part of a wider project of re-creating contexts. Peace claims he gets 'a lot structurally from music, in terms of rhythm and timing, repetition and phrasing'.[5] Employing music as a diegetic tool, songs and lyrics are often embedded in the quartet to offer an additional commentary on events.

Characters are haunted not only through visitation, but through audio-spectral interference which disrupts the sounds of reality to convey a constant reminder that the past can move freely throughout the present. As the quartet develops, familiar lines of pop classics return to haunt characters, helping us understand the complex ways in which individuals cope with fraught issues of memory. Journalist Eddie Dunford paraphrases the Don McLean classic 'American Pie' to communicate the inevitability of defeat when taking on the West Yorkshire Police – 'thinking this'll be the day that I die' [*1974*, 292] – while single lines from musical hits of the period regularly intersect narratives to reveal context, internal tensions or wider political associations. Journalist Jack Whitehead is chased by lyrics evoking his dead wife Carol, while solicitor John Piggott notes that the radio seems constantly to play a 'record about ghosts' [*1983*, 109] and frequently complains about the 'terrible tunes and words in my head' [*1983*, 253].

The way the present remains haunted or possessed by the past is illustrated through the recurrence of specific events, phrases and lyrics which come to bear on future narrative events. The psychological effects of the past penetrate the present at will, shocking characters into recognition of the long shadow it casts over the future. Music is employed as an ironic reference to narrative time in *1974*, with '*We've Only Just Begun*' [*1974*, 19] and '*Don't Forget To*

Remember' [*1974*, 20] quickly outlining the concerns of the quartet. The power of time and memory form an audible backdrop as we hear '*Yesterday Once More* on the jukebox' [*1974*, 218] and '*Always On My Mind* on the radio' [*1974*, 219]. Recalling the deceased through acts of performative memory, this musical sense of a psychic 'time out of joint' grows as its refrains play like a broken record. Through compulsive repetition, disturbances come to the surface and interrupt the present, filling gaps and intermittences with chants and rhymes. Their persistent presence signifies the refusal of loss or, as we see in policeman Bob Fraser and his lost lover Janice Ryan, a self-destructive inability to detach from that which is no longer there.

Movement between past and present is audibly notable in the crackles and hisses of the hoaxed Wearside Jack Tapes. The song which bookends the Wearside Jack Tapes, '*Thank you for being a friend*' [*1980*, 57], suggests an intimate, if unwanted, triangle of intrigue between businessman Richard Dawson, Peter Hunter and the Ripper. Its haunting chorus recalls Charles Manson's question, 'Can the world be as sad as it seems?', a query which resonates spectrally across the quartet. The final words of the tape, '*Spirits Will Kill Hunter!*' [*1980*, 374], demands that these ghosts be recognized as an active and influential force in the present. Hunter himself becomes 'Hunter. Hunted. Haunted.' [*1977*, 343], the gradual breakdown of language reflecting the increasingly obsessed state of the Assistant Chief Constable.

The structural function of musical refrain is most obvious in the concluding section of *1983*, entitled '*Total Eclipse Of The Heart*'. This 'total eclipse' is subject to a structured crescendo as characters anticipate the ultimate end to their world and its dark woes. The present is haunted by an image of what is to come, an image of the future in its full apocalyptic glory, through a bleak soundtrack of Bonnie Tyler, Simple Minds, Elvis, Lulu and Cliff Richard. Remixing history through musical, linguistic and factual 'samples', Peace utilizes a sonic hauntology to foreground the centrality of music to the way in which we remember periods and experiences. In his own novels, musical echoes function as cultural reference points, ways of reconfiguring events or illuminating previous associations. Hauntology foregrounds this return, manipulating boundaries between the conscious and unconscious, dreams and reality, to create a patchwork of disconcerting visitations.

At his trial in 1981, Yorkshire Ripper Peter Sutcliffe told the jury that he heard the voices of the dead while working as a gravedigger and later claimed that the voice of God told him to murder his victims.[6] In the *Red Riding Quartet*, these oral hallucinations are actualized through a series of transmissions that vocalize the voice of the Ripper as well as the voices of his dead and should-be-dead victims. The 'transmissions' feature exclusively in the third novel, *1980*. Prefacing the beginning of each chapter, they appear on a single page opposite the central narrative, each transmission chronicles the fate of one of the Ripper's victims.

The transmissions initially offer an 'official' police account of events, relayed in a formal register using third-person reportage. These are gradually intercut with transmissions from victims of the Ripper, alive and dead. We also hear the Ripper's own version of events, told in the first person, attempting to justify his *modus operandi*. The Ripper's voice is characterized by a pronounced accent – 'e' replacing 'I' – acting as a physical marker of difference between his stream of communication and the numerous other accounts that penetrate and cross over his words. These are broken by competing perspectives from other 'sources' in the investigation that appear through repetition and refrain. Songs, tapes, letters and police witness statements conspire to challenge the validity and coherence of each of the versions offered by these very different voices.

The transmission series exists to convey new evidence and perspectives as well as contextualizing, contesting or countering accounts offered by the novel's central narratives. The final transmission provides us with 'one final picture from the atrocity exhibition from the shadows of the sun out of the arc of the searchlight' [*1980*, 362]. Like J. G. Ballard's 1970 novel *The Atrocity Exhibition*, Peace's compact and repetitive micro-narratives communicate a media-ated violence, offering their traumas as immediate and relatable. Collectively, the transmissions contain material which appears in various novels across the quartet. This unites in *1980* to form a sustained communication between the worlds of the living and the dead. Voiced by a host of chance survivors and their motivated killer, the transmissions enact a reiterated invocation of the past in opposition to received histories of the Ripper case.

The Ripper and his victims appear to present themselves through these textual visitations. Central to this is the concept of 'coming back'. We all speak of times when our actions or words have 'come back to haunt us', but through the transmissions victims come back to haunt the central narrative with a burning desire to articulate new perspectives on past events. The transmissions function to honour these perspectives, giving them voice, power and presence, as well as offering the reader a chilling insight into the sensations, reactions and perceptions of being attacked by the Yorkshire Ripper.

Through the transmissions, the dead address us directly and interrogate us with their voice and gaze, drawing us into an often unwanted dialogic implication in events. These uncanny apparitions make a simple demarcation of past and present impossible, encouraging the reader to listen to and communicate with ghosts of the past and providing a much-needed forum for the marginalized. Via a meeting between the spiritual and the actual we are reminded that the immanence of ghosts as spectres disrupts any closure of the present, opening up new possibilities and alternative histories.

This uncanny internal displacement highlights the policing of textual space, of interior and exterior narratives, as well as the violent exclusion of marginal voices within the central narratives of historical testimony. The transmissions series inhabits the very margins of *1980*. This physical separation can be seen to echo the 'virtual space of spectrality' described by Derrida. Setting the transmissions against the opening of each chapter, Peace creates an 'opposition between what is present and what is not' [*SM*, 11], effectively enabling the space of the novel to become framed by untold stories. Through this spectral economy the transmissions can be regarded as a form of textual resistance, evidencing the way in which a society can be 'regularly visited, haunted, inhabited by what it thought it had excluded'.[7] As phantom texts, the transmissions visibly haunt the official space of the novel. Meaning is created through dialogue between these narratives, a flash of recognition illuminating hitherto unseen connections. Forcing us to bear witness and animated into being, these spectral manifestations are ghosts of the real, their seemingly 'uncanny' exterior leading us to what was actually 'known' and long familiar. They are concerned with a history of concealment and deceit, with 'something which ought to have remained hidden but has come to light'.[8]

The transmissions series suggests that spectres can never be completely exorcised or ignored. Keeping the reader in a state of constant 'haunt', they systematically expose memories of historical trauma. Their shifting, entwined and slippery voices re-create the horrors of recent history not through allusion, but through direct imagery. As dispersed traces of deceased people, these voices cannot simply disappear. The transmissions are full of movement but without life, repeatedly evoking the absent and lost. Relaying in unending and hard-to-distinguish voices transmitted from 'nowhere' to no one, they signal that the quartet at large is infested with ghosts whose presence may disturb or distress, but who also offer hope, reminding us of the victims and promoting the need for justice.

The Spectre of the Past

The *Red Riding Quartet* is concerned with 'the place of recent history in an age of forgetting'.[9] However, for some of its characters, the liberation associated with forgetting is appealing. Surviving Ripper victim Ka Su Peng argues that 'I don't want to remember, I want to forget, but I can't forget, only remember. That's all I do – remember' [*1977*, 128]. Those who attempt to blank out the past are punished through the haunt. The past is a time which these characters must come to know and acknowledge. Although 'the recent past is the hardest to know and understand', the *Red Riding Quartet* denies contemporary readers the right to 'put the past behind' them.[10] The past is subject to an ongoing re-evaluation in these novels and is presented as a perpetual state of conflict. History is disembodied – like the Ripper's victims: torn from its holdings, it lives on as a spectre haunting the present. Contextual news of the apparent discovery of Hitler's diaries regularly cuts into the quartet, alerting us to the danger of false accounts of the past. Voltaire is revived in *1983* to develop this idea. His relative summation of the temporal nature of truth – 'There are truths which are not for all men, nor for all times' [*1983*, 256] – sheds light on the evolving nature of the past on offer. The past is never whole or finalized in this work – it is '*Unending*' [*1977*, 120], without conclusion and subject to constant rewriting.

The quartet opens with an epigraph, 'The only thing new in this world is the history you don't know' [Harry S. Truman, *1974*]. This quotation suggests an interest in illuminating a past we do not know, as well as preventing us from forgetting a history we would rather not know. The four novels draw on a very public past, but do so to foreground marginal voices, focusing on people at the periphery of conflict rather than at the centre. Collectively, their form and contents disrupt perceptions of the past, hybridizing provocative and frightening narratives. Rewriting the historic legacy of a people and place, Peace illuminates the diverse ways in which perspectives can permeate the historical consciousness. Eddie Dunford's musings on 'Mystery, History' [*1974*, 110] attempt to align these various versions, while Detective Chief Superintendent Maurice Jobson is finally left to witness the legacy of the past, observing how and why:

the lies survived, those little fictions we called history –
History and lies –
They survived us all. [*1983*, 38]

Scarred by '*bad memories and history*' [*1983*, 334], characters rely less upon temporal boundaries and instead invest their belief in truths drawn from 'Futures and pasts . . . Futures past' [*1980*, 155]. A sense of time shifting, of temporal flow, suggests that the past is not gone, but finds new forms and articulations in these texts.

The quartet highlights that we are most closely connected to the recent past, but it does not initiate us into a shared past. Instead, it gives the present meaning through reference to our immediate history. Memories and emotional experiences return in the form of the spectre to challenge the 'pastness' of the past. Questioning historical representations handed down as 'fact', Peace reappropriates this inheritance to reaffirm its significance. The haunt as repeated time demonstrates that the past cannot and will not be 'fixed'. Its traumas are so profound that they cause characters to re-imagine time and space, to submit to a chrono-consciousness of the displaced and invaded. The dissidence of these competing voices may unsettle readers and challenge the capacity of the novel to represent such subject matter, but at the end of *1983* the past remains troubling, unresolved and spectral. As a result, the inco-herent interactions between past and present stimulated by these texts disclose more fully the many unrepresented pasts that haunt the present.

Throughout the *Red Riding Quartet*, hauntology is offered as a way of conceptualizing the past and foregrounding the act of return; spectrality – the ghostliness of history – participates in wider histo-riographic debates to illuminate struggles over knowledge, language and power. In this work, to be truly haunted is to deny your own past. Johnny Kelly's claim that 'it never goes away' [*1983*, 315] perhaps best sums up these experiences. While Margaret Thatcher emerges haunted by the nostalgia of Victorian values and Churchillian warmongering at the close of *1983*, the characters of *Red Riding* attempt to exorcise a past that seeks to impose itself upon them at every available opportunity.

This return is part of the nightmare of a very specific history. As Robert Mighall argues, 'specters [. . .] are shaped by historically specific circumstances'.[11] The circumstances shaping the returns in Peace's quartet are specific in the sense that they illuminate a very particular period. Marx argues that such consciousness of the past is a precondition of transformative social action. In Peace's writings, the past returns as a spectre to remind the reader that in order to heal the present and transform the future we must acknowledge the ever-present influence of history. Something of the past always remains, even if only as a haunting presence. In performing this presence, the spectre offers itself as a re-animated or regenerated form, recalled or revived as intertextual representation or memory. Despite this, the quartet is not a work of nostalgia. Peace's hauntology documents a history of gaps, erasures and abductions, a bloody interaction with a beast of a history that will not lie down and die. The past is just as dark as the present in these texts; it is not waved off, but is re-ignited as a source of illumination in the present.

Raising a range of 'sources' and intertextual 'haunts', the *Red Riding Quartet* highlights how the history of a particular period is imagined and transformed into the poetics of the past. The texts provide space for the articulation of alternative voices that sit along-side existing accounts. As Mary Carruthers argues, 'In this way reading a book extends the process whereby one memory engages another in a continuing dialogue [. . .] not a "hermeneutical circle" (which implies mere solipsism) but more like a "hermeneutical dialogue" between two memories.'[12] In an inherently hauntological dimension haunted by haunting itself, the spectre functions to rupture collective amnesia, a perceived disorder of memory.

Hauntology is then not only about the return of the past, but a recognition that the past itself is always spectral. Through the fictional reorganization of his alternative past, Peace raises an evocative ghost-work of counter-memories that fragments the boundaries of the possible. The world of *Red Riding* is one of absence and disappearances, but also one of remembrance. The past daunts the contemporary which desires to exercise its presence, but cannot. Characters seek to disavow memories that nevertheless continue to assert themselves. As a series of novels, the quartet itself may be viewed as a historically marginal, spectral version of the past perched on the periphery between fact and fiction. In this phantomatic reality full of spectres, the present is a time of haunting which seeks to defamiliarize recent horrors, asking readers to re-evaluate the relevance of these events in the present, and for the future.

chapter four
Yorkshire Noir

*'I believe the crime writer, by their choice of genre, is obligated
to document these times and their crimes.'*
[David Peace, 2009]

No-one even looked

The *Red Riding Quartet* looks back to the 1970s and 1980s as a
period in which the darkness of the past returned to impose itself
violently on a present in crisis. The 'inevitability' of crime created by
the social, political and economic circumstances of the period manifests itself in Peace's novels through a thick, dark 'Yorkshire noir'.[1]
'Noir' is an established genre, often stylized and regularly subject to
knowing pastiche. Sourced in Gothic traditions, it is concerned with
shadowy desire, real crime and social disintegration. Set against an
alienating urban world, Peace's own strain of 'Yorkshire noir'
concentrates on the underside of 1970s and 1980s society, the
disruption of the present and challenges to the established social
order. The graphic and fictional child murders of *1974* are the most
overt exploration of this noir-driven polemic. Documenting 'horror
on horror' [*1974*, 51], Clare Kemplay's autopsy reveals that, '4 LUV
had been cut into the victim's chest with a razor blade [. . .] the
palm of each hand has also been pierced through, possibly by a large
nail or a similar metal instrument [. . .] internal tears to the vagina
had been caused by the stem and thorns of a rose inserted into the
vagina and left there [. . .] two swan's wings had been stitched into
her back' [*1974*, 51–2]. The repeated finding that 'None of the
injuries were post-mortem' [*1974*, 52] underscores the dark
brutality of this crime. The murder is used by Arnold Fowler to cast
a wider claim for social responsibility. His claim that 'we've made a
world where crucifying a swan is seen as a prank, not a crime' [*1974*,
140] suggests that the causes of criminality lie at the very heart of
the society that condemns it. Peace's work charts an ongoing

attempt to reconcile imagined crime with real crime and the ethics of using any crime – real or imaginary – as a form of entertainment. Since the publication of *1974*, Peace has made a conscious decision to avoid writing about fictional crime, having 'realised I don't need to make things up. We've created a society with enough real horrors.'[2] Increasingly critical of *1974*, he now claims that it 'represents some of the things I don't like about crime writing, violent, voyeuristic, overdone'.[3] By *1977* his quartet is fully focused on the real atrocities of the Yorkshire Ripper, an increased compassion for the victims of crime fuelling a concerted focus on crime in context.

Introducing contemporaneous concerns such as serial killing and child abuse, new forms of criminality feed the fears underpinning the *Red Riding Quartet*. Moving away from imaginary crimes and grand narratives of the past, the series draws attention to local, personal histories. Illuminating relationships between real life and real crime, Peace highlights the criminality of ordinary people through the modes and motifs of genre fiction. While genre fiction can offer a familiar and satisfying form of literature to contemporary readers, it also functions to reveal conflicts in the social order and explore the ways in which society attempts to reinstate that order. Deploying the characteristic settings, tone and protagonists of crime fiction as part of a wider interrogation of the social, political and economic systems of the 1970s and 1980s, the *Red Riding Quartet* mobilizes the popularity of genre fiction to form an effective pathway into complicated and long-standing tensions.

Peace openly defends genre fiction as a literary form, celebrating its capacity to articulate new voices and perspectives. Asked whether he could align his use of the crime genre with his own literary status as a contemporary novelist, Peace retorted:

> Dostoyevsky wrote crime; Kafka wrote crime; Brecht wrote crime; Orwell wrote crime. Dickens. Greene. Dos Passos. Delillo [. . .] The best work is always done in the margins and the genres: Burroughs and Ballard in Science Fiction; Iain Sinclair and Alan Moore; and I'm proud to share the same section of a shop as Ellroy, Mosley, Pelecanos and Rankin.[4]

Exploding the perceived confines of his chosen genre, Peace aligns the concerns of his quartet with a wider international body of authors who use crime fiction as a means of interrogating troubled social, political and economic contexts.[5] Relating law and legality to the human condition, his defence foregrounds the alienating effect of a contemporary world in which tensions between human values and state control create poverty, crime and prejudice. Exposing the senselessness of criminal convictions and searches for redemption and theological meaning, Peace's quartet is suggestive of the necessary social consciousness of the successful crime writer.

Concerned with the way in which crime affects society and the way society responds or reacts to crime, Peace foregrounds time and place as key factors in any challenge to the social order. Suggesting that 'crimes take place in society, not in a vacuum', his novels situate crimes in their context in an attempt to understand not only how the victim died, but why.[6] Recognition that the *'victims are everywhere'* [*1977*, 72] fuels this broader consciousness of crime as a pervasive social and political problem. One caller to *The John Shark Show* quotes from official statistics: *'crimes fully brought into the open and punished represented no more than fifteen percent of the great mass actually committed . . . and that was in 1964'* [*1977*, 38].

Positioning crime fiction as a generic choice with profound consequences for both writers and readers, Peace argues:

> Crime fiction has both the opportunity and the obligation to be the most political of any writing or any media, crime itself being the most manifest example of the politics of the time. We are defined and damned by the crimes of the times that we live in. The Moors Murders, the Yorkshire Ripper, and the Wests, Rachel Nickell, Jamie Bulger, and Stephen Lawrence: I strongly believe that these crimes and their victims, these investigations and trials (or lack thereof) did not just happen to anyone in anyplace at anytime: they happened to very specific people in a very specific place at a very specific time and this is what crime fiction should be documenting, these dispatches from the front; because we are constantly at war and there are some very, very bad people on the rise. I believe the crime writer, by their choice of genre, is obligated to document these times and their crimes, and the writer who chooses to ignore this responsibility is then simply exploiting, for his or her own financial or personal gratification, a genre that is itself nothing more than an entertainment industry constructed upon the sudden, violent deaths of other, innocent people and the unending, suffering of their families.[7]

Peace's novels use crime to offer a wider examination of the social, political and economic conditions of the 1970s and 1980s. The crimes they represent are not offered as commonplace events but as extraordinary, defining occurrences. Instead of shying away from the brutality and horror of real crime, Peace seconds entertainment in favour of a serious indictment of an era. Connecting 'More crimes and more lies, more lies and more crimes' [*1983*, 402], his quartet encourages recognition and consideration of the agents and motivations of crime. This examination is motivated by a belief that 'crime fiction should be every bit as brutal, harrowing and devastating as the violence of the reality it seeks to document. Anything less at best sanitizes crime and its effects and at worst trivializes it.'[8] Placing the Yorkshire Ripper in the context of a series of contemporaneous atrocities, the *Red Riding Quartet* offers a perspective on misconduct as an expression of its age, foregrounding the materiality of crime and the concrete structures that create the conditions necessary for deviance.

Peace has cited James Ellroy and Raymond Chandler as predecessors in socially conscious crime writing. Fellow author Ian Rankin has called Peace 'the English James Ellroy'.[9] Peace is open in his praise for Ellroy, claiming that '*White Jazz* is possibly the best crime novel ever written, that is the book I'm trying to beat, I want to write a better book than *White Jazz*, with that book he changed crime fiction forever [. . .] I wanted to take that and go on further – in *1974* it's quite obvious he was a big influence on me.'[10] *White Jazz* is the final part of Ellroy's series of crime novels documenting 1940s and 1950s America, its 'darkness, hidden history' and 'perversion behind closed doors'.[11] These unforgiving representations of a place and its prejudices are nowhere better expressed than in the *LA Quartet*.[12]

Both Ellroy and Peace use crime fiction to focus on the dark side of contemporary life, mobilizing sprawling plots with complicated conclusions to outline institutionalized lawlessness. Navigating a fine line between criminality and respectability, the *LA Quartet* follows deeply flawed protagonists operating in an unstable society. Set against the rise of big business, corrupt housing developments and a society built on 'a foundation of lies', both Peace and Ellroy use their respective series to offer counter-narratives on twentieth-century history.[13] Their reconstructions locate crime and the historical record in 'preposterous, testosterone-fueled male power games' using crime fiction as 'the perfect vehicle for social commentary'.[14]

Like the *LA Quartet*, the crimes of the *Red Riding Quartet* reflect the deviance of the society that produced them. From the Box Brothers' robbery of the Edinburgh mail train to Raymond Morris and Cannock Chase, the UK is quickly established as a country characterized by corruption. Before *1974*, Eddie Dunford makes a name for himself exposing the true horrors of The Ratcatcher, 'Graham Goldthorpe, the disgraced music teacher turned council Rat Man who had strangled his sister Mary with a stocking and hung her in the fireplace' [*1974*, 61]. As well as implicating Mary in a childhood friendship with Michael Myshkin, this case is suggestive of the familial, social and political intrigues that shape the crimes of the quartet.

As a microcosm of the UK during the 1970s, Yorkshire is presented as a county founded on criminality. Peace's victims meet their fate on wastegrounds and playing fields, in disused garages and down mineshafts. Sites of crime like the Ashburys are described as 'cursed and godless' [*1980*, 139], places void of hope or morality. God's presence cannot be conceived at such places, cannot sit alongside such evil. These isolated spaces reflect the marginality not only of the victims but also of the killer. The Yorkshire Ripper operates alone, usually at night, within the sites created by post-industrial fallout. Writing in the context of an established public consciousness of these scenes, Peace defamiliarizes infamous sites of crime. During his research he asked himself, 'If Francis Bacon had painted these crime scenes, what would it look like, and how would I write that?'[15] Famously described by Margaret Thatcher as 'that man who paints those dreadful pictures', Bacon offers bleak snapshots of the human condition that share many concerns with Peace's quartet.[16] Mobilizing the uncanny nature of the crime scene, Peace echoes a shared interest in isolated masculine figures and the mutilated female body. Foregrounding the bold and violently nightmarish nature of nondescript backdrops, his novels draw attention to the socio-economic and political circumstances that function to perpetuate the conditions necessary for expressions of deviance. The *Red Riding Quartet* provides a damning analysis of the conditions that conspire to produce specific crimes. Examining humans in extreme situations, the four novels offer a stark portrait of crime as a product of late twentieth-century British society. Unashamedly occupying 'a dark period in the history of West Yorkshire' and the UK, Peace's work explores how and why the challenges of crime and policing can come to define a time and a place and why the genre of crime fiction functions so effectively as socio-political critique.[17]

Peace Man

Historically, UK police forces have fought for regional as opposed to national control and the forces of the *Red Riding Quartet* are no exception. In 1836 Leeds formed a new police force from local funds and in 1850, at the request of the public, the practice of prostitution was brought under police control rather than being banned outright.[18] During the late twentieth century a permanent police presence withdrew from many rural regions of the UK and outpost police stations were replaced by telephone boxes as hotlines to the new, town-based headquarters. In 1974, the Leeds and Bradford forces amalgamated, creating a new single West Yorkshire police force covering two million people. The merger had been anticipated for fifty years and was eventually authorized by the Local Government Act of 1972. Within a few years the new force had to tackle two major national law and order incidents – the Chapeltown riots and the Yorkshire Ripper.

In its heady mix of police procedural, revenge tragedy and hard-boiled fiction, the *Red Riding Quartet* explores connections between reading and detection as part of a wider critique of UK policing during the 1970s and 1980s. Peace argues that due to 'the way crimes are reported [...] policemen are faced with things ordinary people don't see'. As a result close attention should be paid to how 'these things affect these people'.[19] As a mark of respect to their efforts, *1977* carries a dedication addressed not only to the victims of the Ripper but also 'to the men and women who tried to stop those crimes'. Across the four novels, police negotiate the most extreme of circumstances and regularly experience first-hand crime and deviance.

Despite these challenges, it is impossible to ignore the fact that in Peace's quartet the new West Yorkshire force is shown attacking women, torturing suspects and seeking to profit from vice. Even Detective Chief Superintendent Maurice Jobson expresses profound disillusionment with the

brand-new West Yorkshire Metropolitan Police Brass in their nice

new suits and polished shoes with the nice new sheepskins hanging
by their trophies and their tankards, the West Yorkshire Metropolitan
Police Brass with their beer guts and their wallets bulging in those
nice new suits. [*1983*, 278]

Set against a region suffering social unrest, the polished image of
this rebranded force is undermined by self-interest and financial
motivation.

In his study of the UK police investigation into the Yorkshire
Ripper, Michael Bilton suggests that all

police forces are like large extended families. They have their own
'black sheep'; the kids that go off the rails and they turn out okay; the
same 'favourite uncles' when they are young. There are intra-family
rows, and they all come together when the family is criticised.[20]

In Peace's fictional revival of the same investigation, duplicity within
and between UK forces leads to clan-like hostilities rather than
familial co-operation and knowledge-transfer. The goal-orientated
environment of the police force is presented as a markedly masculine world in which 'all the best men' [*1974*, 28] vie for attention and
attainment. Petty jealousies reveal the inner mechanics of an organization whose hegemony is severely under strain. Morale is low and
status is everything, as men at every level ceaselessly battle to undermine one another. In this 'small world' [*1980*, 174] highly regarded
officers are measured by the 'trophies and tankards' of their past
achievements. With the advent of the Yorkshire Ripper, these men
find themselves under pressure from claims that they 'haven't
nicked anyone since Michael bloody Myshkin' [*1980*, 98]. The reputation of the new West Yorkshire force and their Detective Chief
Superintendent is consequently staked firmly in the apprehension
of 'their' killer.

Played against an ironic musical backdrop of the band *The Police*
[*1983*, 13], the old guard of the West Yorkshire force is set against a
new breed of media interest in their policing of a series of major
criminal investigations. Journalist Eddie Dunford's first encounter
with George Oldman details 'a face from before, a big man amongst
big men, thick black hair plastered back to look like less, a pale face
streaked beneath the lights with a thousand burst blood vessels, the
purple footprints of tiny spiders running across his bleached white
cheeks to the slopes of his drunken nose' [*1974*, 4]. Oldman is remi-

niscent of an earlier style of policing, physical discomfort in the media spotlight causing his veneer of command to melt. The fear that those in authority have lost control leads to the introduction of Peter Hunter, Assistant Chief Constable of the Greater Manchester force, to head up a covert Home Office enquiry into the Ripper murders. The presence of the 'most unpopular copper in the North' [*1980*, 8] fuels paranoia that the West Yorkshire force is under internal investigation. As Craven argues, 'It's not just about the Ripper, is it? It's about seeing how many of us you can take down with him' [*1980*, 86–7]. Hunter does not hide his contempt for the West Yorkshire force and has little regard for the old regime of 'Angus, Oldman and Noble', 'Hiding and already beaten, standing between their sandwiches and their better days, their Black Panthers and their M62 Coach Bombings, their A1 Shootings and their Michael Myshkins, those better days a long time gone' [*1980*, 21].[21] Connecting this trio to a series of dubious convictions and coerced confessions, Hunter's assessment casts doubts on a police force sustained by past glory, unable to cope with the 'recriminations and the blame, looking for lambs, a scapegoat –' [*1980*, 24]. His growing unease at the failure of the West Yorkshire Police to apprehend their killer echoes as a losing game – '*Ripper 13, Police 0, 13–nil, 13–nil, 13–nil, 13–nil*' [*1980*, 57] – one that positions the Ripper at home in relation to the investigating team.

Examining the lives of police under pressure, the *Red Riding Quartet* presents a local and national force characterized by homophobia and racism. Journalist Eddie Dunford is warned that 'Oldman's got a thing about gypsies [. . .] and the Irish' [*1974*, 54]; police dogs are accordingly named 'Nigger and Shep, Ringo and Sambo' [*1983*, 80]. Casual prejudice is shown as rife in the West Yorkshire Police and is regularly employed to prey on individuals already in states of extreme vulnerability. On duty and in the community, Peace's policemen display an eagerness to abuse the power of their authority. Petrified detainee Steve Barton is slow-hand-clapped by a ring of police officers as they force him to masturbate into a cup [*1977*, 81], while Mrs Ridyard, mother of missing schoolgirl Hazel, reports to Eddie Dunford that 'They sat in this house for two weeks, George Oldman and his men, using the phone [. . .] And they never paid the bill [. . .] Phone almost got cut off' [*1974*, 32]. Detective Chief Superintendent Maurice Jobson makes a petulant civilian drink a pint of Guinness for calling him a 'Mick' at a bar, flashing his warrant card as a means of intimidation,

Michael Myshkin's appeal is based on the claim that a police officer forced him to confess, while Jimmy Ashworth apparently hangs himself while in police custody. As one copper reminds Eddie, 'Big Brother's watching you [. . .] Always' [*1974*, 90]. The omniscient nature of policing and police corruption extends to the personal lives of officers. In these novels police families are deeply dysfunctional, the many and varied pressures of the job leading to fractured marriages and alienated children. Maurice Jobson's daughter pointedly declares to her father, 'I'll never marry a policeman,' while the broken cry of PC Rudkin's wife – 'Never marry a copper!' [*1983*, 222] – resonates across the personal and professional relationships depicted in the quartet.

In the claustrophobic and intensive organization of the West Yorkshire Police, lies and deception are commonplace while interactions are signalled by casual violence. As Oldman warns Eddie, 'These are violent bloody times, son' [*1974*, 23]. This threat is quickly brought to bear on Eddie's own narrative as he reports that the West Yorkshire Police 'beat me unconscious', 'urinated on me' and 'dragged me by my heels'. Eddie goes on to claim that the police 'took photographs, stripped me, cut the bandages off my right hand, took more photographs, and fingerprinted me' and then 'hosed me down with ice water until I fell over on the chair' [*1974*, 251]. This violent questioning forms a blueprint for the subsequent police interrogations of George Marsh and John Piggott, in which the burning of a cigarette on the back of the hand, a twisted blanket around the face, a fake shot from a gun and the threat of attack from an animal are used to encourage the detainees to repeat false claims until they are accepted as confessions.

Across the quartet, police stations become physical manifestations of covert law enforcement. Policeman Bob Fraser recalls descending 'into the dungeons, keys and locks turning, chains and cuffs rattling, dogs and men barking' [*1977*, 17], while Eddie Dunford notes 'a noose' [*1974*, 262] above the door of his cell. Some of the most graphic displays of police violence occur at Millgarth police station in an unofficial interrogation room known as the 'Belly – the huge fucking hole of a cell right down in the gut, all strip lights and wash-down floors' [*1977*, 77]. Other acts of police violence occur in the full and symbolic gaze of the community. Fraser, Rudkin and Ellis enter the home of the Spencer Boys with 'a shotgun, a sledgehammer, and an axe' [*1977*, 75], Bob Craven, John Rudkin, Dick Alderman, Jim Prentice, Bill Mulloy and Maurice

Jobson raid Jenkins Photo Studio, while the Strafford shootings are completed by senior police officers in the moments after the initial attack. Professionally and morally undermined by the innocent image of the 'Peace Man' [*1977*, 198] imagined by his young son, policeman Bob Fraser comes to regard his colleagues as little more than the state's 'own sponsored fucking monsters let loose on the wind' [*1977*, 15].

In these novels, police vice is often motivated by corrupt opportunities and easy solutions.[22] Obsessively covering up, leaking information and conspiring with criminals, the West Yorkshire Police are shown using their professional power to obtain money and sexual favours. The source of police corruption in Peace's Yorkshire is 'Controlled vice', a scheme designed to bring crime 'off the streets and out of the shop windows, under our wing and in our pocket' [*1983*, 227]. The 1970s were marred by a national scandal involving sections of the London Police making similar gains from organized crime. Centred on the illicit activities of the Obscene Publications Squad and the Drugs Squad, police malpractice extended to a series of controversial miscarriages of justice, most famously involving the Birmingham Six and the Guildford Four.[23] In the *Red Riding Quartet* this historical context is revived and debated by callers to *The John Shark Show*:

> Caller: *This bloke Moody, he's the Head of Scotland Yard's Obscene Publications Squad right?*
> John Shark: *Was, yeah.*
> Caller: *And all the time he's accepting bribes and doing favours for these Porn Barons, Un-bloody-believable.*
> John Shark: *All a far cry from Dixon of Dock Green.*
> Caller: *Fuck, he was probably at it and all. Bloody coppers. Make you sick.*
> *The John Shark Show*
> Radio Leeds
> Saturday 4th June 1977
> [*1977*, 112]

Mobilized and woven into Peace's novel, the internally networked corruption of the new West Yorkshire force is presented as symptomatic of a wider internal corruption in the national police body. Retold through increasingly apoplectic callers, details of the case are reiterated until a wider picture of police corruption has been unquestionably established: '*And all the cannabis they were taking off darkies they were nicking, this other copper he was selling back to other dealers, and I read this copper who was doing it, he was something to do with A10, that lot that are now Complaints Division*' [*1977*, 232]. While the media revel in these findings, the British public become deeply disheartened with both the press and police. As one radio caller notes, '*none of it would have come to light if it hadn't been for the bleeding press. Not very bloody reassuring that, is it? Relying on your lot*' [*1977*, 138].

The voice of the UK media becomes increasingly obsessed with crime and police corruption as the quartet develops. The unregulated nature of policing and police actions becomes a central concern as members of the public turn to the new interface of the radio phone-in show to protest against internal corruption and an apparent absence of accountability. Playing in the background to events, every radio programme is 'about the Yorkshire Ripper' [*1980*, 19], while the television plays an endless range of documentaries that attempt to get inside the '*Mind of the Ripper*' [*1980*, 9]. This presence reaches a peak in *1977* as *The John Shark Show* takes policing as the focus of its phone-in debates. The contentious topic of police pay raises pulses through these exchanges, as callers rhetorically ponder whether anybody would notice if society started to lock up coppers instead of criminals. As part of this ongoing debate, Part Two of *1977* is entitled 'Police and Thieves', as radio reports of police corruption and the mysterious circumstances of prisoner suicides gradually come to dominate the airwaves.

In an attempt to harness media interest, a police publicity campaign mobilizes images of the serial killer as a potent press weapon. Letters purporting to be from the Ripper are printed and sold on 'to *The Sun*' [*1977*, 267], while claims that the force will '*paper every surface with a thousand posters saying*: The Ripper Is a Coward' [*1980*, 19] do little to satisfy a public eager to see the killer brought to justice. Complaints that police have spent four million pounds on 'bloody publicity' [*1980*, 6] overshadow their efforts, limiting the impact of a campaign designed to encourage revelation and dialogue. Emphasizing the ever-present danger of the Ripper, a heady combination of posters, adverts and press conferences refuse to let the story die, constructing a wider narrative built on speculations between unrelated items of evidence that ultimately work to alienate further the man they seek. Once apprehended, the Ripper actually claims to have 'changed my methods because the press and the media had attached a stigma to me. I had been known for some time as the Yorkshire Ripper and I didn't like it. It isn't me. It didn't ring true' [*1980*, 354].

The hunger of the West Yorkshire Police to engage the media as a weapon against crime backfires most notably through the figure-head of George Oldman. In a statement that leads to his demotion, Oldman confesses to the *Yorkshire Post*:

> *Every time the phone rings I wonder if it's him. If I get up in the middle of the night I find myself thinking about him. I feel after all this time, I feel that I really know him [. . .] If we do get him, we'll probably find he had too long on the left breast and not enough on the right. But I don't regard him as evil. The voice is almost sad, a man fed up with what he's done, fed up with himself. To me he's like a bad angel on a mistaken journey and, while I could never condone his methods, I can sympathise with his feelings.* [*1980*, 6]

In his desperation for knowledge, Oldman's sense of familiarity with the Ripper leads the senior police officer to humanize the actions of a killer as error rather than evil. Marked by an all-consuming desire for communication and contact, an open relationship with the media and increasing identification with deviance is ultimately his undoing. Like Oldman, Peter Hunter also identifies the shared humanity of the Ripper, openly asserting that 'He's the same' as the people who hunt him, a man who suffers the 'same patterns we all have, same pressures, rhythms: work, the wife, kids, holidays' [*1980*, 82]. As a result, Hunter becomes frustrated that the 'Ripper Room are looking for a hunchbacked Geordie with hairy bloodstained hands, flesh between his teeth and a hammer in his pocket' [*1980*, 83].

Throughout his quartet, Peace demonstrates that the order imposed by the state is not so easily separable from the disorder against which it is apparently arrayed. The police are as delinquent in these novels and share many facets with the monsters they track. Confusion caused by claims to moral righteousness foregrounds a shared humanity as the police begin to show a primitive relation to the objects of their hunt. Mobilizing the mafia-like influence of authority, Peace represents a police force motivated by money, an investigation founded on rumour and a public gripped by terror. Turning fear to political advantage, the police manipulate emotion to revive pressure on the public psyche, imposing the politics of insecurity and new threats on collective efforts to reinforce their authority over public space. Detective Chief Superintendent Maurice Jobson's final statement to solicitor John Piggott – 'Not guilty? We all are' [*1983*, 390] – provides an effective summation of the precariously thin line separating criminality and law enforcement in the quartet.

Asked whether he thought the new West Yorkshire Police actually were like this, Peace replied:

> Yes, or I wouldn't have written the books in the way that I have. The cases of Stefan Kiszko, Judith Ward and Anthony Steel – all of which involved detectives from the Ripper Squad – offer nothing to contradict my fictions and even a cursory examination of the Ripper investigation itself reveals a monumental degree of failure on the part of senior detectives. Recent revelations (for money) in regard to killing kits only further prove that we do not know the whole story. The survivors and families of the victims, and the communities that were terrorised still do not know the whole truth and that in itself is corrupt.[24]

Implicating the West Yorkshire force in a history of cover-ups, concealments and corruption, the *Red Riding Quartet* presents British police as professionally and morally bankrupt during the 1970s and 1980s. Leonard Marsh's final claim that 'No-one even looked' [*1983*, 398] throws a wider relief across the many unseen crimes of the quartet, as well as a wider, endemic blindness to illicit forms of deviance during this period. Identifying the silent victims and perpetrators of crime, Peace's novels reveal the internal deviance of law enforcement and the intrinsic corruption of the country. Marked by misogyny and Masonic connections, the lawless anti-heroes of the West Yorkshire Police stand as the ultimate examples of the corruption operating at the heart of both Yorkshire and the UK during this period.

Peace has complained that in most contemporary crime fiction 'there doesn't seem to be much debate about where we're going as a society'.[25] This would be a difficult claim to level at his own work, which is concerned not only with personal encounters with crime, but with the social, political and economic conditions that conspire to produce criminal acts. Drawing from and challenging nostalgia about familiar and recent periods, his fictions further an ongoing examination of society using crime fiction as a literary form intricately related to the condition of the social world.[26] Taking the reader on a journey into a socio-political heart of darkness, the many crimes of his quartet combine to underscore the role of politics and culture in influencing the way individuals operate in contemporary society.

Adopting an anti-sanitization approach to crime and charting shifting definitions of deviance and morality, the *Red Riding Quartet* suggests that the line separating good and evil, hunter and hunted, is precariously thin. Reviving the past through the conscious incorporation of real people, places and events, Peace rejects sterilization in favour of uncensored and uncompromising representations. Focusing on how media dynamics construct the reality of crime and crime control, he re-examines a range of contemporary crimes to identify not only the cultural construction of deviance, but its impact on identity and social space. Rejecting the construction of crime as entertainment, his novels are concerned with the relationship between crime, power and control. Consequently, the Ripper, like the many other criminals of the quartet – from the Ratcatcher to Raymond Morris, George Oldman to George Marsh – is finally presented not as an uncanny 'Other' but as a familiar and logical manifestation of the hate, prejudice and greed underpinning the period. Mixing real crimes and locations with fictional reworkings, Peace perverts the expectations of the standard police procedural as well as the generic framework of the crime novel to create a series of texts that engage – in a manner befitting the New Labour discourses circulating in Britain during the twenty-first-century context of their publication – not only with crime, but with the causes of crime. Using this socio-cultural framework as the basis for a scathing critique, his *Red Riding Quartet* mobilizes generic conventions to produce a series of crime fictions in which history itself becomes a subject of detection.

chapter five

From the Picket Line to the Page

'Faction:
1. A small group of people working together in a common cause against the main body; dissension within a group.
2. A book based on facts but presented as a blend of fact and fiction.'
[Oxford Dictionary of English, 2005]

The Novel and The Strike

Although it marks the beginning of a new 'inverse post-war trilogy', *GB84* is, in many ways, a 'natural continuation' of the *Red Riding Quartet*.[1] Like the hunt for the Yorkshire Ripper, the 1984–5 UK miners' strike was divisive and created a widespread mistrust of the British police.[2] In 1984, Margaret Thatcher's Conservative government announced that it intended to close twenty UK coal mines because they had become 'uneconomical'. This would lead to mass job losses, since mines had been the primary source of employment in many towns and villages for generations. Fearful of the impact these measures would have in their own areas, miners at other pits began to come out on strike as concern grew for the future of the industry and rumours of further closures spread. The ensuing year-long conflict which National Union of Miners' (NUM) leader Arthur Scargill dubbed 'a social and industrial Battle of Britain' led to the wholesale destruction of the nationalized coal industry, the erosion of industrial relations and the extinction of a way of life. In his 2004 novel *GB84* Peace revisits the 1984–5 miners' strike twenty years on to defamiliarize another contentious time in twentieth-century British history.

The post-strike period has seen several professional authors with little or no direct experience of the coal dispute produce novelistic accounts of the events of 1984–5.[3] Peace's fifth novel follows this established path, taking the miners' strike as its central narrative concern. What is of interest is the history of the strike proposed by this novel. *GB84* re-examines the coal dispute to 'reveal' hitherto 'unseen' factions within political and social collectives, yet it also gives authority to these representations through its use of 'faction' as a literary style. Reconstructing the past through a pseudo-historical approach, the novel fabricates an effect of polyphonic, multi-sourced novelistic dialogue, incorporating re-animated forms and manipulating literary and linguistic systems.

Michael Williams argues that novels addressing the miners' strike are above all else 'necessary novels', because 'much of the country is still in the dark about the real story behind 1984'.[4] Peace himself has argued that his main aim in writing *GB84* was to 'stop people forgetting what happened [in 1984–5]. Especially younger people.'[5] Although *GB84* aims to stop us forgetting the strike, it is the question of what it encourages us to 'remember' which is more significant. Beckett argues that while reading *GB84* 'you see events and their causes entirely Peace's way'.[6] This statement highlights the power of the author to shape historical narratives. Peace, quoting from Harry Truman, states in *1974* that, 'The only thing new in this world is the history you don't know' [*1974*, 84]. In Faber's press release for *GB84*, this translates into the need to confront an 'occult history' of the strike. The idea of the strike's history as an occult account, a secretive, closely guarded and hidden record, is one at which the novel arrives after a seemingly exhaustive, and exhausting, exploration of events.

The hybrid of fact and fiction offered by *GB84* is undoubtedly distinctive and ambitious. Traversing the spaces left by the historical record, it 'dramatises the gaps that always exist between what is told and the telling of it', constantly experimenting with social, discursive and narrative asymmetries (the formal teratology that led Henry James to call some novels 'fluid puddings').[7] As Russian linguist Mikhail Bakhtin asserts, 'the boundaries between fiction and nonfiction, literature and nonliterature and so forth are not laid up in heaven'.[8] Despite this there remains the need for a caveat, a critical footnote, regarding the responsibility of the writer in highlighting the conscious combination of the factional and fictional. *GB84* carries an author's note on the subject which states that Peace's 'characters are a fiction in a novel based on fact'. However, in this obscure statement lies the implication that there exists somewhere between the two a gap, a difference, between the fictional characters and the factional world they inhabit.

Critics have attempted to grapple with an appropriate critical framework for 'faction'. Terry Eagleton has labelled *GB84* 'documentary fiction', a form which 'combines the maximum flexibility with the maximum realism'.[9] The rise of faction has also been celebrated by some critics. Writing on the publication of *GB84* in the *Guardian*, fellow factional author Eoin McNamee praised Peace's novel, claiming:

> There is something out there in the world of fiction, not defined enough to be a trend, a genre or even a sub-genre. Something akin to the first visual artists who put down their paintbrushes and picked up the real material of the world and started to wonder what they could do with it. It is writers looking to engage with real people and real events, and stitch them into their fiction in a way that is hard-nosed, relevant and edgy.[10]

Peace has admitted that in writing any novel he first puts himself in the past, then imagines, but in *GB84* this imaginative version is doubled with historical fact to create an illusion of the past.[11] As a result, the publicity surrounding this novel mirrors the claim and counter-claim culture of the strike itself. Peace's inconsistency – simultaneously claiming fictional amnesty while also asserting that '95% of *GB84* is true', and asserting that the stream of consciousness narratives of striking miners Martin and Peter in particular are near-verbatim records of oral accounts – leaves the representations of his text in a literary limbo somewhere between the infirm assertions of fact and fiction.[12]

Factional Polyphony

In *GB84* the strike remains as a spectre, a ghost in a world of copies, spoofs and spins. Characters are not only fictional but functionally fictional, engaged by the author in an attempt to confuse the fiction/non-fiction dichotomy through a range of 'alternative' forms and voices. In his study 'Epic and the Novel' Bakhtin outlines the way in which the novel uniquely embraces and ingests other genres.[13] Since the 'generic skeleton of the novel is still far from having hardened, and we cannot foresee all its plastic possibilities', the novel can incorporate various forms of extra-literary and extra-artistic authorial speech into its body.[14]

This 'intimate interaction [. . .] with living rhetorical genres' does not damage the status of the novel, but rather reaffirms it.[15] Exercising its protean capability to cannibalize other forms, styles and languages, each of which 'possesses its own verbal and semantic forms for assimilating various aspects of reality', the novel is able to document movement and change, an essential interplay between past and present.[16]

Peace's strike novel mobilizes a variety of sources – party political documents, press photographs, police reports and personal diaries – in order to persuade the reader that each narrative represents what Bakhtin describes as 'the discourse of a whole incorporated genre'.[17] In this way Peace pushes the novel form to its limits in order to bring to life not only the era but also its characters and histories. Within *GB84*, a variety of narrative forms – records, accounts, interviews and reports – compete for the attention of the reader. In chronological accounts of calendrical particularity, dates and diary entries disturb borders between fact and fiction, imaging the intense, repetitious and demanding nature of the strike itself. Through photographs, songs, newspaper cuttings and journal entries, the reader is placed suggestively in the role of archival voyeur, an unseen witness to character confessions recorded through an amalgamation of previously 'confidential' evidence collated by the author.

GB84 tells the story of the strike from six different narrators, from top to bottom, left to right. These multiple perspectives combine to show the complexity of the strike, defying the capacity of a single narrative point of view to convey the magnitude of the conflict. The novel's chapters contain the third-person narratives of four central characters. Two are mainly italicized and detail the lives of David Johnson ('The Mechanic'), who works freelance for security services, and Malcolm Morris, an MI5 counter-insurgency operative trained in Northern Ireland. The remaining two narratives detail the experiences of Terry Winters, a senior management figure at the NUM, and Neil Fontaine, a security agent working for government adviser Stephen Sweet (whom he consistently calls 'The Jew'). In addition to these narratives, Peace includes the story of Martin and Peter, two striking miners. Their individual accounts are far more personal and intimate than the multiple voices offered by the novel's weekly chapters. Presented as a form of contemporary journalism, their story is columned, clipped and divided into 'days'. These 'days' are offered at the beginning of each chapter on a single page, forcing the reader to follow another voice intersecting those voices already on offer.

In a similar fashion to Walter Brierley's 1935 [1983] *Means-test Man*, contextual newspaper reports and headlines are consumed by characters and related to events as they unfold. Peace overtly extends the literary device of newsprint in the presentation of Martin's and Peter's narrative.[18] The presentation of their fictional accounts in print encourages the reader to become immersed in the perspectives they propagate, experiencing news and views as they 'happen'. In this way Peace offers us an artificial 'News 24' of the period, flitting between reports, contradictions, music, montage and statistics. Individual stories compete, complement and at times directly contradict the narratives offered to us elsewhere in the text. As separated first-person accounts of day-to-day suffering and conflict, the voices of Martin and Peter are put in direct competition with third-person accounts from NUM management, government advisers and intelligence service agents. Repeatedly suggesting divisions, even in alliances on the right, these competing narratives unite to evidence a profound lack of communication between the public and private worlds of the strike, a mosaic of perspectives confusing and challenging our understanding of characters and the dispute itself.

Incorporated literary forms gradually become symbolic as characters turn to canonical texts in order to make sense of the strike. *GB84* features a Zola novel, a favourite book of Arthur Scargill:

> The President carried Zola everywhere. *Germinal.*
> Terry had a copy too. He couldn't get into it. [95]

Here literature is revelatory, foreshadowing Terry's ultimate betrayal of the union. Zola is employed again towards the end of the novel with a section entitled simply 'Terminal'. Unlike *Germinal*, there is no hint of rebirth or regeneration at the end of *GB84*. Zola's works come to figure as a sign of commitment: a commitment that ultimately neither Terry nor the strike can sustain. Popular novels are employed by Peace to reflect Terry's increasingly duplicitous nature. The reader witnesses him cutting up *The Secret Agent* 'to make new codes', using *England Made Me* 'as a football', and throwing *The Spy who Loved Me* 'at the wall' [284]. This choice of texts reflects the heightened romantic and political tensions within the novel at this point, as Diane and The President compete for Terry's waning loyalty and affection. The ultimate literary revelation of the novel – that the strike itself is not a simple linear narrative but an existential drama, 'a play within a play' which demands critical detachment – is left to Sweet, 'The Jew', who, as a result of this epiphany, sharpens his focus on the conflict as a Shakespearean 'Revenger's Tale' and all this implies [418].

In *GB84*, a revisiting of the historical record is aided by the employment and manipulation of established images and tropes from the strike period. Visual art and photographs become ways of reflecting on history as well as 'capturing' it. A sense of aesthetic retrospection encourages Peace's striking miner Martin to see that 'every generation creates its own Year Zero' [24]. Photographic images simulate this 'Year Zero', accelerating and intensifying the development of the coal dispute.[19] Converging with infamous press photographs from the period, a hybrid of words and pictures functions to blur historical memories, accentuating the sensory quality of narrative accounts and encouraging identification between the reader and the novel's factional past.

In *GB84* music plays an equally decisive role in rewriting the story of the strike. Incorporated to foreshadow historical events written 'factionally' into the narrative, classical music fills the offices of both The Jew and The President (Tchaikovsky's Serenade in C and Shostakovich's Seventh Symphony respectively), reflecting their moods and intentions. Peace claims that music 'helps me get the feeling of the year somehow, and even how people spoke, it's immersion research'.[20] From Frankie Goes To Hollywood and WHAM to '99 Red Balloons', music forms an effective backdrop to significant events as the popular hits of the 1980s reflect, taunt and confound the lives of characters.

Music takes on a more significant role as the novel develops, with Peace freely sampling from popular music in repetition and refrain. The biggest musical event of the decade, Band Aid, controversially takes centre stage in this text. Striking miner Peter openly questions the timing of Band Aid and its political implications for the miners' strike. His narrative suggests that the UK government manipulated the situation in Ethiopia to detract attention from its own internal tensions: 'Make miners look greedy next to little brown babies dying of starvation in Africa' [400]. The idea of Band Aid as a deliberate political strategy is echoed by many characters and indeed by the structure of the text itself. Shadowy political agents use Band Aid to intimidate Terry by phone – '"It's Christmas time", sang the voice on the end, "There's no need to be afraid"' [377] – while Part IV is forebodingly entitled 'There's a world outside your window and it's a world of dread and fear' [349].

Adding depth to characterization, music enables the reader to access aspects of personality which are revealed unwittingly through musical taste. Although Sweet's opinions on miners initially toe the party line, it is his humming of the *Snow White* tune 'Hi ho, hi ho, it's off to work we go' that reveals his stereotypical ignorance of mining culture [261]. The Jew's songs are a sign of his success. When miners are seen returning, he 'whistles Waterloo' and sings along to the radio, tapping out the corresponding rhythms of the tune and those of the march back to work. This novel actually extends the musical theme begun in the *Red Riding Quartet*, the concluding chapter of which is titled 'Total Eclipse of the Heart'. Arguably, *GB84* is the dreadful realization of this apocalyptic eclipse, finally rendered in the blasé tones of a throwaway pop song. Popular culture is reworked throughout the novel as a metaphor for power relations, symbolic imaginaries functioning to communicate concerns beyond the confines of the coalfields.

The notion of impending historical judgement is made manifest in *GB84* through an obsession with language and rewriting the past. Characters struggle with 'the question of history – the history essentially of a troubled and terrible century, of how to see it and how to write it'.[21] Peace chooses to confront head-on the problems of authoring history. Neil Fontaine is seen selecting and collecting newspaper cuttings to form his own understanding of the strike [69]. Peter's young daughter is also compelled to cut up newspapers and form a scrapbook entitled 'True History Of The Great Strike For Jobs' [330]. This history is primarily designed to counter the manipulation of the 'truth' by the media during the strike: as 'under all the lies she cut out, she'd then write the truth of the matter' [330]. In her rewriting of history, this little girl not only shows us the value placed on historical account, but also draws attention to the necessarily subjective nature of notions of accuracy and 'truth'. Narrative attempts by characters to author their own accounts of the strike directly mirror the efforts of young Bert in Robert Tressell's novel *The Ragged Trousered Philanthropists*, who presents family and friends with his own history of working-class conflict across the ages.[22] Through these attempts to make order, readers bear witness to the difficulties in authoring and crafting a historical narrative, as characters highlight the power of the written word to redefine, shape and ultimately distort accounts of the past.

Through these extra-literary intrusions we 'see both the collecting and the attempts to make narrative order'.[23] Each narrative effectively constitutes a witness statement, a confessional pared down to the essentials of immediate reality. Through an array of plots, sub-plots, subterfuge and sacrifice, *GB84* becomes as chaotic as the strike that it depicts, its narratives harsh and confrontational, its concoction of voices disorientating. Peace admitted during the writing of *GB84* that 'even I don't actually know what is going on [in the novel]'.[24] His text offers us a cultural scrapbook of the strike: a collection of accumulated material and evidence from deteriorating 'sources', broken narratives fractured and fragmented almost to the point of confusion, often making us feel as if we are reading the working notes of the novel rather than the finished text.

Fragmenting language, voices and a wide range of contemporary social, political and cultural discourses through the intrusion of extra-literary forms, Peace creates the illusion of a host of polyphonic characters operating in participative dialogic exchange. The characters who populate his factional striking world are divided among and within themselves, highlighting the 'unseen' divisions within apparently cohesive units during the strike. *GB84* chooses to focus on a fractured police force at odds with both the strikers and themselves. This notion of a police force divided within itself is extended through recollections of friendly encounters with the police on picket lines. Martin recalls sharing soup with the police: 'not that they'd put that on television or in the papers' [10]. Internal divisions are further developed as readers encounter miners worn down by the strike and near to breaking point:

> I don't
> know how much more of this I can
> take. I really don't. I know there were
> them that thought it was the best thing
> that ever happened to them. First few
> months. Especially some of them with
> kids – Time in house with them . . . I wonder
> how they feel about it all now. After
> nine months. Nine bloody months –
> Nine months of toast for their break-
> fast. Nine months of soup for their din-

ner. Nine months of spaghetti for their
tea. Nine months of their kids without
any new gear. Nine months of their
kids on handouts and other folk's
cast offs. Nine months of their wives
trying to make ends meet. Nine
months of their wives trying to hold
them together. Nine months of them
slowly falling apart. Nine months of
them watching every single news programme there was. Nine months of
them talking about nothing else. Nine
months of them arguing and arguing
and arguing and arguing and arguing.
Nine months of them going up to the
bedroom. Nine months of them lying
on their backs. Nine months of them
staring up at the ceiling. Nine months of
them wishing they were fucking dead. [330]

This re-plotting of the historical chronicle is brought to the textual surface in fragmented form as Peter's story becomes impounded in historical event. Ingesting infamous incidents from the strike, this deployment functions to undermine the strike movement, suggesting divides and defaming existing historical accounts through a 'revelatory' rewriting. Evoking and engaging with living witnesses, Peace's novel appropriates personalities, objectifying people and their experiences to encourage a recomprehension of the past.

The need to dramatize the strike for the latter-day reader and construct a human face for a collective struggle is evident in the heavy connotations of violence, division and struggle suggested by the novel's title. *GB84* draws on an organization established in 1975 by far right, secret service and British army officers, disillusioned with the way the UK was being run, called 'GB75'. As the novel develops, the world of the strike becomes a reflection of this context, a bleak and futile dystopian nightmare. A sense of division and dissatisfaction is reinforced by the characters who inhabit this factional world. Linda Hutcheon has suggested that 'the characters of historiographic metafiction are anything but proper types: they are the ex-centrics, the marginalised, the peripheral figures of fictional history'.[25] The characters of *GB84* occupy 'non-places' – roads, hotels and train stations. As ex-centrics they operate alone, distant and scared, forming connections only through blood, broken bonds or intrigue. Those in positions of power are particularly alienated and dehumanized. Their titles – 'The Chairman', 'The Jew', 'The President' – strip each of their humanity and reduce them to pawns in a wider political game. As in a Zola novel, these characters are isolated in an indifferent world, marginalized by a sense of powerlessness against the wider state machinery. A gloss of factional polyphony is further accentuated by the intrusion of real characters into fictional narratives. *GB84* contains 'guest appearances' from David Hart and Tim Bell (advisers to MacGregor and the NCB), from Joe Gormley and Roger Windsor (respectively, Scargill's predecessor as leader of the NUM and the NUM's chief executive), and from Scargill and Margaret Thatcher.[26] Peace develops the suggestions made after the strike that Hart and Bell were informants for MI5 during the conflict, their apparent assertions of dissatisfaction with the collective animated here in an alternative commentary on the historical record.

The multiplicity of voices in operation throughout the novel signals a wider fragmentation of individuals in an alienating political landscape. As Bakhtin asserts, 'language in the novel is always a particular way of viewing the world, one that strives for social significance'.[27] This metanarrative collapse into what appears to be 'authentic polyphony' is made manifest through the adoption of complex, multilayered styles.[28] As a postmodern form of historiographic metafiction, *GB84* reflects on 'thoughts about thought, experiences of experiences and words about words'.[29] Peace underscores the significance of forms of language in this novel, claiming:

> In the original manuscript of *GB84*, there was much, much more old English [. . .] I wanted to conjure up sleeping ghosts and also the unbroken thread of history, the echoes and the repetitions. Thatcher's treatment of the miners, for me, echoed William the Conqueror's Harrowing of the North – when Norman troops killed every male in Yorkshire and salted the earth – following his victory at Hastings [. . .] And so, yes, these languages matter – they are who we are, where we came from.[30]

Mobilizing contemporary echoes of harrowing and death, Peace encourages these discourses of conflict to infiltrate the language of his characters. As the novel develops, language becomes a means of confusing and complicating, clarifying as well as defining:

Words –
The air full of them. Everywhere. Heard but not seen –
Expressions. Assertions. Declarations. Statements. Utterances.
Asseverations. Designations. Locutions. Affirmations. Pledges. Promises.
Guarantees. Assurances Commitments. Reports. News. Information.
Accounts. Intelligence. Advice. Tidings. Greetings. Phrases. Secrets.
Passwords. Catchwords. Watchwords. Shibboleths. Signals. Calls. Signs.
Counter-Signs. Codes. Commands. Orders. Announcements.
Enunciations. Proclamations. Pronouncements. Judgements. Rows.
Polemics. Quarrels. Feuds. Altercations. Contentions. Debates. Arguments.
Shouts. Questions. Answers, responses. Facts. Figures. Messages.
Interactions. Interplay. Intercourse. Transmissions. Connections, contacts.
Intercommunications. Communications. Interchange. Notifications.
Telling. Discussion. Articulation. Rhetoric. Vocalisation. Dialogue.
Discourse. Speech. Comment. Remark. Observation. Opinion. Critique.
Wisecrack. Prattle. Conference. Confabulations. Chatter. Rumours.
Gossip. Hearsay. Tattle. Scandal. Suggestions. Hints. Undertones.
Murmurs. Grumbles. Mumbles. Whimpers. Lies. Cries. Whispers. Talk –
Talk. All Talk. Nothing but talk –
Language. The air full of it. Everywhere – [27–8]

This polymorphous mass suggests that every word spoken by Peace's characters is subject to manipulation, misappropriation or suggestion – that there is no single meaning to any sentence, action or narrative. When words fail, the characters of *GB84* turn to numbers, statistics and figures to communicate, 'talking and talking' [388] without resolution. The title of the novel comes to represent a final synthesis of numbers and words, language pushed to its limits, contested to the point of confusion. The alternating use of standardized and italicized font visually accentuates the appearance of a profoundly dialogic narrative structure. Reminiscent of foreign translation, this presentation foregrounds ideas about language, its manipulation and meaning, and the potent process of 'othering' in operation throughout the dispute.[31] Through this plurality, the division and confusion of the strike is emphasized, presenting apparently innovative and revelatory accounts articulated by the voices of the previously 'unheard'.

The Authority of Reality

All too often in the drama of factional novels, 'fact' rarely makes more than the briefest of cameo appearances. Although marketed as a form of 'info-fiction', *GB84* does not even provide a 50/50 balance of fact and fiction. Through a covert manipulation of factional styles, it documents 'the struggle between the creator and external reality, the urgent demand to master and re-create that reality'.[32] In attempting to re-create the material reality of the strike, Peace acts as ventriloquist for living characters in order to reframe established readings of the period.

While historical fiction can never offer an objective account of the past, *GB84* offers a controversial form of hypo-history, an under-the-surface version of events melding history and fiction. Peace has expressed hope that through 'fictional reinterpretation, fiction can illuminate the facts maybe and make them more compelling perhaps'; yet, rather than represent the voice and experience of those who suffered most, his own novel rejects a distinctly anti-authoritarian heritage to reinforce the hegemonic relationships of an unequal society.[33] Stratified by officialdom, the language of Peace's novel functions to cohere a socio-political unity of hierarchical relations between discourses.

Hutcheon argues that postmodern fictional rewritings of history should 'open it up to the present, to prevent it from being conclusive and teleological'.[34] In contrast, *GB84* directs its narratives to an end point: a marked finalization of events. In doing so, this counterfactual construction provides a neat closure to an inherently open-ended dispute. Instead of offering readers the unrealized and unrealizable finale that Bakhtin considered vital to the novel form, *GB84* culminates with an 'end stop', inscribing a conclusive culmination to narrative events and to the conflict itself. The narrative overtly refers to its own conclusion as a return to 'Year Zero', the ultimate end 'of everything – master narratives, the subject, history'.[35] Unlike the ending of the *Red Riding Quartet*, Peace suggests that he 'didn't want [*GB84*] to offer a sense of redemption, because as a country we haven't got it. And we don't deserve it.'[36]

The more the 1984–5 miners' strike passes into history, the more contemporary authors will seek to reclaim, readdress and reshape it to communicate truths about the present. However, the past can never be fully 'rediscovered' or recorded in these new writings. *GB84* presents the reader with a coded history of the strike, represented suggestively through a hybridity of mobilized popular cultural markers from the period. Imbuing these forms and voices with an apparent authenticity of attribution, the novel lays claim to a factional history, employing a facade of authenticity to ventriloquize official documents. Beneath its 'innocent' veneer of art and literature, bubblegum pop and classical music, lies the sceptical voice of the author, woven subtly through 'factional' narratives as a background noise, an authoritative referee to the manifest conflicts of the strike itself. As a retroactive attempt to resuscitate alternative perspectives on the miners' strike, *GB84* merges reality effects through the representative power of narrativity. Framing a composite package of fiction and faction within a context of historical documents and popular culture, it encourages contemporary readers to acknowledge and 'authorize' a 'factional' history of the events of 1984–5.

chapter six

The Life of Brian

'I haven't done things according to the book.'
[Brian Clough, 1976]

DUFC

After tackling the weighty subjects of the Yorkshire Ripper and the 1984–5 miners' strike, David Peace approached *The Damned United* as a 'respite book' about 'something and nothing', the forty-four days spent by manager Brian Clough at the helm of British football club Leeds United FC in 1974.[1] Peace claims that watching Clough's first game in charge of Leeds inspired a life-long interest in the iconoclastic figure. He recollects: 'my grandfather, father and I were all Huddersfield Town fans and I actually went to Cloughie's first match in charge which was at [Huddersfield] Town's old Leeds Road ground. It was a pre-season friendly and my father probably thought it would be a safe game for the young me to see. I can distinctly remember seeing Clough getting off the coach and ruffling a kid's hair on the way into the ground. And it was that match that gave me the germ of the idea for the book.'[2]

The Damned United was originally conceived as an epic exploration of Leeds United and British football during the 1970s, in which the figure of Brian Clough would play a relatively minor role. Peace had plans for a novel called:

DUFC – an Occult History of Leeds United; a secret grimoire of the Dirty Whites – told through a chorus of voices; Don Revie on his deathbed; Albert Johanneson in his tower-block flat; Brian Clough during his 44 days at Elland Road in 1974; David Harvey in his Sanday caravan on the Orkney Islands, his malt dreams as United Spectres of Leeds past, present and future; a choir of the Damned, conducted by Luchino Visconti. Or something like that [. . .] I went back to Tokyo and I began to read; the history of Leeds United and

the life of Brian Clough, all the football books and all the local newspapers. And also all the novels that I wanted to pay homage to: *Room
at the Top, Saturday Night and Sunday Morning, A Kind of Loving,
This Sporting Life*, Christie Malry's *Own Double-Entry* and Alma
Cogan. And then there came a point, when and where I stopped
reading and I started writing; different lives, different voices [. . .]
There was a very lengthy and very noir prologue entitled 'I, Brian
Clough, Having Slaughtered Alf Ramsey'; there was also a shifty
little character called the Irish Shit-house, a man trapped in a glass
box, endlessly giving his commentary and his opinion; and then
there was that ghostly voice of troubled-Don.[3]

As one voice emerged from this competing chorus, Peace found that
the real Brian Clough came to alter his original plans for the text.
'The more I listened to this voice,' Peace recalls, 'the more I read
about this life [. . .] the more and more I both admired and feared
this Brian Clough; a man of two-halves (at least), as we are all men
of two-halves (at least). But always a character. A genuine character.'[4] Peace's Clough is undoubtedly an engrossing protagonist
and as the eventual sole narrator, this 'man of two-halves' emerged
to dominate Peace's novel.

Historically, Brian Clough's time at Leeds was already a highly
contentious subject. A turf war for the 'truth' had been fought out
across biographies, histories, documentaries and interviews for
some thirty years prior to the publication of *The Damned United*. As
Ray Fell, chairman of the Leeds United Supporters Club, suggests,
'Much has been written and said about the period, a good propor-
tion of it fictional, lots of it guesswork.'[5] During his research, Peace
found that 'nearly every source contradicted the other', leaving him
'faced with at least fifteen versions of "the truth"'.[6] Focusing on a
particular time and set of characters that already fascinate the
British public, Peace's novel contributes to this established range of
opposing sources. However, Peace remains adamant that *The
Damned United* does not seek to enter into any ongoing battle for

'the truth' because no book, whether it is a work of fiction or nonfiction, can ever claim to be 'the truth'. Any writing, whatever its genre,
will always be subjective. To me, *The Damned United* is like a
painting, a portrait of the man, as opposed to a photograph.[7]

Offering an artistic impression rather than a definitive snapshot in his consciously constructed selection of materials, Peace maintains that a 'biographer is choosing which bits to put in and which bits to leave out. So I actually think a novel is more honest. Maybe I was being naive. I felt it was all a matter of public record. I put it together and dramatised it, but nearly all of it was out there.'[8] Conscious of his own subjectivity and working with knowledge of an existing canon on Clough, Peace believes that, of all his novels, *The Damned United* is 'not controversial. I've written about police corruption, the miners' strike, Tokyo in the aftermath of defeat and I could accept that those might be seen as controversial. But the life of a football manager?'[9]

Despite this confident claim, *The Damned United* did prove controversial. The novel was greeted with criticism of its factional representations, particularly by those who feared that readers might 'think there's a grain of truth in it'.[10] Johnny Giles – a former Leeds midfielder under Clough – even took legal action to have sections of his dialogue removed from the novel with the objection that: 'You can't have it both ways, using real names in a factual setting but then writing fiction about them.'[11] This chapter suggests that *The Damned United* sets out to challenge 'fact' and 'fiction' in its refusal to represent historical events through a simple linear narrative or in balanced shades of black and white. Instead, Peace's novel recognizes the darkness and shades of grey that define the past, seeking to draw from the Clough/Leeds episode to examine the wider social, political and economic discourses that informed the development of late twentieth-century British society.

A man of two-halves

The 1970s is perhaps most notable as the period in which feminism began to bloom into the popular consciousness. It was also at this time that concepts and discourses of masculinity came under critical review. Read with this context in mind, *The Damned United* offers a culturally specific form of masculinity. Set against a decline in British heavy industry and social, political and economic crisis, the novel offers football – a game rooted in working-class communities – as a significant source of male identity. *The Damned United* is concerned with the situations and activities of men and the production and expression of masculinity. From the dressing room to the board room, the manager's office to the pitch, space is clearly gendered. Male imperatives direct decisions made in these spaces, feeding into the construction of male identity. Offering his own masculinity as performative, a discourse expressed through repetition and fuelled by sport and routine, Peace's fictional Brian Clough is in many ways an archetype of the 1970s male.[12]

Peace's protagonist measures and validates his own masculinity through the power games and political machinations of the beautiful game. In his role as manager, control is the foremost source of masculine expression, especially territorial control. For Clough, control is implicitly connected to the rules of football in which total governance over the pitch, players and club is of paramount importance. Sociologist R. W. Connell argues that football instructs men in two aspects of power: the development of force through 'the irresistible occupation of space' and the power of skill through 'the ability to operate on the objects within that space, including other humans'.[13] Peace's Clough demonstrates force through his control of people and skill through his ability to enact change. In turning around the fate of Derby County, Clough is always ready to remind himself, '*You have built an ocean liner out of a shipwreck*' [87]. Since his occupation as football manager is well suited to exercising control, football becomes an extension and expression of his own masculinity as absolute operational mode.

However, during his time at Leeds, Clough struggles with events that conspire to undermine his masculinity. On arrival, Clough quickly becomes literally and metaphorically 'damned'. He finds Leeds United equally 'damned' – detestable and loathsome in their complete refusal to accept his authority and values. The inability of either side to form the single entity suggested by their professional title creates an obvious irony in their marked absence of any harmony and, refusing to join together in common purpose or endeavour, Clough and the Leeds team become the epitome of the novel's original title 'DUFC'.

Peace confronts the challenge of representing two very different periods in Clough's professional life by altering the narrative voice to establish a 'man of two-halves' through 'the first person present; present in those 44 days in 1974. And in the second person present; present in the memories that brought him to those 44 days in 1974. Present and incorrect.'[14] This technique not only foregrounds the obviously invented voice of Clough as a fictional character, rather than as a resurrected factual figure, but also challenges readers to confront his paranoid and tormented inner monologues.[15] Peace asserts that, as an author, 'the second person narrative voice [. . .] is the voice I feel most comfortable writing in', because the 'way we remember ourselves is strange – it's me but it's not me, how do you express this? It's him remembering himself, but it's not a "he" or an "I" it's a "you".'[16] During the writing process Peace claims he usually experiments with different tenses, but with *The Damned United*, 'it seemed in order to drive the momentum of the 44 days it needed to be in the present tense [. . .] if he had been looking back it would have altered the paranoia, the immediacy, the momentum [. . .] in the first draft the "you" was written in past tense but I switched it to second'.[17] Using italics to indicate this second-person narrative, Peace creates a clear visual demarcation between the former glories and current struggles of his narrator. Contrasting two periods in Clough's working history, Peace uses the second person to access memories, looking back to explain how Clough arrives at the position where he begins his first-person narrative at Leeds.

Opening with 'Day One', *The Damned United* is comprised of forty-four chapters detailing a day-by-day account of Clough's time at Leeds. Divided into a series of seven 'reckonings', each section is preceded by a table of First Division Football League results for the period, with the results of Leeds United highlighted in bold.[18] These tables visually chart the descent of Leeds under Clough from the echelons of top-flight football to the despair of defeat. Juxtaposing words and numbers, Peace sets success against failure, placing Derby's performance in a Football League Cup third round replay with Chelsea – '*easily the best performance since I have come to Derby*' [69] – against a shocking later defeat with Leeds. Clough's second-person narrative at Derby and first-person narrative at Leeds also arrive at the point of his departure within a few pages of one another, encouraging parallels between past and present, Clough's struggle to stay at Derby and, conversely, to flee from Leeds.

In the opening pages of *The Damned United* the reader is drawn back to Clough's early fear of failure in his career-ending injury at the age of twenty-nine, an event that Clough reflects upon in the second person as '*The worst day of your life*' [7]. His subsequent managerial career is viewed as an extension of this failure, since management is

> *no substitute. Still second best –*
> *Your future. Still second best.* [12]

Inspired by the scenes of another classic British sports novel, David Storey's *This Sporting Life*, and developing an interest in failure and defeat established in his earlier work, Peace employs this injury as a means of informing his character's later choices.[19] At Leeds Clough confesses, 'I hate injured players. I don't want to hear their bloody names. I don't want to see their fucking faces. I stay out of the treatment rooms. I stay out of the bloody hospitals. I can't stand the fucking sight of them' [129]. His reaction echoes an enduring sensitivity to the injury that ended his own career, suggesting a connection between conceptions of the able body and effective masculinity. In an expression of role strain, the dual pains of memory and realization finally force Clough to confront his transformation from player to manager. Distancing himself from injured players and hospitals, he makes a concerted effort to avoid any reminder of past failure that might function to undermine his current authority and success.

At Leeds, Clough's formerly celebrated expressions of masculinity, his energy, spirit, monstrous ego, humour and wisdom, are not viewed as strengths in his personality but as weaknesses. His arrival is described as an ambush by '*Men who want you to fail. Men who want you to lose. Men who wish you were dead*' [51]. Confronted by the '*red eyes and the sharpened teeth*', a 'Finger in my face' [7] and a host of disinterested players, Clough's immediate response is not revenge but rejection: '*Screw them. Bugger them. Fuck the bloody lot of them*' [9]. At social events he is made to feel 'like a bloody intruder at a party' [61], while his speeches meet with a silence that speaks volumes: 'I listen for the sound of a pin drop, drop, dropping' [62]. In his infamous instruction to the inherited Leeds team that

> as far as I'm concerned, the first thing you can do for me is to chuck all your medals and all your caps and all your pots and all your pans into the biggest fucking dustbin you can find, because you've never won any of them fairly. You've done it all by bloody cheating. [29]

Clough demonstrates both masculine authority and a fear of emasculation, dismissing the club's former glory in an attempt to rebuild it in his own image.

These actions betray a vulnerability and lack of confidence that is contrary to the prior reputation of the new manager. On match days at Leeds, Clough is reduced to a state of impotent fear that forces him to 'hide in the office [. . .] I hide and listen to the feet above me' [177]. An increasing paranoia that 'No one understands my position. No one understands the mess Revie left them in and put me in' [116] is mirrored by the wider context of 1974. Clough picks up newspapers to distract himself, but is faced with further failures:

> Nixon and resignation, resignation, resignation:
> *'I have never been a quitter. To leave office before my term is complete is abhorrent to every instinct in my body ...'*
> I put down the paper and I switch on the telly, but there's nothing on except documentaries and news programmes about Cyprus, Cyprus, Cyprus:
> *Deceit and division; division and hate; hate and war; war and death.*
> [126]

Like Clough, Nixon was an outsider who hated elites and who became rightly paranoid that his enemies were out to destroy him. Both men shared a suspicion of those in authority and, once they had achieved a position of power, set out to react against the elitism of the past. As Peace's novel develops, media representations of Nixon's failure and subsequent resignation as a result of the Watergate Scandal pre-empt Clough's own professional fall.[20] Set against the political backdrop of Turkey's military invasion of Cyprus, Clough not only identifies with, but is ultimately unable to escape from, an overarching context of personal, social, national and international conflicts during his time at Leeds. Reflecting his own internal divisions and hates, contextual disagreements are raised by Peace as a backdrop to Clough's personal and professional crises.

The Damned United functions as a further stage in the author's ongoing development of an occult history of Yorkshire and the UK during the 1970s and 1980s. Prior to the novel's publication, Peace expressed concern that *The Damned United* would not offer 'any departure at all; 1974, Leeds – sounds very familiar'.[21] Constructing an occult history of the region's most infamous sporting event, Peace draws on the hostile landscape of 1970s Yorkshire as a living reflection of the psychological torment and deflated confidence of his central character. Informed by previous experiences as a visitor, Clough arrives with an established view of Leeds as a '*Hateful, hateful place, spiteful, spiteful place ...*

Elland Road, *Leeds, Leeds, Leeds*' [5]. Although he reassures himself that 'I am no longer a visitor' [5], his first day at the club undermines this assumption as he arrives to find 'No place to park. No place reserved' [7]. For Clough, 'The sun never shines at Elland Road', there is only 'wind and shadow, mist and rain; dogshit and puddles, purple tracksuits and purple faces' [96]. Repelled by the hostile masculinity and 'West Riding charm' [146] of '32,000 [. . .] *Tetley Bittermen*' [179], Clough is condemned by these 'Yorkshire zombies' [301] and left to the mercy of 'the dark, empty Yorkshire night' [50].[22]

As in the *Red Riding Quartet*, the power of the 'haunt' functions to undermine the manager's already fractured self-belief. The death of Clough's mother during his time at Derby constitutes a significant ordeal for the young manager. He confesses:

> It hits you anew every day. Every time you close your eyes, that's all you ever see, her face in the kitchen. In the doorway. In the garden. In her hat. In her nightie. In the hospital. You wish you had buried your mam, not cremated her. Now there is no grave, no place to go. But if you had buried her, if there had been a grave, you'd go every Sunday. [210]

Each reminder of his mother repetitively returns Clough to trauma, endlessly turning over events until the past reappears and '*Haunts you here. Haunts you now*' [24]. The notoriously verbose manager is reduced to repetition, unable to say or think anything but '*You've lost your mam. You've lost your mam. You've lost your mam*' [200].

'Repetition, Repetition' are the first words of the novel's epigraphic 'Argument' and, as with every David Peace novel, the technique forms a key feature of *The Damned United*. Enhanced by the 'repetitive, hard, insistent, worked' language of his protagonist, an incantatory rhythm of assertion creates an almost blank verse through which the linguistic brutality and primally obsessive nature of Clough's perceptions can be related.[23] Beating out the same phrases in quick succession, repetition articulates the fears and doubts ceaselessly circulating in Clough's mind. Through these internal monologues Peace captures the fear and loathing that rages across Elland Road and gradually comes to erode Clough's confidence. Emphasizing the ritual nature of his sport as well as the increasingly hostile chants of the terraces, repetition even extends to physical events as Clough leaves 'for my final game, same as my first game:

Hudderfield Town vs Leeds United' [323].

The lingering presence of Don Revie, combined with the absence of his mother, family and long-term colleague Peter Taylor, foregrounds Clough's vulnerable position at Leeds. His enduring relationship with Taylor becomes a frequently noted absence, as Clough is left to reflect on '*Peter Taylor. The only friend you ever had . . . He brought out the best in you*' [17]. Only once he is parted from 'Your only friend, Your right hand. Your shadow' [18] does Clough recognize his need for allies. In abject isolation at Leeds, he finds himself unwanted, without confidant, without '*The applause. The adoration. The love*' [9] of his previous ventures. Perceived as a wicked stepfather to Revie's doting patriarch, Clough is unable to disguise his hatred of '*All his sons, his bastard sons. Their daddy dead, their daddy gone*' [9]. Unsettled by the enduring presence of an ex-manager, Clough becomes acutely sensitive to 'The empty desk. The empty chair. *Don's desk. Don's chair*' [10]. His attempts to remove 'The photographs on the walls. The trophies in the cabinets. The ghosts of Elland Road' [8] form part of his concerted efforts to exorcize 'the ghost of troubled Don' [35]. Plagued by dreams of 'empty cities after the A bomb' in which 'I am the only man left alive', Clough's time at Leeds becomes characterized by a potent combination of presence and absence. Like many of Peace's characters, Clough is haunted by the presence of absence: 'I pick up the phone –

The line is dead' [101]. His paranoia is punctuated only by the sinister refrain 'Are you there, Brian? Are you still there?' [279], a question that betrays Clough's continuing inability to contend with loss and let go of the past.

In another motif extended from the *Red Riding Quartet*, Clough's lost watch becomes a reminder of the pressures of time as well as his inability to impose order and authority on Leeds. Offering time as a masculine instrument of control, the civilizing presence of Clough's watch is foregrounded through its absence. Clough loses the watch on his second day at the club – 'I look at my watch. It's not there. I look in my pockets. But it's bloody gone' [23] – and repeatedly notes its absence throughout his forty-four-day tenure. His desire to find the watch grows into near obsession, until he finally orders his players to 'get down on your bloody hands and knees and look for my fucking watch!' [72]. After he loses the dressing room, Clough is reduced to scrabbling around 'on my hands and my knees on the training ground, looking for that bloody watch of mine in the grass and the dirt' [124]. When

the watch finally resurfaces [177], its return is (mis)interpreted as
a potential change of fortune: 'my watch that is back on my wrist
[. . .] maybe, just maybe this might work out' [179]. This response
not only brings into sharp relief both the desperation of the manager and the finite nature of time at this point in the novel, but also
marks a change in Clough's previously rational rejection of superstitions.

The Damned United charts a growing series of bad omens that
echo the presence of 'magick' in Peace's earlier work. At Derby,
Clough is contemptuous of Don Revie's pre-match preparations –
'*The rituals observed, the superstitions followed*' [49] – and chooses to
ignore a series of magpies that foreshadow his own later sorrow
through physical conflict with Peter Taylor.[24] As a man of reason,
Clough does not respect the '*Curses, History. Tradition*' [39] of Leeds
United, believing only in 'Ability and application. Discipline and
determination' [52–3]. Once at Leeds, Clough is subject to further
superstition from chief coach Syd, who regularly utters vague
threats under his breath. The position of Leeds manager itself
appears '*As if by magick*' [169] at a point when Clough is vulnerable
and desperate to maintain his top-level position. Clough's own first-
person narrative unfolds against a set of escalating curses prefacing
each of the novel's seven 'reckonings'.[25] Finally, surrounded by
multiple portents of doom – from broken mirrors and pictures of
peacocks [201] to spilt salt [211] and big black dogs [212] – Clough
is literally unable to ignore a reflection of 'the writing on a wall –

TUO HGUOLC' [212].

Through these increasingly uncanny instances, the first signs of
a crisis emerge. Each incident functions to undermine Clough's
faith and confidence in the past as a foundation on which to build
his future success. Engaged in a persistent internal dialogue with his
demons, Clough struggles to maintain his identity and reputation at
Leeds. As part of this struggle, Peace's protagonist finally realizes
that he is fuelled by his relationship with other men. To resolve this
struggle, he is forced to acknowledge and concede power to Don
Revie, 'as the King Pin, as the Father Figure, as the Man who Made
Everything Tick' [340]. From the haunting presence of Don Revie
and the absence of Clough's watch to the doomed landscape of
Leeds and the superstitious curses of shadowy Northern detractors,
Peace mobilizes established motifs from his existing canon to
explore how and why loss, defeat and failure combine to challenge
identity. Establishing a further dimension to the author's occult

history of a specific time and place, the motifs of the *Red Riding Quartet* are extended in *The Damned United* to show that although '*The scenery changes. The pain remains*' [11].

Football manager one week, prime minister the next

Setting the socialist ideals of Brian Clough against the Thatcherite individualism of Don Revie's Leeds team, *The Damned United* pits two opposing ideologies in battle both on and off the football pitch. Clough sets out with a keen sense of social justice and an understanding of the political importance of honest and clear language. His early career demonstrates the lost social mobility of pre-big-money football as he proceeds on the basis of merit to the top of his chosen industry. Watching his eldest son play football in the 'potholes and the puddles' of the Leeds United car park, Clough is reminded of his humble beginnings as 'A boy with a ball. A boy with a dream' [9]. Clough begins the novel as a 'football socialist', advocating a fair and accessible game for all. During a period of decline for British primary industry and manufacturing, Clough promotes football as an important means of maintaining social inclusion and solidarity. As an expression of this belief, he canvasses for the Labour Party [325] and gives away free tickets to striking miners. These examples of social engagement lead to the tongue-in-cheek claim that he could be '*Football manager one week, prime minister the next*' [134].

Pig-headed, belligerent and brilliant, Peace's protagonist takes inspiration from the angry young men of 1950s British literature. From *Room at the Top* to *The Loneliness of the Long Distance Runner*, his factional characterization is underpinned by a history of fictional working-class male protagonists who achieve against the odds and '*Don't let the bastards grind you down*' [133]. In a pertinent reminder that 'What ever people say you are, that is what you're not' [87], Clough references Sillitoe's 1958 novel *Saturday Night, Sunday Morning* to align himself with the defiant rebels of previous decades. Fuelled by pride and faith in the values of common sense and loyalty to his country, Clough comes to believe that leadership of the national football team

is your destiny. It is your fate –

Not luck. Not God. It is your future –
It is your revenge. [92]

He plots this revenge by empowering those around him with a desire
to rebel against authority. Pierre Bordieu has argued that 'sport, like
any other practice, is an object of struggles between the fractions of
the dominant class and between the social classes'.[26] For Clough,
sport becomes a constant struggle for power as an extension of
historical class conflict. Railing against management and media,
secretaries and star players, Clough is engaged in a constant and
confused war of defiance. Excited by 'The Siege of Derby' [275], in
which his newly ex-players stage a sit-in to have his resignation
refused by the Board, Clough goes on to oversee the Derby County
Protest Movement, a wider programme of agitation including
marches through the town centre [276] and a national campaign
called '*B.B.C! Bring Back Cloughie!*' [280]. This rebellious pride is
underpinned by the belief that Clough is an autonomous and self-
made man whose socialist values cannot be swayed. The desire to
struggle against authority figures is a common aspect of Peace's
central characters, but constitutes an especially essential element of
his fictional Clough.[27] In his dealings with authority, Clough's first
response is always rebellion. He infuriates the League, offends the
FA and alienates chairmen, leading to fines for his clubs and bans
for his players. Since '*There's only one winner; only ever one winner –*
Brian Howard Clough' [105], he must do and have everything, as
in his hero Frank Sinatra's classic song, 'My Way' [36].

For a man who perceives the board room as 'The battlefield' [12],
Clough's desire to overcome authority becomes as significant as his
desire to beat opposition teams. During his first spell in management at Hartlepools, Clough repeatedly clashes with the Board until

Mr Ernest Ord, millionaire chairman of Hartlepools United,
resigns –
Your first coup.Your first blood –
1 – 0. [23]

Dismantling authority to extend his own influence over the club,
Clough's time at Hartlepools becomes marred by constant struggles
and political power games. Even at Derby he is incapable of operating as an effective member of a team, eventually rebelling against
those closest to him:

*You don't ask Pete. You don't ask the chairman. You don't ask the board
–*

You are the manager. You are the man in charge. You are the Boss –
You sign the players. You pick the players. Because it's you who sinks if
they don't swim. No one else. That's why you don't ask. That's why you
just do it. [121]

After this point Clough's 'you' becomes a kind of prayer-like voice,
as the manager rejects formal religion in favour of worship at the
altar of football, even ending his 'sermons' to players with '*Amen*'
[29]. Initiating a '*Golden Age, a Second Coming at Derby County*' [98],
Clough is elevated by the club and its supporters as a saviour figure
of quasi-religious authority and accordingly paid '*an annual salary
of £15,000; double that of the Archbishop of Canterbury*', since '*the
Derby ground is full, but the churches are empty*' [101].

Clough's hatred of authority becomes particularly explosive
during his time at Leeds, where he quickly establishes himself as '*a
dynamite dealer, waiting to blow the place to Kingdom Cum*' [24].
Driving up the M1 with his youngest son, Clough aligns his journey
with a revolutionary march northwards to face 'The press. The fans.
The steady, grey rain. The endless, grey sky –
The emperors and the kings. Oliver Cromwell and Brian Clough'
[18]. Within days of his arrival at the club, Clough stages his own
personal revolution, overthrowing staff and players in a
Cromwellian act of defiance:

> *you sack sixteen of the playing staff, the chief scout, four groundsmen, the
> secretary, the assistant secretary, a couple of clerks and the tea ladies. You
> take down the photographs of Jack Nicholas, Raich Carter and Peter
> Doherty –*
> *No more tradition. No more history. No more curses –*
> *You want a bloody revolution. You want a future. You want it now.* [40]

His desire to enact transformation betrays a destructive impatience
and, as a result, the certainties of the past – for both Clough and
Leeds United – are undermined by rash decision making and impul-
sive actions. Instead of building on a golden age of stability, Clough's
arrival at Leeds begins 'The Derby Express' [165], transferring
allied players from his old club to Leeds. Such expressions of
absolute power are underlined through demonstrations of ownership. In the now infamous decision to break and burn the desk of his

predecessor Don Revie, Clough imposes authority in a symbolic act of defiance and destruction. Even Revie's secretary is forced to concede that she is 'Yours now, Mr Clough' [11].

As part of this drive for ownership, Clough's socialist ideals begin to wane in the face of increasing individualism, financial motivation and media interest in the young manager. During the late 1970s and early 1980s, British football became an expression of a particular type of politics. Former links between social origin and the sport came under attack from media moguls and cash-hungry directors, encouraging capitalism to dominate a game previously distinct in its working-class roots and promotion of social solidarity. *The Damned United* uses the character of Brian Clough to foreshadow these developments and locate their origins. Setting a 1970s working-class male against the new money and new individualism of a Thatcherite dawn, the novel interrogates issues of income and access that would come to dominate the 'beautiful' game. As Barney Ronay argues, the 1970s and 1980s 'saw the emergence of a new strain of rightwing footballer [. . .] with his golfing sweaters, his sponsored Rover and his first intimations of the spiralling financial rewards that would reach frantic levels in the decades to come'.[28] Peace's novel deliberately locates itself at a point where there is a 'shift whereby sport as an elite practice reserved for amateurs became sport as a spectacle produced by professionals for consumption by the masses'.[29] Although Peace's Clough sets out as a man principled in the values of socialism, rebellion and change, he gradually becomes distracted by money and power and finds himself working at a club whose values are the opposite of those he set out to honour.

As Clough climbs higher up the managerial ladder, he becomes deeply undemocratic and establishes himself in a position where his word is law. While Peter Taylor previously negotiated financial settlements and stressed the need for money to be a factor in all professional decisions, Clough becomes increasingly distracted by financial reward and personal power during his time at Derby. The failure of his sporting marriage to Taylor and his decision to take the job at Leeds are the first signs of the way in which this will impact on his later career. Although he claims that the move from Derby to Brighton and then quickly on to Leeds is '*not about the money*' [299], Clough's failure at his new club means that he eventually becomes concerned with getting his 'slice of the pie', culminating in the demand for a £25,000 settlement for forty-four days' work. As a critique of the kind of working-class aspiration that led to

Thatcherism, *The Damned United* uses the figure of Brian Clough to explore a change in football and politics during this period. Moving away from a sport played by and for the people to one owned and controlled by capitalists with little direct interest in, or experience of, the game, Clough ultimately contributes to, rather than prevents, the erosion of the relationship between socialist values and football and the corporatization of sport by the media and business in the late twentieth century.

Twenty-first-century readers approach *The Damned United* from a time in which the role of the media and public awareness of the football manager is key to the modern game. In fact, this media presence and concept of the superstar manager are relatively new. The real Brian Clough was one of the first football managers whose engagement with the media not only influenced the development of the game, but also turned him into a celebrity in his own right.[30] As an outspoken and often outrageous commentator, Peace's Clough follows this historical lead, providing the press with good copy and consequently enjoying a high profile in the media. A potent combination of fame and infamy encourages him to believe that his authority extends to control over the press and he comes to pride himself in an ability to benefit from their relationship. Clough confidently claims:

> I already know their faces, already know their names and their papers; what time they have to have their copy in by and what time their presses roll; what they like to drink, when they like to drink it and how much they like to drink of it. And they already know just what to ask me and what not; what to write and what not; because I practically write their sodding copy for them; do their bleeding jobs for them –
> *And they bloody love me for it. Fucking love me –*
> Every time I open my mouth. [99]

In a mutually beneficial agreement built on an implicit understanding of power and representation, Clough and the media work together to forge a new image of football during the 1970s. Both print and visual media expanded during this period to meet an increased demand for commentary on sport. In *The Damned United*, this contextual development enables Clough to extend his authority to fill these new forms. He is astutely conscious that:

It is a new world. It is a new England –
The colour supplements, The colour television. The brand-new papers. The
Sun. The columns and then panels. The columns and the panels that need
opinions. Minds with opinions. Mouths with opinions –
A mind and a mouth like yours, open wide. [107]

Through his early dealings with the media, Clough transforms himself into a highly coveted face of the game, a figure capable of wielding considerable personal power. Convinced that although *'They might kick the screen, they might kiss the screen, but you know no one switches it off while you're on. They bloody watch it. The same with your columns in the newspapers'* [209], he is able to forge *'A new name for yourself –*

Cloughie' [107]. Moving from football to popular comment, Clough mutates into a mouth-for-rent, is sent by the *Daily Mail* to meet Muhammad Ali in 'the Meeting of the Mouths – Ego vs Ego' [323], and quickly becomes a familiar face in British popular culture.

A media presence underscores Clough's authority, but also offers the distracting belief that adoration can be found away from the football pitch. Through his close relationship with the press and frequent appearances in the media, Clough effectively furthers the commodification of his formerly working-class sport. *The Damned United* exposes the role of the media in splintering the solidarity and class connections that had previously defined the game, distracting managers with money and the cult of celebrity. Warned by Derby board member Jack Kirkland to *'Stay off the bloody television and cut down the newspaper work'* [228], Clough is eventually forced to concede that it was a *'Fucking shame you only trained with the team for thirty minutes that week. Fucking shame you spent most of that week on the motorway or on the train, up and down to London Weekend Television'* [168]. As a result, Derby County become 'Fallen Champions' [162], while Clough rises to the media spotlight.

During his time at Leeds, Clough's control of the press slips further as he finds himself unable to direct the media as easily as he had at Derby. In a foreshadow of his own eventual clashes with the press, Clough sees

Bestie by the side of the road, larger than life, any life –
His head full of demons; his own throat cut . . .
To sell them Brylcreem. Double Diamond beer and pork sausages. [52]

Distracted by adverts featuring fellow iconic footballer George Best, Clough glimpses in these hoardings shadows of his own fate.[31] Like Best, Clough finally comes to realize that he cannot control the media and is left to reflect helplessly that '*You are not on the back pages of the papers, you're on the front*' [325]. As a consequence of Clough's media presence, his Leeds players also find themselves 'put on trial by television' [193] as the Bremner and Giles incident is repeated until it escalates far beyond its original magnitude. Clough's knee-jerk reaction, 'Ban the television!' [194], is met with little more than ironic reflection from the Leeds Board – '"Those who live by the sword", laughs Bolton' [194] – as a rebellion against a wider issue of the period, of sport becoming a mediated event. Confirming Clough's realization that his former 'control' over the media was simply an illusion, *The Damned United* charts developments in relations between the media and football that would come to direct representations of, and engagements with, the game for the rest of the twentieth century.

Dramatizing Brian Clough's forty-four days at Leeds as an important event in recent British social history, Peace adds to Clough's own self-mythologizing of this period through autobiographies and accounts penned during his lifetime. Ending his own novel with a clear affirmation of Clough's abilities through his later European Cup wins with Nottingham Forest [343], Peace does not simply create a Brian Clough simulator, instead focusing on the man behind the words.[32] As a result, *The Damned United* is more than a simple historical football book. It is a novel 'about fact and about fiction, about dreams and about nightmares, about defeat and about revenge, about tragedy and about farce, about wings made of wax and rays made of sun'.[33]

Peace's Clough demonstrates the courage and idealism of a hero and is very much aware of the myth that has built up around him. However, this becomes his undoing. His fatal attraction to the Leeds job betrays a compulsive rivalry, one that ultimately undermines his masculinity and success. Events become almost Aristotelian in their scale as readers witness a reversal of fortune caused not only by a mistake, but by a fatal flaw in the nature of Clough as tragic hero. Through Clough's quasi-Shakespearean monologues, readers witness the traits responsible for both his rise and his downfall. Carried along by one voice, in two periods, an overarching sense of doom betrays the inevitability of an approaching fall.

Although Peace set out to write a novel that was 'an antidote' to his previous texts, 'something lighter and quicker', *The Damned United* is not simply a respite book about 'something and nothing'.[34] Instead it offers a significant continuation and ongoing interrogation of key events in the history of Yorkshire and the UK as part of the author's wider construction of an occult account of the 1970s and 1980s. Addressing universal themes of rivalry, tragedy, love and ambition, Peace reaches beyond the traditional confines of the sports novel to destabilize notions of 'fact' and 'fiction' through an intense, singular focus on an already familiar public figure. As 'another fiction, based on another fact' [345], *The Damned United* does not offer football as a mere game of two halves, but as an expression of, and meditation on, the social, political and economic discourses of late twentieth-century British society.

chapter seven

Occupation and Defeat in the *Tokyo Trilogy*

'One of the things I've realised is that the books all deal with defeat ...'
[David Peace, 2010]

Defeat

The writings of David Peace are haunted by the occult presence of the past, an alternative history that remains untold in recent accounts of historical events. As a series of novels concerned with occupation and defeat, the *Tokyo Trilogy* moves towards a broader awareness of the role of the past in authoring the present and future of twentieth-century Japan.[1] Set in the wake of a particularly savage conflict that marked the final stages of World War II, the trilogy interrogates social, political and economic manifestations of defeat and occupation, employing extremes of time and place to document the rise of Tokyo from post-war ruin in 1945 to a city 'regained' in 1964.[2]

In the final months of World War II, Japan was faced with an increasingly slim chance of victory. Subjected to an unprecedented ordeal from the air, the country suffered a heavily depleted defence and a rapidly declining population. Japan's largely wooden residential and factory buildings experienced severe damage, with forty percent of built-up areas in more than sixty cities destroyed as a result of the Allied aerial bombardment.[3] Despite this devastation, the West continued to perceive an unbending defiance in the enemy and, assuming that Japan would carry on fighting until the very end, responded on 6 August 1945 by dropping an atomic bomb on Hiroshima.[4] The decision to drop the atomic bomb on a city rather than on open land functioned as a gesture to the Japanese leadership that Tokyo could, and perhaps would, be next. With the capital city already devastated, fear began to grow that the Western threat of atomic war could lead to the outright extermination of the Japanese race.

In the wake of Hiroshima and under threat of further atomic attacks, the Japanese Emperor unconditionally surrendered to Allied powers on 15 August 1945. Forced to concede to the Potsdam Declaration that defined the terms for Japanese surrender – to end the war or endure 'prompt and utter destruction' – on what became known as 'VJ day' (Victory in Japan), Japan's surrender brought an end to World War II. Written by President Harry S. Truman of the US, Chinese leader Chiang Kai-Shek and Prime Minister Winston Churchill of the UK (in one of his final agreements before handing office to Clement Attlee the following day), the Potsdam Declaration was initially rejected by Japan. However, after the horrors of Hiroshima, the Emperor broadcast a national declaration of peace, warning his people to prepare for a future 'enduring the unendurable and suffering that which is insufferable'.[5]

Led by the supreme command of General Douglas MacArthur as SCAP (Supreme Commander of Allied Forces), Japan was occupied for the next eight years by Allied forces from the US and Australia, but also from India, New Zealand and the UK. Although the occupation was formally ended on 8 September 1951 by the San Francisco Peace Treaty, it did not come into force until 28 April 1952 when Japan was returned her free country status.

The years 1945–52 marked the first time in history that Japan had been occupied by a foreign power. During this period its people were forced to contend with conflicting feelings of guilt and relief, pain for the past and hope for the future. As historian Conrad Totman reflects, 'the Japanese public in August 1945 was torn between powerful grief over the lost cause and equally powerful relief that the bombing, slaughter and sleepless nights had ended'.[6] As a result of this tension, the post-war period became a highly contentious time in which the Japanese struggled to come to terms with change.

The first phase of the Allied occupation focused on social and cultural revolution as well as political and military reform. The occupiers sought to eradicate the militarism that had defined Japan's past. This was achieved through the promotion of Western democratic ideals as a viable path forward from the ruins of defeat. On 2 September 1945, the Japanese Instrument of Surrender was agreed, which aimed to eliminate the war potential of Japan and establish the country as a pro-Western power. The old regime was readdressed through war crimes tribunals, the reduction of the powers of the emperor and the authoring of a new constitution.[7] An initial period of 'retribution and reform' was followed by a second phase of 'recon-struction'.[8] This change was partly influenced by early developments in the Cold War, but was also fuelled by the growing financial cost to the US of sustaining post-war Japan. The 1964 Olympics provided a useful stimulus to this programme of recon-struction, offering much-needed urgency, a sense of direction and a chance to celebrate the change engendered by the occupying forces.

The socio-cultural history of reconstruction was one of reform from above with an emphasis on the Japanese people and their responsibility for the past. Negotiating the values and identity of another nation, the occupiers sought to instil new hopes and dreams in a people largely locked in old habits and dispositions. Coping with the shock of defeat and the aberration of loss, the Japanese popula-tion was encouraged to use the end of the war as a point of demarcation. In reality, the pain of defeat became an informing influence on the character of a country in mourning. Confronted by 'one hundred million people in a state of trauma', the occupiers were forced to navigate the hopelessness and exhaustion of post-war Japan.[9]

The first two novels of David Peace's *Tokyo Trilogy* open in *media res* amidst these scenes of social, economic and political ruin. Both *Tokyo Year Zero* and *Occupied City* demonstrate sympathy for subjects materially, physically and mentally broken by a legacy of total war. Trapped in a seemingly endless purgatory, a landscape scarred by death and retribution, expressions of compromise and desperation come to define the occupation period as depicted by these novels. United by a shared sense of loss, confusion and despair, characters inhabit a world shaped by dislocation and displacement. Foregrounding the ruin of the present, the weight of the past hangs heavy over the occupation period as an uncomfortable reminder of a city rebuilding itself for a second time (after a first rebuild as a result of the 1923 earthquake).

Underscoring his literary images with grainy black-and-white photographic images of post-war Japan, Peace creates a layered focus on defeat through the eyes of the losers rather than the victors, using landscape as a starting point from which to conduct a wider investigation of the many and varied ways in which defeat can come to define a time and place. Refusing to shy away from graphic representations, Peace's novels go some way to capture the 'terrible misery of that time and the desperation of honest men and women to make a living'.[10] The opening pages of *Tokyo Year Zero* immerse the reader in a post-apocalyptic world of despair where '*They are handing out potassium cyanide to the women, the children and the aged, saying this latest cabinet reshuffle foretells the end of the war, the end of Japan, the end of the word*' [*TYZ*, 3]. The novel's epigraph – '51. Defeat' – from *A Fool's Life* by Akutagawa Ryunosuke, foregrounds defeat and occupation as central concerns of a country trying to pull itself up off its knees. To counter the effects of his own 'defeat', Ryunosuke's writer takes the sleep-inducing barbiturate Veronal in an attempt to gain 'clarity', foreshadowing Detective Minami's own reliance on Muronal [*TYZ*, 3] to endure the defeated world of *Tokyo Year Zero*. In the '*hot and dark, hidden and cowed*' [*TYZ*, 3] city of post-war Tokyo, society has become a ghost-town where everyone is either 'evacuated or absent' [*TYZ*, 4]. At a time when '*Everything is lost*' [*TYZ*, 35], Minami is left to reflect:

> If you've never been defeated, never lost –
> If you've never been beaten before –
> Then you don't know the pain –
> The pain of surrender –
> *Of occupation* . . . [*TYZ*, 70]

Forced to destroy past allegiances, but unable to forge new connections with a changed place and time, the population of post-war Tokyo is haunted by memories of recent defeat. Minami continues to recall vividly the public response to Japanese surrender, people 'howling, now prostate upon the floor in lamentation, weeping in the dust' [*TYZ*, 23]. The 'sounds of one hundred million weeping, howling, wounded people borne on a wind across a nation ending' [*TYZ*, 23] forms a soundtrack to his existence as a once great city is transformed into a living '*Hell*' [*TYZ*, 25] of despondence and disease.

As Minami passes through a landscape of defeat he notes 'Buildings of which nothing remains but their front walls; now only sky where their windows and their ceilings should be [. . .] Bomb after bomb, fire after fire, building after building, neighbourhood after neighbourhood until there are no buildings, there are no neighbourhoods and there is no city, no Tokyo' [*TYZ*, 6]. In a non-space marked by absence and loss, defeat is literally in the air, as Boss

Matsuda notes the old regime 'burning all their documents and their records. That's the smoke of surrender' [*TYZ*, 8–9]. Although the 'storm has now passed' [*TYZ*, 2], the war is a continued and felt presence. Minami works from a police office behind 'blackout curtains' with the 'toilet blocked. No water. Nothing' [*TYZ*, 3], while his force operate with 'only one working car for the whole division' [*TYZ*, 30]. Surrounded by 'impotent telegraph poles' [*TYZ*, 47] and wearing 'the same shirt and the same trousers I have worn every day for the past four or five years' [*TYZ*, 51], the detective comes to represent the reality of defeat in post-war Japan.

The landscape of the *Tokyo Trilogy* is used to question the status of those surviving as '*the lucky ones*' [*TYZ*, 38]. Detective Minami and Murata Masako, the young woman who survives the bank massacre of *Occupied City*, interrogate the value of survival in a period of defeat. Refusing to accept that 'Those who survive are stronger' [*OC*, 58], characters endure war and poisoning only to remain trapped in the ongoing horror of life under occupation. The miracle of their survival is consequently set against the horrific reality of living in the shadows of 'The defeat and the capitulation. The surrender and the occupation. The ghosts all here today' [*TYZ*, 33]. Through the pervading presence of the past, post-war Tokyo is quickly established as a place in which the living and the dead co-exist on a transitory plain. Amidst the apparent progress of the occupation, the return of the past manifests itself in the numerous war dead that re-enter the country for burial under the chilling reminder that 'the day will soon come when the ashes of the war dead will have to be returned to their relatives in ordinary plain brown wrapping paper'. In a world where 'men talk about ghosts and demons in their sleep', the past impedes the progress of the present, trapping ordinary men and women in an occupied stasis. Even Minaimi is forced to concede that there will be 'No new mornings here' [*TYZ*, 125].

In this state of stasis, time itself becomes defeated as characters 'lose track of the time' [*TYZ*, 14] and note that time has become 'disjointed' [*TYZ*, 25]. Like many of Peace's protagonists, Minami is not only aware of, but increasingly obsessed with time – repeatedly reflecting, 'I glance at my watch' [*TYZ*, 41]. In a world in which change appears to have stopped dead, 'Everyone [is] talking about the minutes that feel like hours. The hours that feel like weeks. The weeks that feel like months. The months that feel like years –

This year that has felt like a decade' [*TYZ*, 70]. Wristwatches become a symbol of this wider spatio-temporal jarring. Minami encounters an old man at a People's Bar who tells him that his watch is stuck at twelve midday [*TYZ*, 158]. The detective later revisits the bar, only to find it in ruins. He is told that the building was destroyed during the war by a bomb which killed over a hundred people. Forced to concede that he previously 'must have been drinking with ghosts' [*TYZ*, 210], Minami becomes increasingly aware that the boundaries of time and space, like much else in post-war Tokyo, are shattered, that nothing in the present can escape from the stains of the past.[11]

Largely discredited in their newly occupied country, the Japanese army and its ex-soldiers return to this ruined landscape to find their former identities undermined by occupiers who are eager to deny Japan's military past. As historian Richard Storry suggests, many Japanese servicemen came back to 'a Japan that no longer cared for them. They had left their homes as heroes. They returned as living ghosts, to be submerged in the anonymous masses struggling for a bare livelihood.'[12] Throughout *Tokyo Year Zero*, returning Japanese soldiers are, like the post-war city itself, both living and dead, past and present, trapped 'between retreat and defeat' [*TYZ*, 2]. One newly returned soldier sits at a new, American-style diner to tell his own narrative of defeat, of a family misinformed of his death, of their staging of his funeral in his absence and conviction that their son is long dead. His post-war return is met with fear and denial – 'They say I'm a ghost' [TYZ, 186] – leaving him, like Minami and Murata Masako, a 'survivor' without a past, present or future.

Capturing the chaos of reconstruction, the *Tokyo Trilogy* sets the shattered identities of the past against an unstable world of the post-war present, following people fleeing or hiding in ruined buildings and under false names. Boss Matsuda is quick to offer Detective Minami 'a new job? A new name? A new life? A new past . . . ?' [*TYZ*, 9] as simply another 'product' available on the new black market. In the occupied city of Tokyo everyone has secrets, nothing is what it seems and no one is immune from deception. Minami quickly becomes obsessed with duplicity and its prevalence in the hierarchies of power. He highlights the case of:

> Chief Inspector Adashi –
> *Adashi or Anjo or Ando or whatever he calls himself this week; he has changed his name and he has changed his job, his uniform and his rank, his life and his past; he is not the only one . . .*

No one is who they say they are . . .
No one is who they seem to be . . . [TYZ, 34–5]

Minami's timely reminder that 'We lost a war. We've all got secrets' [*TYZ*, 65] functions as an early warning of his own hidden past, as well as that of his father's, as a Kempei solider who succumbed to a post-integration mental breakdown. Serial killer Kodaira hints that he is aware of Minami's previous identity during police questioning [*TYZ*, 141], using this information as a weapon against the detective whose own sense of self becomes increasingly fractured.

The advent of the occupation and the trauma of defeat return Tokyo to a time at which

'the hour is zero; the Year Zero –

Tokyo Year Zero' [*TYZ*, 26]. This assertion ends the introduction to the first novel of the trilogy, effectively establishing an overview of events leading up to the one-year commemoration of Japanese surrender. Minami is very conscious of this anniversary – regularly noting 'It has been one year' [*TYZ*, 33] – and its relationship to a developing series of serial killings. However, this marker of time also inspires frustration and anger. The detective battles a constant desire to scream '*Get off your knees!*' [*TYZ*, 54] to those around him and challenges 'the progress of reform and the gains of democracy' [*TYZ*, 29] achieved in the initial twelve months of US occupation.

Repetition is a key feature of Peace's work and the *Tokyo Trilogy* is no exception. In *Tokyo Year Zero* the technique is taken to a breaking point of cyclical incantation and replication. Peace argues that, as an author, repetition 'works for me on two levels: every day we do the same things and we say the same things and there is very little variation [. . .] people live quite repetitious lives. Fiction never seems to pick up on this. I want the books to be realistic.'[13] In his *Red Riding Quartet* this literary style is developed across four novels, but in the *Tokyo Trilogy* Peace begins at an end point, not only for a city at 'Year Zero' but for his own use of repetition and refrain.

In a series that highlights the significance of the past to the present, repetition is used to warn against the dangers of forgetting and to help characters hold on to a precarious grasp of reality. Rather than creating a cumulative effect, this technique quickly becomes relentless as repetition interjects the narrative with flashbacks to previous conflicts and the broader background noise of society. Through an economy of expression, repetition adds to the pace of the narrative, encouraging readers to race through events and encounters. As characters make the same mistakes, repeat the same routines and turn over the same problems, repetition becomes an effective means of reflecting this internal rhythm as well as the everyday sounds and events of post-war Japanese society. Drawing on the necessarily repetitious nature of genre fiction, the trilogy highlights the intensely repetitious nature of crime. Minami and Dr Nakadate are painfully aware of this haunting repetition of crime, and their shared fear that *'We've both seen this before'* [*TYZ*, 114] becomes a significant breakthrough in the pattern of the Kodaira killings.

After writing the first novel of the trilogy, Peace claims to have realized he had 'gone as far as I can go with what I was trying to do with the repetition and one lines' and promised that *Occupied City* would be 'a different kind of book'.[14] Although the intensity of narrative repetition undoubtedly reaches its zenith in this first novel, the brutality of repetition in *Tokyo Year Zero* is transformed in *Occupied City* into an interweaving of chants from various speakers connected by a writer whose incantations frame the text. As the second novel develops, language begins to crack under the strain of competing narrative perspectives. Leaving the reader 'In this place – no place / un-place', the novel ends *'In-caesura, in-difference'* [*OC*, 17], a pause reflecting a wider lack of clarity in which nothing is determined and no single voice can be considered authoritative.

The rhythm of the first two novels not only echoes the ancient languages and songs of Japanese culture but, when read aloud, carries its own incantation, a soundtrack to the surface narrative, drawing upon music and memory, language and life. Throughout *Tokyo Year Zero* and *Occupied City*, background noises combine to create an obsessive effect, encouraging the reader to hear, taste and smell the landscape of post-war Tokyo. Peace claims that he is 'very conscious of the sound' of his novels.[15] This acute awareness transforms the narratives of his *Tokyo Trilogy* into a series of audio spectacles. Peace employs the evocative *'smells of rotten apricots'* [*TYZ*, 79] and the noises of the occupation to create a powerful sonic landscape. From the *'Chik-taku. Chiku-taku. Chiku-taku . . .'* [*TYZ*, 29] of a ticking watch and the incanted prayer 'Namu-amida-butsu. Namu-amida-butsu. Namu-amida-butsu' [*TYZ*, 32] to the *'Potsu-potsu'* of continuously falling rain [*TYZ*, 364], an auditory dimension layers experience of time and space.

Above this repetitive soundscape, detective Minami is acutely aware of a constant

'*Ton-ton. Ton-ton. Ton-ton. Ton-ton. Ton-ton. Ton-ton* . . .
The sound of hammering and hammering –
Ton-ton. Ton-ton. Ton-ton. Ton-ton . . . ' [*TYZ*, 29]. The concrete
poetry of this repetition is suggestive of the concrete reconstruction
of post-war Japan, while in *Occupied City* the sound of hammering
functions to highlight another empty attempt to restore order, as
characters note 'the sound of hammers, the hammers and nails to
hide the stains' [*OC*, 112] of the Shiinamachi bank massacre. Peace
claims the inspiration for the insistent sound of hammering 'came
from a story about the sound of hammering set in the reconstruction years'.[16] In this story the sound of hammering, and the yellow
wood used in the construction process, become symbols of home
and hope. However, for Peace's own post-war characters, the same
sound becomes a depressing metronome for their post-war existence. Influenced by the drumbeat of Noh theatre that resembles a
death ritual or funeral rite, the sounds of the reconstruction offer
little more than a masked intonation of despair. Surviving in spite
of, rather than because of, these repetitive noises, the sonic landscape of the trilogy becomes an increasingly irritating reminder of
the empty constitutional promises of the occupiers.

Intertextual Occupation

Both *Tokyo Year Zero* and *Occupied City* use true crime as a starting
point to investigate social, economic and political manifestations of
defeat. The novels suggest that understanding the fractured,
defeated and occupied nature of post-war Tokyo is vital to understanding the nature of the crimes that came to define this particular
time and place. *Tokyo Year Zero* re-examines the case of Kodaira
Yoshio, a serial killer who raped and murdered ten women between
25 May 1945 and 6 August 1946 in Tochigi and Tokyo. After the
fifth murder, he began to commit necrophilia with his corpses and
raped around thirty women in addition to his murder victims. On
20 August 1946, Kodaira was arrested. The Supreme Court
sentenced him to death on 16 November 1948 and he was executed
on 5 October 1949. In *Tokyo Year Zero*, Detective Minami works in
the First Investigative Division of the Tokyo Metropolitan Police
Department and is put on the Kodaira case.[17] In the opening pages
of the novel, Minami's colleagues appear reluctant to investigate the
evolving series of murders – 'Take our time, walk slowly and hope

we're late' [*TYZ*, 5] – and are quickly distracted by the murder of Boss Senju and the implication of fellow detective Fujita in the events leading up to his death. Initially, Minami's motto is also '*Hear nothing, see nothing, say nothing*' [*TYZ*, 86], but as a pattern of murders involving the ritual strangulation and rape of young girls emerges, he realizes that repetition – 'The good detective visits the crime scene one hundred times' [*TYZ*, 173] – rather than reluctance is the key to finding the killer and usurping the criminal occupation of Tokyo as '*Kodaira country*' [*TYZ*, 273].

The victims of Kodaira Yoshio are found strangled, raped and left to die among the bodies of the war dead. As extensions of the wider debris of conflict, these defeated women come into close focus through candid and vivid descriptions of their wasted bodies. Minami describes Kodaira's first victim as '*Bloated, punctured, flesh and bones, hair and teeth*' [*TYZ*, 13] and seems fascinated by the decaying corpses of a growing series of broken women [*TYZ*, 37]. Throughout the novel, Kodaira's crimes are offered as a product of the socio-economic conditions of the period. Manipulating the defeated and occupied state of post-war Japan to prey upon vulnerable women who will 'fuck for bread' [*TYZ*, 189], the Kodaira case is raised as a broader political comment on gender and power relations.

In the second novel, *Occupied City*, the Shiinamachi bank massacre is also used to suggest connections between the causes of crime and the condition of occupation. The novel reveals that on Monday 26 January 1948 a killer entered the Shiinamachi branch of the Teikoku bank and told the acting manager that there had been a dysentery outbreak in the local area. He claimed that, since a person from that area had made a deposit in the bank earlier in the day, every member of the bank staff had to be vaccinated against the disease and that he had been sent by Lieutenant Parker, the man in charge of the disinfecting team for the area, to ensure this was carried out. The poison he administered killed twelve of the staff. Little money was missing when police arrived on the scene, leading to rumours that the killer might have had political motivations. The *modus operandi* of the crime is offered as a statement in itself, a warning from disgruntled members of the old Japanese biological research Unit 731 who felt abandoned in a post-war period of reconstruction. Disease is rife in post-war Japan and, as a result, fear motivates the bank staff to drink the medicine offered by their killer. Their trust is generated by his promise to cure them as well as by his uniform that represents the authority of the occupation.

The narrative device used to structure *Occupied City* is based on the short story 'In a Grove' by Japanese writer Akutagawa Ryunosuke, perhaps best known in the West as the story that provided the inspiration for Akira Kurosawa's film *Rashomon*.[18] Intertextually 'occupying' the ancient Shinto tradition of story-telling, Peace's novel follows a writer's attempts to use a medium to summon up twelve witnesses, who each relate their tale in a single chapter before extinguishing a candle to signal their conclusion. These witnesses include the twelve victims of the Shiinamachi bank massacre, one female survivor, two detectives working on the case, a journalist from a local paper, a gangster, an occult detective, an American chemicals expert, a Russian investigator, a ferryboat man, the accused Hirasawa and the character Peace offers as the real killer.[19] As the unlucky thirteenth member of this group, the writer is left in darkness to piece together their statements.[20]

In Peace's novels it is the case that dictates the way in which the tale is told. Historically, these cases have been plagued by conspiracy and complicity. Peace's narratives attempt to reflect this through their spectrum of competing truths and lies told by a collection of contradictory witnesses. Having spent a long time researching the Shiinamachi bank massacre for *Occupied City*, Peace 'didn't think it was a story that could be told with one narrative voice, I wanted to show competing versions of the truth'.[21] The resulting novel allows Peace the chance for a more formal experiment in form than in *Tokyo Year Zero*, drawing on his own intertextual occupation of the established traditions of Japanese narrative structures to interrogate forms of political, social, historical and cultural occupation in post-war Japanese society. Through a wider exploration of the writer's relationship with narrative, voices of the dead are raised as a form of exorcism. At the end of its séance, the novel closes with a corre-sponding plea for 'no more stories and no more lies' in a 'book always, already written,

written and abandoned' [*OC*, 288].

Marred by conflicting information and a lack of co-operation, the characters of *Occupied City* circle around the hunt to locate a killer, as each narrative attempts to shed new light on the events informing one fateful day. Although 'The First Candle' does this most directly, communicating the collected voices of the twelve victims of the Shiinamachi bank massacre – 'And so again tonight we are Takeuchi

Sutejiro, Watanabe Yoshiyasu, Nishimura Hidehiko, Shirai Shoichi, Akiyama Miyako, Uchida Hideko, Sawada Yoshio, Kato Teruko, Takizawa Tatsuo, Takizawa Ryu, Takizawa Takado and Takizawa Yoshihiro' [*OC*, 7] – an alternative perspective is offered by 'The Tenth Candle – The ~~Protestations, Denials~~, Confessions of the ~~Accused, Convicted~~, Condemned Man in the Cell, *as it really was?*' [*OC*, 239]. Here, the voice of the accused Hirasawa Sadamichi confesses that although he is guilty of arson and fraud, he is not the murderer.[22] In *Occupied City* narrative sections are often crossed out, highlighting the imposition of censorship in a supposedly democratic post-war Japan, as well as the editing process intrinsic in the writing of historical accounts. As the novel develops, readers are forced to read past this visual editing to penetrate the words beneath. In the eleventh candle many of these 'edited' words are the confessions of the man the novel positions as the real killer. The 'Last Words of the Teikoku Murderer, or a Personal History of Japanese Iniquity, Local Suffering & Universal Indifference (1948)' [*OC*, 257] give voice to the killer, who describes his employment during World War II in the 'Death Factory' [*OC*, 257] at Pingfan as part of the infamous Unit 731.[23] Although the Killer writes to Lieutenant General Shiro Ishii, the former head of the Japanese biological research programme, complaining that '*defeated Japan has not been very cordial in welcoming us back*' [*OC*, 262] and asks for a money loan to help his post-war rehabilitation, he does not receive a reply and 'goes hungry and cold while night after night, the men the Killer once followed, the men the Killer once served, retire well fed and warm' [*OC*, 265]. A sense of injustice motivates his final actions in the Shiinamachi bank massacre as an act of protest at a past denied, a history erased and a people left destitute.

Expanding the individual consequences of crime to wider universal concerns, the *Tokyo Trilogy* revisits notable cases in the history of post-war Tokyo to explore 'why these two murders happened there, why in Tokyo'.[24] Despite claiming that he had a piece of paper that 'had anti-crime novel above the desk' while he was writing this trilogy, Peace explores the many conspiracies that have formed around these two infamous cases and in doing so reveals the key role played by the condition of defeat in perpetuating an underlying paranoia and complicity in crime demonstrated by both the occupiers and their occupied people.

Exploring how crimes come to define the society that produced them, the *Tokyo Trilogy* uses the specific circumstances of the occupation to explain the crimes of the period. The epigraph to *Occupied City* sets the promises of the occupiers against the pain of life under occupation, presenting Tokyo as a world turned upside down in which no one is who they seem to be. In the first two novels of the trilogy readers encounter murderers who pose as officials, journalists who act as doctors or policemen, and war criminals like Ishii who *'despite having staged a mock funeral was alive & well & living in Japan'* [*OC*, 90]. Murata Masako is left to reflect that in this new unstable world, 'the war is not over. A cup is not a cup. Medicine is not medicine. A friend is not a friend, a colleague not a colleague. For a colleague here yesterday, sat in the seat at the counter beside me, that colleague is not here today. Because a doctor is not a doctor' [*OC*, 60]. Sifting through the 'ashes of meaning' [*OC*, 69], characters quickly realize that time and identity – once familiar anchors to truth and reality – have been occupied by new forces in a post-war world.

Political Occupation

The Allied occupation of post-war Japan has been widely cited as one of the 'most harmonious occupations of one great country by another that has ever been known'.[25] Historian Richard Storry suggests that 'the Americans did not behave like demons at all', while E. O. Reischauer argues that 'the disillusioned and demoralized Japanese, instead of reacting to the army of occupation and its leader with the normal sullen resentment of a defeated people, regarded the Americans as guides to a new and better day'.[26] Peace's novels do not subscribe to these existing perspectives and instead offer an alternative account of the occupation period through the eyes of the people in post-war Japan.

As the lead occupying force, the US enjoyed a far greater free hand in Japan than had originally been foreseen. They swiftly enacted widescale social change with the aim of achieving political stability and economic regeneration in the ruined country. Post-war social historian John Dower argues:

> While the victors preached democracy, they ruled by fiat; while they espoused equality, they themselves constituted an inviolate privileged caste. Their reformist agenda rested on the assumption that,

virtually without exception, Western culture and its values were superior to those of 'the Orient'. At the same time, almost every inter-action between victor and vanquished was infused with intimations of white supremacism. For all its uniqueness of time, place and circumstance [. . .] the occupation was in this sense but a new mani-festation of the old racial paternalism that historically accompanied the global expansion of the Western powers.[27]

Peace claims that he was drawn to write about this period because 'everything in Japan [. . .] goes back to the US Occupation, because in this period the Americans gave a political Constitution to Japan'.[28] However, the new post-war constitution was not greeted with enthusiasm. The American occupiers imposed the new consti-tution before the ruins of Japan's past had been fully cleared, pursuing 'policies designed basically to advance home-country interests while insisting on the benevolence of its motivation'.[29] Many Japanese people complained that they were effectively 'forced to be free' and highlighted tensions between claims regarding their new 'freedoms' and the strict censorship, strike-breaking and curbs on popular protests introduced by the occupiers. The effects of these new limitations were profound. Under the new constitution:

> Japan had no sovereignty and accordingly no diplomatic relations. No Japanese were allowed to travel abroad until the occupation was almost over; no major political, administrative or economic decisions were possible without the conqueror's approval; no public criticism of the American regime was permissible, although in the end dissi-dent voices were irrepressible.[30]

A memo from General MacArthur's command even claimed that post-war Japan could 'only be considered a vast concentration camp under the control of the allies and foreclosed from all avenues to commerce and trade'.[31]

In Peace's novels, SCAP (Supreme Commander of Allied Forces) and the new constitution are represented as foreign impo-sitions and expressions of the wider promotion of Western values in the East. Peace's American characters maintain a shadowy presence in post-war Japan and make virtually no attempt to engage with the people or place they occupy. Entering into this heart of darkness, Peace focuses on 'the judgement of the Victors and the punishment of the Losers' [*TYZ*, 29–30]. Detective Minami sees 'The Capital

City of the Showa Dead, the Losers on their hands and knees, the Victors in their trucks and jeeps –

No resistance here' [*TYZ*, 30]. Throughout *Tokyo Year Zero* and *Occupied City*, American '*jeeps with their big white stars and their big white teeth*' [*TYZ*, 38] break through everyday life to function as an unremitting reminder of the presence and power of the occupier.

Tokyo Year Zero explores the immediate and practical implications of the occupiers' new democratic capitalism as set against the reality of life on the ground in a defeated city. Miniami attempts to board a train and finds 'two empty carriages reserved exclusively for the Victors, one second-class hard-seat carriage for the privileged Losers, and a long string of run-down third-class carriages for the rest of us' [*TYZ*, 52]. Reflecting a wider Americanization of Tokyo during the period, the detective tries to buy food but finds that while they 'have no white rice [. . .] they have white bread' [*TYZ*, 185].[32] Although conscious of 'rumours of purges and SCAP's so-called reforms' [*TYZ*, 55], characters nevertheless fail to experience the impact of these changes in their own lives: '*I don't feel free. I don't feel I have rights . . .* ' [*TYZ*, 69]. The old Japanese nobility and the new American occupiers are even said to hunt together [*TYZ*, 76], popularizing the belief that the occupation simply involves 'new uniforms but the same old politics' [*TYZ*, 153].

As part of their drive for democratic capitalism, the American forces act decisively to eradicate political divisions. The warning throughout *Occupied City* is that 'Americans are colluding [. . .] To destroy and to bury socialism' [*OC*, 209]. Forging ahead with a vision of a democratic united Japan, the occupation forces insist that 'all internal differences must be forgotten, all labour disputes postponed' [*TYZ*, 153]. The homogenization of Japan by its occupiers becomes a more palpable threat as this second novel develops, until the fear that 'EVERYWHERE IS AMERICA' [*OC*, 211] breaks through as a repetitive and pervading concern of its multiple narrators. The Eighth Candle 'Martyr-Log of a Homo Sovieticus' – the journals of Comrade Andrei Kaidanovsky – even likens post-war Tokyo to 'post-revolutionary Petrograd in that eerie winter of 1917–18, when the city and its people seemed to have broken free of their moorings, when the city and its people seemed to be floating off somewhere unknown' [*OC*, 179].

In response to these oppressive and uncertain conditions, subcultures begin to develop – from prostitutes to black marketers – to cater to the needs of an occupied society. Through the architecture of the trilogy, the gangster becomes a symbol of the disease corrupting post-war Japan. In a newly capitalist society driven by material gain and commercial wealth, Boss Matsuda Giichi, 'in a new silk suit [. . .] with a Panama hat in one hand and a foreign cigar in the other', is raised as '*The brand new Emperor of Tokyo*' [*TYZ*, 8]. 'Shimbashi New Life Market' functions as another symbol of this new entrepreneurial spirit. Minami reflects that 'every single rag and every single morsel has a market value' [*TYZ*, 169]. Trade is conducted on the basis of 'one law; buy or be bought. Sell or be sold. Eat or be eaten' [*TYZ*, 42]. Engaged in a ritual of 'endlessly buying and selling, selling and buying', the New Life Market is offered as an epitome of 'the New Japan' [*TYZ*, 52] promoted by the occupation period.[33]

As an extension of the values of democratic capitalism, Japanese women become another commodity to be traded and exploited. The 1945 occupation commenced amidst fears that the Americans would be savage and aggressive to the women of Japan. Japanese historian Takemae Eiji suggests that during the post-war period 'much of the violence was directed against women, the first attacks beginning within hours after the landing of advance units'.[34] In an attempt to curb attacks, the Allied occupiers quickly established the Recreation and Amusement Association (RAA).[35] The RAA encouraged prostitution as a subculture of defeat as well as an apparent expression of democratic capitalism and the American pleasure principle. As a political, social and economic system underpinned by an ideology of free market economic pluralism, democratic capitalism formed part of the core of the new Japanese constitution, mirroring its central role in the US economic system which celebrated individual liberties. The occupiers argued that many post-war Japanese women celebrated their own new-found liberties by agreeing to engage in legalized prostitution. In fact, many women most likely joined out of a sense of national duty, as well as to feed their families. These 'comfort women' were organized into brothels as an apparent 'filter' to protect ordinary women and girls from the sexual repression that occupiers feared would be unleashed. Although rape cases in post-war Japan remained low, in *Tokyo Year Zero* it is suggested that there was a corresponding rise in the same period 'from 20 missing persons a month to 2–3000 a month of which forty percent are young women 15–25 years' [*TYZ*, 57]. This context informs the sexual and gender relations that characterize Peace's representations of post-war Japan. Through his active engagement with the local community, Detective Minami becomes aware that everyone is 'Talking about the GI who raped and sodomised a thirteen year-old girl, the two other Victors who kidnapped and raped a girl on her way home from a flower-arranging class, talking about the Japanese man who attacked and beat up two Girls in Kamata' [*TYZ*, 69–70]. This latent sexual conflict reaches a logical pinnacle in the Kodaira case as an expression of underlying tensions released in the wake of the war.

Peace states that he has 'a very very low opinion of men [. . .] There's never any who-dunnit is there? It's always a fucking man and the victims are always women and children.'[36] In the *Tokyo Trilogy* women are regularly cast as suffering victims. When police attention turns to the 'ladies of the Salon Matsu' [*TYZ*, 117] and the International Palace in their hunt for Kodaira, its Mamma claims that the victim represents 'all of us [. . .] Every woman in Japan' [*TYZ*, 120]. The trilogy focuses on the things women are forced to do to survive in post-war Japan and examines how this compounds their status as victims. Although this status is historically true of the crimes and times Peace interrogates, his novels nevertheless make the reader conscious of women as absent or marginal in these worlds. *Occupied City* marks the first occasion Peace uses a female narrative voice, but, like many of his female characters, Murata Masako is a victim of male aggression as a survivor of the Shiinamachi bank massacre. The women of the *Tokyo Trilogy* are savagely murdered like Kodaira's victims, unrealistically idealized like Yuki, or nameless and subservient like Minami's wife.[37] Minami himself is incapable of seeing women in any other way than as idealized angels or helpless victims. The subservience and gratitude of his own wife makes Minami 'want to slap her face. I want to beat her body.' His frustration at his wife's acceptance and passivity – "'Please don't think about us," she says. "We will be fine. Please just think about solving the case"' [*TYZ*, 49] – motivates an anger that increasingly alienates him from his home and children.

In this defeated and depleted world, Yuki 'is the one splash of colour among the dust' [*TYZ*, 45]. Minami comes to obsess about Yuki as a means of escape from trauma and hopelessness. As he lies with her post-coitally, he reflects:

> I have waited hours to lie again here upon the old tatami mats of her dim and lamp-lit room. *I think about her all the time*. I have waited hours to stare again at her peeling screens with their ivy-leaf designs.

I think about her all the time. I have waited hours to watch her draw
her figures with their fox-faces upon these screens –
I think about her all the time . . . [TYZ, 46]

The repeated image of Yuki as 'She dips her fingers in my come [.
. .] She puts her fingers to her lips' [*TYZ*, 46] comes to 'haunt'
Minami as a constant reminder of the solace he finds in this strain
of *femme fatale*. As the novel develops, Minami's irresistible desire
for Yuki increasingly exposes him to compromising situations, yet
Yuki, like Minami, is also a victim, stuck in a situation from which
she cannot escape. Engaged in an asymmetric relationship with his
wife, Minami becomes trapped between two very different women.
As the Kodaira case reaches a climax, his affair with Yuki drives him
to the point of obsession, exhausting him and clouding his ability to
make rational decisions about the case and his own sense of self.

Asked whether he has a tendency to include idealized women like
Yuki in his novels, Peace replied:

Unfortunately there is, kind of. What I mean is quite evident in the
book. I don't agree with this idea of a woman, but that's how a lot of
men think when they idealize a woman. I think it's difficult to write
about this, because, for example, with this book, sometimes I was
accused by female critics, in America, of using stereotypes, but the
difficulty is that the stereotype exists, so you can't ignore it.[38]

Through Minami's complex guilt-ridden relationships with his wife
and Yuki, readers are exposed to the hierarchical masculine society
of Japan and the tensions that emerge between the sanitized and
sexualized female. The danger of these gender roles is suggested by
Minami as he sits in the ruins of the city and watches

two little boys spread out my newspaper. I watch them crease and
fold the paper into two GI hats. The three little girls stand among the
rubble and call to the two little boys. In the ruins, the two little boys
march up and down with their dog-ends in their mouths and their
paper hats on their heads –
  '*Asobu?*' call the three little girls –
  '*Asobu* . . . ? *Asobu* . . . ?' [TYZ, 177]

Imitating the gender roles acted out as part of everyday life in
defeated Tokyo, this childish game is seen by Minami as a sinister

expression of the imbalanced power relations and empty constitutional changes of a country under occupation. Sexualized by association, the call of these little girls – 'do you want to play?' – is actualized in the reality of the International Palace where Minami witnesses girls prostrate on mats in oppressive heat, a dedicated PRO station 'where the Victors get their prophylactics' and a 'company store where the girls buy their cheap cosmetics and their shoddy clothes on borrowed money at expensive prices' [*TYZ*, 163]. Comprised of women 'found or bought among the ruins of the cities and the countryside', the International Palace offers an alternative perspective on the reality of MacArthur's institutionalization of prostitution in post-war Japan, a reality in which 'the toll is heavy and the turnover high –

Most of the first girls were hospitalised –

Many of the rest committed suicide' [*TYZ*, 159]. Perhaps the most overt comment on the reality of 'comfort women' comes through a slow reveal, more reminiscent of a movie than a novel, as Peace opens the narrative lens to show:

> There is a girl in the corridor. There is a naked girl in the corridor. There is a naked girl in the corridor on all fours, no older than fourteen. There is a naked girl in the corridor on all fours, no older than fourteen, being penetrated up her backside by a Victor as she stares down the long, long corridor at Nishi and I with tears running down her cheeks, down her cheeks and into her mouth, saying, 'Oh, very good Joe. Thank you, Joe. Oh, very good Joe. Thank you, Joe. Oh, oh, Joe . . . '
> *She is better off dead. I am better off dead . . .*
> This is America, This is Japan. This is democracy. This is defeat. I don't have a country anymore. On her knees or on her back, blood and come down her thighs. *I don't have a heart anymore*
> . . .
>   Her legs apart, her cunt swollen with pricks and pus –
>   *I don't want a heart.* I don't want a heart . . .
>   Thank you, Emperor MacArthur. [TYZ, 166]

As each detail builds, the reader is left to realize this vision as the ultimate image of occupation and defeat. Peace describes this horrific scene as representative of 'the whole point of the book. That girl is every girl, every woman and that GI is every man, everywhere.'[39]

The *Tokyo Trilogy* attempts to explore 'the social and economic conditions and the sexual politics between the way men and women interact' in post-war Japan.[40] In the first two novels, 'Death is a man' [*TYZ*, 373] and the 'city is a woman' [*OC*, 287] who is regularly raped, defeated and occupied. In a world where nothing is as it seems, Minami soon realizes that 'The men are the women. The women are the men' [*TYZ*, 126]. After a year of assaults and murders, reforms and purges, he is left to reflect:

> Things never change. There are wars and there are restorations. Things never change. There are wars and there are victories. Things never change. There are wars and there are defeats. Things never change. There are occupations and there are elections. *Things never change.* Because there is always a second meeting. *Things never change.* There is always a second meeting to discuss the first – *Never change. Never change. Never change . . .* [*TYZ*, 205]

The fear of the occupied is that their American occupiers 'will re-write history –
Their history. Your history, My history, Our history [. . .] Until everyone believes this history' [*TYZ*, 194]. Secure and confident in the knowledge that 'They can do what they want, when they want, to who they want, how they want' [*OC*, 225], the Allied occupiers dream of transforming Tokyo 'From Defeated and Ruined City, Surrendered and Occupied City, to Olympic and Future City, in less than twenty years' [*OC*, 162]. However, their vision is authored completely independently of – and in the case of Japanese women, in spite of – the needs, culture and history of the occupied people. In the post-war Tokyo of Peace's trilogy, the occupied people of Japan are engaged in a constant battle with the innate tensions of democratic capitalism promoted by their new US-imposed constitution. From the Occult Detective to the entrepreneurial gangster, individuals constantly struggle with the occupiers and each other for ownership and occupation of 'their' city.

While 'America does not know invasion. America does not know siege. America does not know surrender. America does not know defeat' [*OC*, 180], Tokyo experiences it for the first time in these novels. Peace claims that while he was writing the *Tokyo Trilogy*, the 2003 invasion of

Iraq was uppermost in my mind. Particularly as various members of the Bush White House constantly held up the occupation of Japan as a 'good occupation'. And certainly I think the readiness with which Bush and Blair went to war, and the support from countries such as Japan shows their ignorance of history, specifically war and its consequences for civilians. I'm not sure we ever do recover. In Japan, I feel the history and the legacy of the Second World War, or the Pacific war as it is more often called here, is very much the elephant in the room.[41]

Tackling another uncomfortable legacy of death, defeat and occupation, his trilogy suggests the need for re-examination in the post-war world. Positioning the novel as a part of a wider project against forgetting the lessons of the past, Peace attempts to retrieve an historical consciousness in danger of being lost in light of the new constitutions, values and ethics imposed by the external occupier during post-war years of defeat and powerlessness. Perhaps this is why Peace expresses 'hope that the *Tokyo Trilogy* works both on a historical level and in the western world [today]'.[42]

Through the intense singular experiences of his occupied characters, Peace presents the fractured and defeated world of post-war Tokyo as a metaphor for the fractured nature of memory and the historical imagination. In reconstructing himself, Minami enables the reader to begin to reconstruct the collective memory of post-war Japan. Tokyo is raised by these novels as a wider representation of our heterogeneous understanding of occupation as personal and political, social and psychological. Revealing the true occupying force to be that of democratic capitalism, the novels draw parallels with other contemporary cities occupied by similar manifestations of this imposed condition.

Peace offers the Allied occupation of post-war Japan as both paradox and symbol, a seemingly contradictory, inexplicable interplay of error and truth. Set in the ruins of the capital, his trilogy foregrounds the function of place in chronicling historical change. Peace believes that many 'cities become charged with meanings over time, and I definitely feel that in Tokyo. I wanted to go down through the layers, like an archaeological dig, to find the meaning of the place. What happened here has been concreted over, but the past reappears and grows out between the cracks.'[43] The map provided at the beginning of *Tokyo Year Zero* documents these geographies of time and place, foregrounding the physical occupation of the post-war city-scape. Concentrating on myth and memory, the first two novels of the *Tokyo Trilogy* access an alternative version of the past that lies just below familiar histories. The first novel introduces a city in defeat, the second a city in occupation. As part of a wider investigation of defeat and occupation as multi-valenced concepts, Peace occupies real crimes, established narrative structures and languages to cast alternative perspectives on the post-war period.

The *Tokyo Trilogy* does not offer readers a conventional 'cherry blossom' vision of Japan. Peace writes as social anthropologist, exploring the various types of new communities, interpersonal relations and cultural divisions created in the post-war years. His fictional Tokyo is a burnt-out shell of a city, suffering the imposition of defeat and occupation. Engaging with this panorama of destruction and decay, the trilogy explores the personal and political after-effects of war, engaging with psychological responses to defeat through acts of destruction and creation. Turning again to fact and raiding it to reveal the fictions inherent in all historical narratives, Peace presents a series of novels concerned with the occupation of places by people but also of people by places, authors with narratives and narratives with authors, pre-empting an unsettling conclusion to the trilogy in the third and final novel, *Tokyo Regained*.

conclusion
His Dark Materials

David Peace offers twenty-first-century readers unique novelized histories of personalities and periods we think we know well, yet his novels do more than simply offer the past for the pleasure of the present. Peace approaches previous times with a profound scepticism and does not allow readers to submit to the gratification of closed narratives or to settle into familiar cultural, political or social geographies. Instead, his novels suggest that 'fact' can never be definitive and should have no greater or lesser role than 'fiction' in directing the ways in which we choose to remember the past. Highlighting the necessarily subjective and selective nature of all narrative accounts – fact, fiction, 'faction' or otherwise – Peace's work points towards the arrogance and dishonesty of any text that claims to offer an authoritative 'truth' about the past. His work churns fact and fiction together, sifting through the ruins of hidden or broken histories in an effort to encourage readers to 'accept nothing and question everything'.[1]

In Peace's hands the novel becomes part of this process whereby the past is constantly fashioned afresh. Although the novel is itself marked by history, it can also be understood as 'one of the ways in which history is made, and re-made'.[2] Engaged in the politics of remaking, Peace's novels offer an apparent illumination of previously disavowed accounts of the past. Setting the facticity of history against the supposed fictionality of literary representation, Peace pushes the limits of the form to explore a wider crisis of representation. As counter-narratives, his novels offer partial, problematic or conflicting accounts. Jolted into post-historical reflection by these competing narratives, readers are encouraged to theorize the contemporary to its historical roots through a persistent and tortuous return of the past to the present. Across his work, Peace constantly strains at the shackles of the novel, challenging its capacity to contain new images and representations. Over the course of his writings, Peace has become aware of the limitations of his chosen form, admitting that he is often forced to 'struggle with the novel' and increasingly finds that 'poetry is the best way for me to reflect mental processes and the way people act and behave'.[3]

In recent years Peace's work has been released from the confines of the novel form through adaptations to television and film. In 2008, owner of Revolution Films Andrew Easton read the *Red Riding Quartet* and was inspired to translate the novels onto the small screen. With the support of FilmFour, Easton commissioned screenwriter Tony Grisoni to adapt the four texts into a trilogy, omitting second novel *1977* due to budgetary constraints. The project produced three made-for-television films that function as self-contained stories with distinct directorial visions, as well as an epic trilogy with recurring themes and motifs. Creating three films, using three directors (Julian Jarrold for *1974*, James Marsh for *1980* and Anand Tucker for *1983*), in three formats (16mm, 35mm and digital film respectively), each worked independently of one another, speaking only briefly at the beginning of the project to negotiate the logistics of sharing the same actors and locations.

Filmed in the wake of the acclaimed BBC 1970s police drama *Life on Mars*, the *Red Riding* trilogy takes a darker perspective on a period that had recently been revisited to popular acclaim by the British viewing public. Interpreting Peace's work as 'Dickens on bad acid', Grisoni's screenplay creates violent, grim worlds dominated by men and casual violence. [4] His Yorkshire is a murky, dark, deceitful place plagued by rain. Despite being part-funded by *Screen Yorkshire*, it is interesting to speculate how much the Yorkshire Tourist Board could have hoped to benefit from these films. In *Red Riding* it is unremittingly 'grim up North'. Disfigured by mist and drizzle, the Yorkshire Moors brood over concrete cities of corruption and run-down housing estates. A million miles from the romantic myth of the Brontës, or the heart-warming local pastoral of popular British TV series *Heartbeat*, the landscape of *Red Riding* is presented through distancing techniques of slit-staging and super 8 to awaken grainy memories of past times.[5]

Released amidst a sustained press campaign by Channel Four and after resounding critical responses from the UK press, Revolution Films secured an American theatrical release for the trilogy in early 2010. Reflecting on the US release of all three films under one ticket – as a back-to-back *Lord of the Rings*-style viewing saga – David Peace warned that Grisoni's new adaptation of his quartet offers 'quite a dark six hours in the cinema'.[6] The haut-noir production does not provide an easy viewing experience, but the three films were expected to prove particularly challenging for American audiences expected to have little or no knowledge of the geographies and histories under examination. Despite this challenge, *Red Riding* was embraced by America and greeted with widespread critical success. Writing in *Variety*, Todd McCarthy celebrated *Red Riding* as 'a world-class dramatic work', while David Thomson of *The New York Review of Books* claimed that the trilogy is 'better than *The Godfather*'. In response to this popular reception, Columbia Pictures acquired the rights to produce their own version of the *Red Riding Quartet* in late 2009.

The transformation of Peace's novels through adaptation was repeated in the same year by Peter Morgan in his screenplay of *The Damned United*. Released in 2009, the motion picture combined with the *Red Riding* television trilogy and the publication of the second instalment of the *Tokyo Trilogy* to mark a period dubbed by Peace's publishers Faber as 'The Year of Peace'. Directed by Tom Hooper with funding from BBC Films and Left Bank Pictures, *The Damned United* film dramatizes Peace's novel to produce a softer, more sympathetic version of Clough's time at Leeds, rejecting the challenge of translating onto the big screen the intense internal monologues that characterize Peace's Clough. Designed to neutralize some of the criticisms levelled at the novel by Clough's family, the film was intended 'to make a slightly different take on Brian Clough than David Peace's', one intended to 'push a lot of the darkness out'.[7] Using Peace's novel as a starting point, the film tells a moving 'buddy story' about the friendship between two men. Concentrating on the rise and fall of Clough at Derby and Leeds, it rejects the occult aspects of Peace's protagonist and even chooses to omit the most infamous event in the novel, the manager's axe-attack on predecessor Don Revie's desk. Producer Andy Harries explains that in the context of a 2009 release date, the production team 'wanted to make a film with an upbeat ending'.[8] As a result, the more controversial aspects of Peace's protagonist were sidelined in favour of a feel-good conclusion.

Consumed in the context of the twenty-first century, these adaptations, as well as the novels upon which they are based, speak as much to the contemporary world of the new millennium as they do to the twentieth-century past they represent. In his timely advice to 'remember the etymology of the word', contemporary author John Fowles stresses that in order to have meaning, a novel 'must have relevance to the writer's now'.[9] Speaking to the 'writer's now',

Peace's fictions look back to the recent past and in doing so invite stark comparisons with our own contemporary world. Peace not only examines the traumas of the twentieth century, but also sheds light on wider issues that resonate with contemporary global events. Offering a very close impression of a past that has all too recently returned to haunt the present day, his novels do not distance us from history, but further implicate us in a shared responsibility for thinking critically about our past and present.

In their contemporary relevance, Peace's fictions offer historical reverberations that resonate darkly across today's world.[10] It is impossible for any politically engaged individual to read a David Peace novel without being haunted by the present-day problems addressed in his fictions. Echoes of the child-abuse ring operating known but unpunished in the *Red Riding Quartet* have recently been felt in the 2008 Haut de la Garenne child abuse scandal, while the mysterious death of Peter Hunter in *1980* can be recalled in the unexplained disappearance and 'suicide' of Chief Constable of Greater Manchester Police Michael Todd in 2008. Elsewhere, the fictional abductions of Jeanette, Susan and Clare are uncomfortably close to the cases of Madeline McCann, Natascha Kampusch and Shannon Matthews.[11] In an international context, savage scenes of police violence in Millgarth can be seen to carry future echoes of the 2004 Abu Ghraib prison abuse scandal, while the horrors of the invasion and occupation of post-war Japan in the *Tokyo Trilogy* bear many similarities to the 2003 invasion of Iraq by America and her Allies. Twenty-first-century readers arrive at novels like *GB84* in a context of rising unemployment and a wider global economic recession, while in sport, the unswerving confidence of Peace's Clough is mirrored in the modern game's own big-heads such as Jose Mourinho. In these contemporary echoes, Peace's novels suggest that repercussions of past corruption and defeat remain seen and felt forces for not only years, but decades to come.

Carving into old landscapes that strain under his new creations and renovations of the recent past, Peace maps (his)story onto existing frameworks to offer an antithetical presentation of order and disorder. Throughout these novels, the past reasserts its role in the present, disrupting narratives to engage readers in a multiplicity of perspectives on recent events. In his chronicle of work to date, Peace drags fiction from facts to illuminate new perspectives on the past that bear relevance to contemporary social, political and economic developments. Encouraging the twenty-first-century reader to look back at the recent past through the corruption of a time and place, the traumas of industrial unrest and competitive treachery, or the horrors of occupation and defeat, Peace mobilizes his dark materials to encourage a critical reappraisal of the twentieth-century world. With the promise of more occult accounts to come, contemporary readers can be certain that there is no end to history in the work of David Peace.

Notes

Introduction: Peace in our Time

1 Born in 1967, David Neil Peace was raised in Ossett, West Yorkshire. Schooled at Batley Grammar, Peace studied for A Levels at Wakefield Sixth Form College and went on to read English at Manchester Polytechnic, now Manchester Metropolitan University. After spending two years writing unpublished novels as an unemployed graduate, he left the UK in 1991 to teach English as a Foreign Language in Istanbul before moving to Tokyo in 1994. Peace has cited the importance of these travels in establishing a voice for his work. While living in Japan in 2003, he claimed that being 'far away now, it is perhaps easier for me to recreate and sustain the places and times about which I write – unimpeded and oblivious to the distractions and changes of the present' (David Peace, "Talking Books: David Peace May 2003", *BBC Online*, http://www.bbc.co.uk/bradford/culture/words/ david_ peace_ intv. shtml, accessed 19 May 2004). Peace lived in Tokyo until 2009, when he returned to Yorkshire with his Japanese wife and family.

2 All references to the novels of David Peace contained in this book refer to the following paperback editions: *1974* (London: Serpent's Tail, 1999); *1977* (London: Serpent's Tail, 2000); *1980* (London: Serpent's Tail, 2001); *1983* (London: Serpent's Tail, 2002); *GB84* (London: Faber, 2004); *The Damned United* (London: Faber, 2007); *Tokyo Year Zero* (London: Faber, 2008); *Occupied City* (London: Faber, 2010). All spacing, fonts, positioning of text and spellings in the quotations raised by this book seek to replicate their presentation in Peace's novels as faithfully as possible. This often involves the use of italics and incomplete parenthetical phrases.

3 David Peace in "A World of Dread and Fear", *KPunk*, http://k-punk.abstractdynamics.org/archives/006370.html, accessed 10 April 2010. Geoffrey Boycott is another Yorkshire sporting legend whose cricket skills propelled him to fame and friendship with contemporary Brian Clough in the 1970s. Like Clough, Boycott is outspoken and often the subject of controversy.

4 Melvyn Bragg, 'The Damned United', *The Southbank Show*, ITV One, 11 May 2008, 22.50–23.50.

5 David Peace, "In Conversation with Kester Aspen", Waterstones Leeds Q&A to launch *Occupied City*, 13 August 2009.

6 David Peace in Nicola Upson, "Hunting The Yorkshire Ripper", *New Statesman*, 20 August 2001, http://www.newstatesman.com/200108200036, accessed 10 April 2008.

7 Jean François Lyotard, *The Postmodern Condition: A Report on Knowledge* (Manchester: Manchester University Press, 1979), pp. xxiv–xxv.

8 Walter Benjamin, "Thesis on the Philosophy of History", in *Illuminations* (London: Fontana, 1973), p. 255.

9 David Peace in Matthew Hart, "An Interview with David Peace", *Contemporary Literature*, 47.4 (2006): 546–68, p. 555.

10 David Peace, "The Red Riding Quartet", *Crimetime*, http://www.crimetime.co.uk/features/davidpeace.php, accessed 10 April 2010.

11 Christopher Booker, *The Seventies: Portrait of a Decade* (London: Allen Lane, 1980), p. 4.

12 *Life on Mars* is a BBC TV series set in the 1970s. Broadcast on BBC One from 2006–2008, it was inspired by a David Bowie song of the same name. The series is part police procedural, part science fiction drama. It follows the fictional adventures of police officer Sam Tyler who is hit by a car in 2006 and wakes to find himself in the Greater Manchester Police of the 1970s. The series was a major critical and commercial success and spawned a spin-off series, *Ashes to Ashes*, following female police officer Alex Drake who is shot in 2008 and regains consciousness to find herself in the London Metropolitan Police during the 1980s. See David Peace in Matthew Hart, "An Interview with David Peace", *Contemporary Literature*, 47.4 (2006): 546–68, p. 556.

13 Alwyn Turner, *Crisis? What Crisis? Britain in the 1970s* (London: Aurum, 2008), p. xiii; Andy Beckett, *When the Lights Went Out: What Really Happened to Britain in the Seventies* (London: Faber, 2009), p. 4.

14 Margaret Thatcher was elected leader of the Conservative Party in February 1975. She was perceived as offering much needed steel in the face of the defiant British unions. Dubbed the 'Iron Lady' by the Russians and the 'milk-snatcher' by the British victims of her social spending cuts, she set out a clear mandate suggesting that the UK had become over-reliant on state support. She promoted a move away from this 'nanny state' to private incentives and fewer public subsidies.

15 Turner, 2008, p. 192.

16 Hilda Murrell was an expert botanist who turned her skills to campaigning for safety in nuclear arms construction. She began to campaign against nuclear power and power stations shortly before her disappearance and death in March 1984. Hilda was abducted in her

own car and three days later police found her mutilated body in a field. A local labourer was later convicted for the crime, but doubts remain regarding the safety of his conviction.

17 The 'Cold War' between the US and the Soviet Union emerged from the aftermath of World War II in 1947 and lasted until around 1991. This economic and military competition between the two countries manifested itself in ongoing arms building, military propaganda and technological competition. In October 1962 the Cold War reached a critical point when the US discovered that the Soviet Union had positioned missiles on the neighbouring island of Cuba. The subsequent political fallout was a key moment in the Cold War and a low point in twentieth-century East/West relations.

18 A war in the Middle East during October 1973 pushed up oil prices leading to a high demand for coal.

chapter one A Very Yorkshire Tale

1 Opening quotation from Martin Wainwright, *True North* (London: Guardian, 2009), p. 10. J. Hill and J. Williams, "Sport and Identity in the North of England", in E. Royale, *Regional Identities* (Manchester: Manchester University Press, 1998), p. 201; A. Mitchell, "Manifesto of the North", in T. Wright, *The English Question* (London: Fabian Society, 2000), p. 46.

2 David Peace, "The Big Issue Event: Q&A with Paul Johnston", *Edinburgh Book Festival*, 22 August 2009; David Peace, "In Conversation with Kester Aspen", Waterstones Leeds Q&A to launch *Occupied City*, 13 August 2009.

3 Roy Wright, "Huddersfield Town fan David Peace is behind TV's darkest tale", *Huddersfield Daily Examiner*, 5 March 2009. Peace claims that 'from William and the Harrowing of the North to the Wars of the Roses [. . .] I think, more than anywhere else in England, people in West Yorkshire know that Official History is only ever written by the winners and that it's always/usually a lie' (David Peace, "Bradford and Yorkshire People: David Peace", *BBC Online*, http://www.bbc.co.uk/bradford/content/articles/2009/03/03/david_pe ace_2009_feature.shtml, accessed 10 August 2009).

4 David Peace, "h2g2 BBC Author: David Peace", *BBC Online*, http://www.bbc.co.uk/dna/h2g2/A3126188, accessed 10 August 2009.

5 David Peace in Nicola Upson, "Hunting The Yorkshire Ripper", *New Statesman*, 20 August 2001, http://www.newstatesman.com/ 200108200036, accessed 10 April 2008.

6 Growing up in Yorkshire, Peace was influenced by the novels, plays and kitchen-sink realism of earlier 'angry young men' including John Osborne, Barry Hines, Stan Barstow and John Braine. Writing about the provincial regions and the marginalized people of Britain during

the 1950s and 1960s, their literature represents the working man as an underdog achieving against all the odds, reflecting a wider disillusionment with society as well as political unease and social alienation in post-war Britain.

John Osborne is a British playwright whose 1956 drama *Look Back in Anger* inspired the label used to describe his dissatisfied grouping of post-war British writers as 'angry young men'. His play drew on contextual tensions regarding social class in post-war British society to make a claim for the ordinary working man. It has since become a cultural reference point for those seeking to challenge the values of the middle class.

Barry Hines is a British author who is probably best known for his 1968 novel *A Kestrel for a Knave* that was later adapted into the 1970 film *Kes*. Both the novel and the film explore the challenges faced by the British post-war working classes in the North of England.

Stan Barstow is best known for his 1960 novel *A Kind of Loving*. The novel follows the fortunes of a working-class hero from humble beginnings in a mining village to life in London. Like Peace, Barstow also lived in Ossett. Peace claims that 'although I have never met him, it was an inspiration knowing that the author of *A Kind of Loving* lived on the next street' (David Peace, "The Red Riding Quartet", *Crimetime*, http://www.crimetime.co.uk/features/davidpeace.php, accessed 10 April 2010).

John Braine is a British author whose 1957 novel *Room at the Top* is considered to be one the key texts of the 'angry young men' canon. The novel tells the story of a working-class boy who rises to success in post-war Britain.

7 Fear and paranoia in the regions gradually extends to the country at large as the crisis becomes national. As Ripper writer Michael Bilton argues, 'You have to live in the North of England to comprehend how such a terrible series of crimes terrified a major part of the British Isles' (Michael Bilton, *Wicked Beyond Belief: The Hunt for the Yorkshire Ripper* [London: HarperCollins, 2006], p. xxxi), since 'vast swathes of the North of England were affected by the complete absence of peaceful communities during the Ripper case' (Bilton, 2006, p. 582).

8 David Thomson in LeftBank Pictures, *The Damned United Production Notes* (London: LeftBank Pictures, 2009), p. 9.

9 Raphael Samuel, *Theatres of Memory: Vol. II Island Stories* (London: Verso, 1998), p. 166.

10 David Peace, "Profile", *Telegraph*, http://www.telegraph.co.uk/culture/tvandradio/4980191/David-Peace-author-of-Red-Riding-and-The-Damned-United-profile.html, accessed 10 August 2009.

11 The 'Moors Murders' were committed by Ian Brady and Myra Hindley between July 1963 and October 1965. The pair killed five chil-

dren, some of whom were sexually assaulted, and disposed of some of their bodies on Saddleworth Moor, north of Manchester in the South Pennines. During the investigation police found photographs of Hindley posing on the Moors. These photographs were used as visual clues suggesting the whereabouts of their victims' graves by police hunting for the bodies of the missing.

12 Hayden White, *Tropics of Discourse: Essays in Cultural Criticism* (Baltimore: The Johns Hopkins University Press, 1978), pp. 151–2.

13 Leeds grew from a Saxon village to a new town in 1207. 'Leeds' derives from 'Loidis', the name given to a forest covering most of the kingdom of Elmet which existed during the fifth century into the early seventh century. During the English Civil War in 1646 Charles I was brought to Leeds as a prisoner while William the Conqueror oversaw campaigns to harrow the Northern lands. His reign marked an end to the quasi-independence of the region, while his scorched earth policy of invasion saw Yorkshire burnt and depopulated (although Leeds was semi-protected from this process due to its ownership by the de Lacy family who were friendly with the new ruler). Leeds has always drawn its economy from clothing and textiles as home to the moors, fells and sheep farming. In the eighteenth century Leeds saw a shift to industrial textiles and 'satanic mills', while the advent of the railways in the nineteenth century played a key role in the Industrial Revolution. Despite being less than twenty miles from the Yorkshire Dales, during the twentieth century Leeds began to bear the scars of overcrowding, dirty industry and poor hygiene. Slums became common and crime rife. In 1974 a government reorganization of the regions meant that the West Riding of Yorkshire ceased to exist. Unlike most counties in England, which historically were divided into hundreds, Yorkshire was first divided into Thrydings, meaning 'Thirds'. Yorkshire's famous three historical Ridings, North, East and West, were aligned with the rest of the country as part of this shake-up and transformed into normal counties, and 1977 saw the expansion of Leeds to include areas like Otley, Garforth and Wetherby. Today Leeds is home to more than 700,000 people known as 'Loiners', or residents of Leeds.

14 David Peace, "Book Munch Classic Interview: David Peace", *Bookmunch*, http://www.bookmunch.co.uk/view.php?id=1341, accessed 10 August 2009.

15 Populated by intimidating buildings, Leeds is presented by the quartet as a demonic site of anger and anxiety. Despite a strong sense of place, it is easy to become disorientated by the relative emptiness of Peace's urban past. In a scared townscape interaction with architecture can often lead to confusion and physical discomfort. Open space is not a source of solace but of fear. For some characters these associations cause agoraphobia, a spatial disease. Mrs Jobson 'hadn't left the house

since that night [. . .] not even to scrub the graffiti off the door, the graffiti that said she liked to suck black men's willies down the bus station' [*1977*, 98]. Mrs Dawson is also fearful of the outside world and remains confined to the hospital or under the controlling influence of her construction magnate husband. Her fear of open natural spaces as well as the inner-city spaces of urbanity is significant. In the *Red Riding Quartet*, the natural world offers no respite from the intensity of city space; both are tinged with terror and threat.

16 The Chapeltown riots occurred in 1975, 1981 and 1987 in the Chapeltown area of Leeds, the same area blighted by the reign of the Ripper. The riots were motivated by racial tension, social deprivation and high unemployment felt most keenly in inner-city areas.

17 The YRA (Yorkshire Republican Army) is a group campaigning for a separatist Republic of Yorkshire. They were widely associated with, and considered sympathetic to, the IRA in Northern Ireland during the 1970s and 1980s.

18 A white heraldic rose is the symbol of the House of York. A red heraldic rose is the symbol of the House of Lancaster. The two houses, based in the North East and North West of England respectively, entered into conflict during the fifteenth century in a battle that became known as the 'War of the Roses'.

19 As Bilton argues, 'The Yorkshire Ripper – entered the lexicon of criminology, making this killer geographically distinct from the fiend who had stalked the Whitechapel district of London's East End' (Bilton, 2006, p. 580).

20 David Peace, "Peace Le Roman Tokyo année zéro payot-rivages", *Payot and Rivages*, http://www.payot-rivages.net/index.php?id=30&selection_auteur=Peace,+David, accessed 10 August 2009.

21 G. J. Ashwork (ed.), *Sense of Plane: Sense of Time* (Aldershot: Ashgate, 2005), p. 70.

22 John Brannigan, *Orwell to the Present: Literature in England 1945–2000* (Basingstoke: Palgrave Macmillan, 2003), p. 174.

chapter two Words Fail

1 Opening quotation from George Orwell, *Shooting an Elephant* (London: Secker and Warburg, 1950), p. 76; M. M. Bakhtin, "Discourse in the Novel", in *The Dialogic Imagination: Four Essays*, trans. Michael Holquist and Caryl Emerson (Austin: University of Texas Press, 2004), p. 276.

2 Bakhtin, "Discourse in the Novel", p. 331.

3 Bakhtin, "Discourse in the Novel", p. 29.

4 The power of the written word also operates through a series of epistolary exchanges from an author purporting to be the Ripper. At other points letters are used to reveal abandonment (such as Janice of Fraser

and Fraser of his son Bobby), while the note found in the mouth of dead girl Karen Douglas relates the killer's '5 LUV' [*1980*, 131] tally to the police. These communications function as essential plot devices, revealing protected or limited information as well as highlighting themes of concealment and intrigue.

5 Issues of language are further problematized through a series of deceptive acronyms, from the shorthand *YR* [*1980*, 164] of the Yorkshire Ripper to the MJM of the corrupt publishing house (mirroring the initials of convicted Michael John Myshkin) and the plot-pivoting blood group B that 'looks wrong' [*1977*, 58] on police records.

6 Eddie reveals his contempt for the overbearing presence of 'a car jammed full of aunties, blood and fake' at his father's funeral [*1974*, 8].

7 However, as Part Three of *1980* pertinently reminds readers, 'We Are All Prostitutes' [*1980*, 259].

8 In interview, Peace claims that 'Yorkshire of the 1970s was a hostile environment to be living in [. . .] especially for women' (David Peace, "The Red Riding Quartet", *Crimetime*, http://www.crimetime.co.uk/features/davidpeace.php, accessed 10 April 2010).

9 Helen Marshall's confidence and career are also undermined by her appearance in *Spunk* Issue 3 January 1975 [*1980*, 367].

10 Ironically, Hunter's prayer is answered by Helen Marshall's pregnancy later in *1980*.

11 As the so-called 'father of the Enlightenment', Voltaire criticized religion as an organized form of superstition, but was more critical towards acts of organized religion than of the concept of religion itself.

12 Alistair Crowley is the figure most closely associated with the term 'magick'. Connected to an underworld of demonic and chaotic forces as well as paranormal and mystical beliefs, 'magick' is popularly associated with acts of banishing, purification, consecration, invocation and evocation.

13 In the vision of the apocalypse described by the book of Revelation there are seven churches of Asia, seven candlesticks, seven stars, seven trumpets, seven spirits before the throne of God, seven horns, seven vials, seven plagues, a seven-headed monster, and the lamb with seven eyes.

14 Echoing across *1977* in spectral tones of '*Jubelo* . . . ' [*1977*, 98] and '*Jubelum* . . . ' [*1977*, 102], the Jubilee is defined by Jack as 'a year of emancipation, a time of remission and forgiveness from sin, an end to penance [. . .] a time of celebration' [*1977*, 164]. However, there are also suggestions in the novel that the Jubilee functions to spark a rise in Christian nationalism. One caller to *The John Shark Show* debates the outrage caused by people hanging the Union Jack upside down at Jubilee parties, suggesting that 'upside down crosses' would produce similar reactions because, after all, '*There's a cross on the flag isn't there?*' [*1977*, 126].

15 The teachings of the Reverend Laws are not always received kindly.
    Peter Hunter punches him in the nose in protest at Laws's counselling
    of Helen Marshall [*1980*, 312], while the Reverend is singled out for
    criticism at the 'Exorcist Killing' trial by both the judge and the local
    bishop.

16 The character of the Reverend Laws is purportedly based on a real
    person. In interview, Peace claimed that 'Back in 1974, in Ossett, this
    is a small town where we were growing up, there was a case that gained
    national notoriety. A guy – his name was Michael Taylor, he was
    married and he had three sons. And his sons were at my dad's school,
    yeah? Where he was a teacher. And this guy was in some kind of group.
    They had formed this bizarre evangelical Christian sect. Michael
    Taylor was a member of this sect. It was still attached to a regular kind
    of church. He became convinced that he was possessed by the devil
    and the priest from the church – and his wife – decided that they were
    going to exorcise him. They took him to the church, and they kept him
    there overnight, trying to expel all these demons. This is recounted in
    my book. They expelled all kinds of demons from him. Anyway, they
    didn't manage to get out the demon of murder. So they were all
    exhausted. They all went home in the early hours of the morning. His
    kids were actually with some neighbours [. . .] They tied him down,
    on the altar of the church, yeah? Man, this is a regular fuckin' priest
    who is doing this. They tied him down on the altar, threw holy water
    on him, said prayers, and cast out the demons. And the demons did go.
    I can't remember, there was like forty-nine or fifty-two demons?
    [. . .] They're all exhausted at this point. They send him back to the
    house. And on the lawn of his house, on the fucking front lawn of his
    house, he killed his wife. He took her eyes out with his bare hands
    [. . .] And then, this guy, who is naked, except for a pair of socks and
    wearing his wife's blood, runs naked down the streets of my hometown.
    That obviously affected my family! Because his kids went to my dad's
    school. This really, really upset my family [. . .] She died from shock,
    and from loss of blood. Yeah. I think he might have stabbed her as well
    [. . .] And a tangent to that is, it led to the banning of the film *The
    Exorcist*, because people seemed to believe that [. . .] well, *The Exorcist*
    was already causing controversy, causing some people to believe that
    they were possessed. They marketed the fucking film as the most
    frightening film of all time, yeah? So people were passing out right
    there in the cinemas. But actually, there's no fucking connection at all.
    Because nobody involved in the case had ever seen the film, in fact,
    they'd never heard of it. Well [. . .] then, you see [. . .] the bishop got
    involved, and the whole fucking thing went to court. The guy is still in
    a secured mental hospital. He's still alive. And the priest was defrocked.
    There was lots of criticism of the priest and the bishop. It always led

me to wonder, what happened to this priest? Whatever became of him? And *that* is where the Reverend Martin Laws came from' (David Peace in Gene Gregorits, "These Endless Fucking End Days: A Chat with David Peace by Gene Gregorits", http://gene-gregorits.com/DAVID %20PEACE.html, accessed 12 December 2008).

17 Dr Papps reports to Hunter, 'In January 1975, a man called Michael Williams believed he was possessed by an evil spirit. A local priest tried to perform an exorcism, however something went wrong and Williams ended up killing his wife and running naked through the streets of Ossett covered in her blood. The woman's name was Carol Williams. She was Jack Whitehead's ex-wife. Williams killed her by hammering a nail into the top of her skull. Worse, Whitehead was there. Saw it all' [*1980*, 150]. In his own account Laws claims that, 'Through thee church, E met Michael and Carol Williams at their house in Ossett in December 1974 where E had been invited to lecture on thee Irvingites. We took communion of ready-sliced bread and undiluted Ribena' [*1983*, 320].

18 William E. Kennick, "The Language of Religion", *The Philosophical Review*, 65 (1956) 56–71, p. 63.

19 David Peace, "The Red Riding Quartet", *Crimetime*, http://www.crimetime.co.uk/features/davidpeace.php, accessed 10 April 2010.

20 David Peace in David Hickey, "Peace follows turbulent times", *The Japan Times*, 6 July 2008, http://search.japantimes.co.jp/cgi-bin/fl20080706x1.html, accessed 13 July 2009.

21 According to Michael Bilton, Yorkshire Ripper Peter Sutcliffe employed time as a central strategy in luring his victims into distraction prior to attack. In the moments before he killed Josephine Whittaker, Sutcliffe told her to look at a church clock to distract her from his weapon (Michael Bilton, *Wicked Beyond Belief: The Hunt for the Yorkshire Ripper* [London: HarperCollins, 2006], p. 512). When another victim, Irene Richardson, was found by the police, Bilton claims that her 'watch [. . .] was no longer working and the hands were stopped at the 8.50 position. Time had literally run out for her' (Bilton, 2006, p. 83).

chapter three Towards a Hauntology of the North

1 Opening quotation from Avery Gordon, *Ghostly Matters: Haunting and the Sociological Imagination* (London: University of Minnesota Press, 2008), p. 3. Pierre Machery, "Marx Dematerialised", in M. Sprinkler (ed.), *Ghostly Demarcations: A Symposium on Jacques Derrida's Spectres of Marx* (London: Verso, 2008), p. 18. Re-reading Marx in the wake of the fall of the Berlin Wall and the so-called 'end of history', Derrida's

Spectres of Marx addresses the decline of the spirit and possibility of revolution in the late twentieth century. Derrida wrote *Spectres of Marx: The State of the Debt, the Work of Mourning, and the New International* as the plenary address for the conference 'Whither Marxism? Global Crisis in International Perspective' held in April 1993 at the University of California Riverside. His arguments were later 'augmented' and 'clarified' in an edited, published version of the lecture which is referenced in this chapter as *SM* (Jacques Derrida, *Spectres of Marx: The State of the Debt, the Work of Mourning, and the New International*, trans. Peggy Kamuf [London: Routledge, 1994]). In the context of the late twentieth century, Derrida argues that the spirit of social and political revolution has become a ghost whose presence we feel but whose physical manifestation is absent. Throughout his work, Marx employs numerous metaphors of spectres and phantoms. The first noun of *The Communist Manifesto* relates specifically to this phenomenon: 'A *spectre* is haunting Europe – the *spectre* of communism.' *The Communist Manifesto* openly appeals to the ghosts of communism, while *The Eighteenth Brummaire* resurrects the dead and proposes history as repetition. In Marx's writings the past itself is offered as a mode of haunting, one that 'weighs like a nightmare on the brains of the living' (Karl Marx, *The Eighteenth Brumaire of Louis Bonaparte* [London: Progress, 1964], p. 152). Ghosts or revenants hang over the continent and its history since 'haunting is historical' [*SM*, 4]. These spectres are plural since they refer both to the pervading spirit of Marx in contemporary society and to the spectres that haunt his writings. This later textual haunt is of paramount importance since the 'spectres of Marx' do not operate alone, 'for there is always *more than one of them*' [*SM*, 8].

The haunt manifests itself as specifically related to the politics of the past. Derrida suggests that 'the essence of the political will always have the inessential figure, the very anessence of a ghost' [*SM*, 24]. This ghost is a phantasmic and anti-essential presence. It causes us to question its ambiguous state which is at once both present and absent, its time passed and present. These conflicting sites place the ghost firmly on the edge of spatio-temporal boundaries. Although it is not of matter the dematerialized spirit still matters and is not divested of influence. Derrida takes pains to distinguish the spirit and the spectres as two different forms of the haunt. The spirit assumes body and incarnates itself in the spectre. What define the spectre are its familiarity and difference: it is recognizable and felt yet at the same time 'altogether other' [*SM*, 10]. Derrida describes this paradox as 'the furtive and ungraspable visibility of the invisible' [*SM*, 7], a presence from the past which causes confusion, doubt and rethinking since 'there is something disappeared, departed in the apparition itself as reapparation of the departed' [*SM*, 6]. A paradoxical incorporation of return and abstraction accentuates the contradictory state of the ghost which is 'neither dead nor alive, it is dead and alive at the same time' [*SM*, 148]. The twin state of the spectre is used by Derrida to argue the need to recognize our cultural past as necessarily ambiguous and varied. The spectre reminds us that 'an inheritance is never gathered together' as a unified narrative, but is expressed 'in different voices' [*SM*, 19]. Through this 'hauntology' – an analysis of 'the real and the unreal, the actual and the inactual, the living and the non-living, being and non-being' [*SM*, 11] – Derrida begins to explore the 'logic of haunting' [*SM*, 10] or why the past returns. In French, the term 'hauntology' is a homophone to ontology. While ontology is concerned with being, hauntology is concerned with a paradoxical state of both being and non-being.

2 David Peace in Gene Gregorits, "These Endless Fucking End Days: A Chat with David Peace by Gene Gregorits", http://gene-gregorits.com/DAVID%20PEACE.html, accessed 12 December 2008. He goes on to assert that the transmission pieces made him cry due to the extremely personal content of their perspectives. He has claimed that having the transmissions set out on a single page was his own idea and one he defended to his initially sceptical publishers.

3 Jacques Derrida, "The Ghost Dance: An Interview with Jacques Derrida", *Public*, 2 (1989): 60–73, p. 61.

4 David Peace, "Ready For War", *Stop Smiling Magazine*, http://www.stopsmilingonline.com/story_detail.php?i=707, accessed 2 December 2008.

5 David Peace, "The Red Riding Quartet", *Crimetime*, http://www.crimetime.co.uk/features/davidpeace.php, accessed 10 April 2010.

6 In his own analysis of the hunt for the Ripper, Michael Bilton claims that once caught, 'Sutcliffe spent many hours detailing how he had come to hear God send him on his Divine mission to kill prostitutes' (Michael Bilton, *Wicked Beyond Belief: The Hunt for the Yorkshire Ripper* [London: HarperCollins, 2006], p. 510).

7 Jacques Derrida, "Desistance", in Philippe Lacoue-Labarthe, *Typography: Mimesis, Philosophy, Politics*, trans. C. Fynsk (Cambridge, MA: Harvard University Press, 1989), p. 27.

8 Sigmund Freud, *The Uncanny* (London: Penguin, 2003), p. 241.

9 Tony Judt, *Reappraisals: Reflections of the Forgotten Twentieth Century* (London: Vintage, 2009), p. 1.

10 Judt, 2009, p. 2.

11 Robert Mighall, *A Geography of Victorian Gothic: Mapping History's Nightmares* (Oxford: Oxford University Press, 2003), p. xviii.

12 Mary Carruthers, *The Book of Memory:A Study of Memory in Medieval Culture* (Cambridge: Cambridge University Press, 1990), p. 215.

chapter four Yorkshire Noir

1 Opening quotation from David Peace, "The Red Riding Quartet", *Crimetime*,   http://www.crimetime.co.uk/features/davidpeace.php, accessed 10 April 2010. Although the description 'Yorkshire noir' has been used widely in relation to the novels of David Peace, the phrase was first employed by Andrew Vine in his review of *1974* in 1999. David Peace, "Snapshot of the Time", *Yorkshire Post*, 4 March 2009, http://www.yorkshirepost.co.uk/features/Snapshot-of-time.5037932. jp, accessed 27 May 2009.

2 David Peace, "Hero or Villain", *Independent on Sunday*, 8 March 2009, p. 54.

3 David Peace, "The Red Riding Quartet", *Crimetime*, http://www. crimetime.co.uk/features/davidpeace.php, accessed 10 April 2010.

4 David Peace in Paul Currion, "Balls to the British Novel", *The Unforgiving Minute*, http://www.currion.net/tag/david-peace/, accessed 27 May 2009.

5 The *USA Trilogy* consists of *The 42nd Parallel* (1930), *Nineteen Nineteen* or *1919* (1932), and *The Big Money* (1936). Like John Dos Passos's series, Peace's quartet weaves fact and fiction, sampling newspaper reports and other non-fictional works to provide a comprehensive portrait of a country at a specific point in time.

6 David Peace in Mike Marquesse, "David Peace: State of the Union Rights", *Independent*, 5 March 2004, p. 17.

7 David Peace, "The Red Riding Quartet", *Crimetime*, http://www. crimetime.co.uk/features/davidpeace.php, accessed 10 April 2010. Fred and Rosemary West were sentenced to life imprisonment for the torture, rape and murder of at least twelve females between 1967 and 1987. Many of these crimes occurred at the couple's homes in Gloucester – most famously at 25 Cromwell Street – between May 1973 and September 1979. On 1 January 1995 Fred West hanged himself in prison. Rosemary West announced her intention not to appeal her imprisonment in 2001. Their crimes shocked the UK, drawing attention to the covert presence of crime in the community. For further details on the Moors Murders, see chapter 1.

   Rachel Nickell was stabbed forty-nine times, sexually assaulted and had her throat cut in front of her two-year-old son on Wimbledon Common in London on 15 July 1992. Colin Stagg was quickly identified as fitting the police psychologists' profile of the killer and a honey trap was established to catch him. Using the limited evidence gained from this and under the advice of the Crown Prosecution Service, the Metropolitan Police arrested Stagg. The case was thrown out of court based on the police deception involved in Stagg's entrapment. He later sued the police for damages totalling £1 million. In 2008, Scotland Yard's cold case review team used new DNA evidence to identify Robert Napper as Rachel's killer and issued a corresponding apology to Colin Stagg.

Two-year-old Jamie Bulger was abducted and kidnapped by two ten-year-old boys – Jon Venables and Robert Thomson – from New Strand Shopping Centre in Bootle near Liverpool, England where he was shopping with his mother on 12 February 1993. His body was found beside a local railway line in Walton on 14 February 1993. The killers were released with new identities on life licence in June 2001 after serving eight years. Then Shadow Home Secretary Tony Blair gave a speech on 19 February 1993 in which he claimed that the crime was an 'ugly manifestation of a society that is becoming unworthy of that name' (Richard Davenport-Hines, "Bulger, James Patrick [1990–1993]", in Catherine Soans and Angus Stevenson [eds.], *Oxford Dictionary of English* [Oxford: Oxford University Press, 2005], p. 1243).

Stephen Lawrence, a black British teenager, was murdered on 22 April 1993. Five suspects were arrested, but none were convicted. The 'Stephen Lawrence Inquiry Report' concluded that the Metropolitan Police had failed to follow up leads, did not arrest suspects and was institutionally racist.

8 David Peace, "The Red Riding Quartet", *Crimetime*, http://www.crimetime.co.uk/features/davidpeace.php, accessed 10 April 2010.

9 Peace also owes a debt of influence to British detective narratives. Inspired by a childhood love of Sherlock Holmes, Peace recalls cutting up newspapers and forming a case history to imitate his detective hero. Conan Doyle wrote several historical crime novels and became fascinated with miscarriages of UK justice, personally investigating several closed cases during his lifetime. Conan Doyle investigated the cases of Oscar Slater and George Edalji, the latter of which is discussed in the Julian Barnes novel *Arthur and George* (London: Jonathan Cape, 2005). Returning to the Sherlock Holmes texts – especially *A Study in Scarlet* – to get a feel for the rhythms of crime fiction before writing his own quartet, Peace is firmly in debt to this tradition of British detective narratives. Ian Rankin in John Morton, "The Criminally Underrated Novels of David Peace", *Guardian*, 9 August 2007, http://www.guardian.co.uk/books/booksblog/2007/aug/09/thecriminal lyunderratednove, accessed 17 May 2009.

10 David Peace in Ludger Menke, "Podcast No. 3: Interview mit David Peace", *KrimiBlod.De*, http://krimiblog.de/447/podcast-interview-mit-david-peace.html, accessed 15 January 2009.

11 Alex Cutter, "The Madhouse of the Skull", *Fluxeuropa*, http://www.fluxeuropa.com/jamesellroy-quartet.htm, accessed 27 May 2009.

12 James Ellroy's *LA Quartet* consists of *The Black Dahlia* (1987), *The Big Nowhere* (1988), *LA Confidential* (1990) and *White Jazz* (1992).

13 James Ellroy, *The Black Dahlia* (London: Arrow Books, 1993), p. 361.

14 James Ellroy in Lee Horsley, "Unpublished Interview with James Ellroy", 7 October 1995; Ellroy in Charles L. P. Silet, "Mad Dog and Glory: A Conversation with James Ellroy", *The Armchair Detective*, 28 (Summer 1995): 236–44, p. 243.

15 David Peace in Nicola Upson, "Hunting the Yorkshire Ripper", *New Statesman*, 20 August 2001, http://www.newstatesman.com/200108200036, accessed 10 April 2008.

16 Margaret Thatcher in Michael Kimmelman, "Francis Bacon, Artist of the Macabre, Dies", *New York Times*, 13 April 1992, http://www.nytimes.com/1992/04/29/arts/francis-bacon-82-artist-of-the-macabre-dies.html?scp=2&sq=man%20who%20paints%20those%20awful%20pictures&st=cse, accessed 1 February 2010.

17 David Peace in Chris Verguson, "Profiles: West Yorkshire Confidential", *BBC Online*, http://www.bbc.co.uk/bradford/ content/articles/2008/06/02/david_peace_2008_feature.shtml, accessed 27 May 2009.

18 Lord Shaftesbury subsequently called areas of Leeds 'a modern equivalent of Sodom' (Michael Bilton, *Wicked Beyond Belief: The Hunt for the Yorkshire Ripper* [London: HarperCollins, 2006], p. 41).

19 David Peace in Ludger Menke, "Podcast No. 3: Interview mit David Peace", *KrimiBlod.De*, http://krimiblog.de/447/podcast-interview-mit-david-peace.html, accessed 15 January 2009.

20 Bilton, 2006, p. 589.

21 'The Black Panther', aka Donald Neilson, was a former builder who turned to crime in 1975 when his business failed. He initially burgled domestic homes, but later progressed to post offices. After shooting three sub-postmasters he became the most wanted man in Britain. His reign came to an end after an unsuccessful kidnap and ransom attempt on heiress Lesley Whittle. After killing Lesley, Neilson was eventually accosted in the early stages of another post office robbery in December 1975.

The A1 and the M62 are two of the busiest roads in the North of England. The M62 coach bombings occurred on 4 February 1974 on the M62 motorway between Bradford and Leeds. A bomb planted by members of the IRA exploded on a bus carrying off-duty British military personnel who were on leave with their families, killing twelve people. Although originally convicted for the crime, Judith Ward later had her conviction overturned due to questionable scientific evidence and the claim that her original confession was forced by investigating police officers.

22 T. Newburn, "Understanding and Preventing Police Corruption: Lessons from the Literature", *Police Research Series*, Paper 110 (London: Home Office, 1999), p. 19.

23 In 1972 it was revealed that a major pornographer had been making illegal payments to seventeen police employees, including officers at the most senior level – the Head of the Obscene Publications Squad DCI George Fenwick, his superior DCS Bill Moody, Head of the Serious Crime Squad Wallace Virgo and Head of the Flying Squad Commander Kenneth Drury. As part of the subsequent investigation the Obscene Publications Squad was disbanded and over twenty detectives were asked to resign or dismissed. At their trial in 1977, Judge Mr Justice Mars-Jones claimed that members of the police had engaged in corruption on a scale which beggared description (Barry Cox [ed.], *The Fall of Scotland Yard* [London: Penguin Books, 1977]).

The men who formed the group that became known as the 'Birmingham Six' – Hugh Callaghan, Patrick Joseph Hill, Gerard Hunter, Richard McIlkenny, William Power and John Walker – were sentenced to life imprisonment in 1975 for a series of pub bombings in the city of Birmingham, England on 21 November 1974 that killed twenty-one people. The crimes were attributed to the Provisional IRA and the six accused Belfast-born Roman Catholic men were taken into custody on 22 November 1975. Their convictions were later found to be unsafe and subsequently overturned by the Court of Appeal on 14 March 1991 due to evidence of police fabrication and forced confessions. The six men were later awarded compensation ranging from £840,000 to £1.2 million. The Court of Appeal stated that 'Dr Skuse's conclusion was wrong, and demonstrably wrong, judged even by the state of forensic science in 1974' (*Home Office, Regina v R v McIlkenney* (1991) 93, Cr.App.R, 53–4).

The Guildford Four were also wrongly convicted of carrying out bombings for the Provisional IRA on 5 October 1974 at two pubs in Guildford, England. Although all four men initially confessed, their statements were later retracted amidst claims of police torture and intimidation of both the accused and their families. In 1989 a detective revisiting the case found that interview notes had been obviously edited and retyped by police during the original investigation. The four men were released on these grounds in the same year. On 9 February 2006 British Prime Minister Tony Blair apologized to the families of the Guildford Four, stating, 'I am very sorry that they were subject to such an ordeal and injustice [...] they deserve to be completely and publicly exonerated' (Tony Blair, "Blair apologizes to Guildford Four family", *Guardian Unlimited*, http://www.guardian.co.uk/politics/ 2005/feb/09/ northernireland.devolution, accessed 29 January 2008).

The collapse of the case and evidence of other miscarriages of justice caused the Home Secretary to set up a Royal Commission on Criminal Justice in 1991. The commission reported in 1993 and led to the Criminal Appeal Act of 1995 and the establishment of the Criminal Cases Review Commission in 1997.

24 David Peace, "West Yorkshire Noir?", *BBC Online*, http://www.bbc.co.uk/bradford/content/articles/2008/05/16/david_pe ace_feature.shtml?page=2, accessed 27 May 2009.

Lesley Molseed, an eleven-year-old schoolgirl from Rochdale, Lancashire, was murdered on 5 October 1975. Stefan Kiszko, a twenty-six-year-old tax clerk, was wrongly convicted of her murder and served sixteen years in what became an infamous miscarriage of UK justice. At the time of the investigation, three local teenage girls came forward. One claimed that Stefan had exposed himself to her before the murder, one claimed he had exposed himself to her after the murder and the third claimed that he had been stalking her for some time. The police decided that Stefan fitted their profile of the killer and stopped pursuing alternative avenues. Significantly, they also chose to ignore evidence including details of the testosterone the accused was receiving for his hypogonadism that might have made him behave unusually at the time of the alleged attacks (further details of this evidence can be found in Jonathan Rose [ed.], *Innocents: How Justice Failed Stefan Kiszko and Lesley Molseed* [London: Fourth Estate, 1997]). After a lengthy series of appeals, Kiszko was released in November 1992 but died a year later. Ronald Castree was eventually convicted of Lesley's murder on 12 November 2007. The senior officer in charge of the original investigation – Detective Superintendent Dick Holland – later came to public prominence as a senior officer on the flawed investigation into the Yorkshire Ripper. At the point of his retirement from the force in 1988, Holland cited Kiszko's and Judith Ward's convictions as being among his finest hours during his thirty-five years with the police. Holland was demoted during the Yorkshire Ripper inquiry four years after Kiszko's conviction. In *Red Riding*, the false confession and imprisonment of Michael Myshkin at the hands of George Oldman arguably draws inspiration from this contemporary event.

Anthony Steel was convicted of murdering Carol Wilkinson on 10 October 1977. He was given a life sentence in 1979 based on contradictory witness statements and unlikely evidence. His case was finally appealed in July 2000 and quashed in February 2003.

In Michael Bilton's book on the Ripper inquiry, he revealed that when Peter Sutcliffe was apprehended he was wearing a V-neck jumper upside down over his legs that allowed him to expose himself while carrying out his attacks (Michael Bilton, *Wicked Beyond Belief: The Hunt for the Yorkshire Ripper* [London: HarperCollins, 2006], p. 577). The jury at his trial was not given this evidence and after his conviction, exhibits officer Detective Constable Alan Foster 'was told to take various items of Sutcliffe's property – including the jumper – to the incinerator because the case was concluded'. Foster held on to the item because 'Sutcliffe was looked at for 47 other offences [. . .] I thought it was wrong to destroy the jumper because you don't know what the future holds – as has been proved by the emergence of DNA' (David Bruce, "Killing Kit of the Ripper", *Yorkshire Evening Post*, 22 February 2003, http://www.yorkshireeveningpost.co.uk/news/KILLING-KIT-OF-THE-RIPPER.239646.jp, accessed 19 January 2009). As well as proving that the original evidence at Sutcliffe's trial was condensed by police, the jumper suggests that his murders were in fact premeditated.

25 David Peace in Nicola Upson, "Hunting the Yorkshire Ripper", *New Statesman*, 20 August 2001, http://www.newstatesman.com/200108200036, accessed 10 April 2008.

26 Peace cites Ian Rankin as a good example of a contemporary writer who successfully occupies genre fiction to communicate lasting truths about a specific time and place. In the Rebus series, Peace argues that Rankin has successfully created a 'portrait of Edinburgh at a time of massive change, Scotland regaining parliament, devolution, asylum seekers, he's taken the opportunity to say something about a time and place'. Bemoaning the lack of critical acclaim received by socially conscious contemporary British crime novelists, Peace argues that in 'twenty, fifty years time, you're not going to read Zadie Smith, you're going to read Rankin and know something about what the United or not United Kingdom was like' (David Peace in Ludger Menke, "Podcast No. 3: Interview mit David Peace", *KrimiBlod.De*, http://krimiblog.de/447/podcast-interview-mit-david-peace.html, accessed 15 January 2009).

chapter five From the Picket Line to the Page

1 Opening definition from Catherine Soans and Angus Stevenson (eds.), *Oxford Dictionary of English* (Oxford: Oxford University Press, 2005), p. 1278. David Peace, "Book Munch Classic Interview: David Peace", *Bookmunch*, http://www.bookmunch.co.uk/view.php?id=1341, accessed 10 August 2009. David Peace in Matthew Hart, "An Interview with David Peace", *Contemporary Literature*, 47.4 (2006): 546–68, p. 568.

2 *GB84* also marked a professional move for Peace from publisher

Serpent's Tail to Faber and Faber. Faber is one of the UK's largest independent publishing houses with a backlist of Nobel Laureates, Booker
Prize winners and literary greats such as T. S. Eliot, Sylvia Plath and
Philip Larkin. It enjoys far greater press, distribution and commercial
power than the smaller Serpent's Tail. In response to accusations that
the publication of *GB84* sought to monopolize the twentieth anniversary of the miners' strike in 2004, Peace argued that it was Faber's 'idea
to publish it to coincide with the twentieth anniversary of the strike'
(David Peace, "The Big Issue Event: Q&A with Paul Johnston",
Edinburgh Book Festival, 22 August 2009).

3 Other novels that tackle the strike include Roger Granelli, *Dark Edge*
(Bridgend: Poetry Wales Press, 1997); William O'Rourke, *Notts: A
Striking Novel* (New York: Marlowe & Company, 1996); Martyn
Waites, *Born Under Punches* (London: Pocket, 2003). The strike is
discussed but not at centre stage in novels such as Tom Davies, *Black
Sunlight* (London: Futura, 1986) and Raymond Williams, *Loyalties*
(London: Hogarth, 1989).

4 Euan Ferguson, "The Last English Civil War", *Observer*, 29 February
2004, p. 34.

5 David Peace in Michael Williams, "No Fucking End in Sight", *BBC
Online*, 12 March 2004, http://www.bbc.co.uk/bradford/culture/
words/david_peace_gb84.shtml, accessed 19 March 2004.

6 Andy Beckett, "Political Gothic", *London Review of Books*, 23
September 2004, 26:18, p. 29.

7 Michael Holquist in M. M. Bakhtin, "Epic and the Novel", in M. M.
Bakhtin, *The Dialogic Imagination:Four Essays*, trans. Michael Holquist
and Caryl Emerson (Austin: University of Texas Press, 2004), p.
xxviii.

8 Bakhtin, 2004, p. 33.

9 Terry Eagleton, "At the Coal Face", *Guardian*, 6 March 2004, p. 23.

10 Eoin McNamee, "Hand-Held Narrative", *Guardian*, 11 April 2004, p.
43.

11 David Peace, "Crisp Sandwiches and Pickets", *New Statesman*, 3
January 2004, p. 25.

12 Phil Sharpe, "GB84: A Powerful Tribute to the Miners' Strike",
Socialist Future, 20 April 2004, http://www.socialistfuture.org.uk/msf/
articles/reviews/GB84.htm, accessed 29 April 2004.

13 Throughout his work, Russian linguist Mikhail Bakhtin aims to define
the uniqueness of the relatively young novel form as distinct from the
historically established epic. Bakhtin cannot provide a comprehensive
theory on the novel since it is a developing form, still evolving into all
it can be, 'the sole genre that continues to develop, that is as yet uncom-
pleted' (Bakhtin, 2004, p. 3). Bakhtin scholars Clark and Holquist
argue that Bakhtin assigns the term 'novel' to 'whatever form of expres-

sion within a given literary system reveals the limits of that system as inadequate, imposed or arbitrary' (Katerina Clark and Michael Holquist, *Mikhail Bakhtin* [London: Harvard University Press, 1984], p. 276). The canonical genres are then associated with whatever is fixed, rigid, authoritarian.

Bakhtin charts the development of the novel during the nineteenth century from devalued obscurity to radical prominence. He proposes that this development may be seen to coincide with the breakdown of cultural boundaries, an increase in popular festivity and the growth of a collective desire to ridicule the claims of universal validity espoused by Aristotelean notions of poetics. Morson and Emerson suggest that while Bakhtin believed that poetry reinforces and reinscribes existing systems, he also believed that prosaics – the theoretical and forensic study of prose – 'invades a tranquil realm to dispute territory, violate generic decorum and upset poetic harmony' (Gary Saul Morson and Caryl Emerson, *Mikhail Bakhtin: Creation of a Prosaics* [Stanford: Stanford University Press, 1990], p. 304). The novel therefore has a greater potential to decentralize official systems.

As a broadly anti-canonical force, the novel breaks and reverses hegemonic relationships, establishing itself as the 'people's' anti-genre, challenging the authority of received tradition and replacing it with a multi-vocal dialogic history. As the primary genre maintaining close ties with folk culture and the 'carnival', the novel is antithetical to the rule of law and order that entails what Holquist describes as a 'presumption of authority' and a 'claim to absolute language' (Michael Holquist, "Introduction", in Bakhtin, 2004, p. xxxiii).

According to Bakhtin, the novel articulates an 'expression of a Galilean perception of language'. Just as Galileo refused to acknowledge his own planet as the centre of the solar system, so the novel 'refuses to acknowledge its own language as the sole verbal and semantic centre of the ideological world'. Instead the novel foregrounds its duty to 'represent all the ideological voices of its era [. . .] all the era's languages that have any claim to being significant' (M. M. Bakhtin, "Discourse in the Novel", in *The Dialogic Imagination: Four Essays*, ed. Michael Holquist, trans. Michael Holquist and Caryl Emerson [Austin: University of Texas Press, 2004], pp. 366, 411). In doing so it necessarily alters the relationship between author and reader. The novel empowers an active understanding by prohibiting us from simply siding with the language of the authorial voice. Instead we are compelled to arbitrate between the languages of different ideological voices.

Antithetical to the spirit of poetics, the prosaic spirit of the novel allows the author to become a dialogic equal with each of these voices (rather than the privileged speaker of a monologue): 'a character's word about himself and his world is just as fully weighted as the author's word usually is; it is not subordinated to the character's objectified image nor merely one of his characteristics, nor does it serve as a mouthpiece for the author's voice. It possesses extraordinary independence in the structure of the work; it sounds, as it were, *alongside* the author's word and in a special way combines with it and with the full and equally valid voices of other characters' (M. M. Bakhtin, "Problems of Dostoevsky's Poetics", in Pam Morris [ed.], *The Bakhtin Reader: Selected Writings of Bakhtin, Medvedev and Voloshinov* [London: Arnold, 1994], p. 8). This discourse allows both the author and the characters to speak in a profoundly polyphonic interaction. Presenting a variety of perspectives, the novel offers a multi-accented artistic discourse of exchange between multiple social voices and languages. The parity of this exchange operates in opposition to the desire for mastery that is inherent in official languages and ideologies.

As a result of this multi-vocal intersection, Clark and Holquist argue that the 'heteroglot novel [. . .] is more sensitive to otherness', is capable of accommodating more voices, more hybrids of language and life (Clark and Holquist, 1984, p. 293). The novel, engaged with the present here and now of reality, according to Bakhtin contains no 'epic distance', only the 'spontaneity of the inconclusive present', which 'keeps the genre from congealing' (Bakhtin, "Epic and the Novel", 2004, pp. 23, 27). Defying generic classification in its constantly evolving nature, the novel synthesizes past and present and looks to a future of open-ended human struggle. Bakhtin describes the novel as 'plasticity itself. It is a genre that is ever questing, ever examining itself and subjecting its established forms to review' (Bakhtin, "Epic and the Novel", 2004, p. 39). Incorporating humour and irony, the form eliminates what Holquist calls 'all one sided, dogmatic seriousness (both in life and thought) and all one sided pathos', reasserting identity and history in dialogic interaction within the 'familiar zone' of the 'openended present' (Holquist, "Introduction", 2004, p. iv.). Bakhtin himself argues that the writer, 'drawn towards everything that is not yet completed', is able to produce a text 'determined by experience, knowledge and practice (the future)' precisely because of this openness to the 'feel' of the present time (Bakhtin, "Epic and the Novel", 2004, pp. 27, 15). Comfortable with its fragmentation and variety of voices, the novel juxtaposes social and historical languages, challenging wisdom and values, unitary representational perspectives and claims to absolute truth.

14 Bakhtin, "Epic and the Novel", 2004, p. 3.
15 Bakhtin, "Discourse in the Novel", 2004, p. 269.
16 Bakhtin, "Discourse in the Novel", 2004, p. 321. Bakhtin later suggests that authors of polyphonic texts employ 'multi-toned narration, the

mixing of high and low, serious and comic; they make wide use of inserted genres – letters, found manuscripts, retold dialogue [. . .] and various authorial masks make their appearance' (Bakhtin, "Problems of Dostoevsky's Poetics", in Morris, 1994, p. 108).

17 Bakhtin, "Discourse in the Novel", 2004, p. 324.
18 Walter Brierley, *Means-test Man* (London: Spokesman Books, 1983).
19 For examples of these images, see Peace, 2004, pp. 1, 117, 229, 349, 451.
20 David Peace, "Q Hero: David Peace", *Q Magazine*, April 2009: 32–4, p. 34.
21 Malcolm Bradbury, *The Modern British Novel* (London: Penguin, 2001), p. 482.
22 Robert Tressell, *The Ragged Trousered Philanthropists* (London: HarperPerennial, 2005), p. 299.
23 Linda Hutcheon, *A Poetics of Postmodernism: History, Theory, Fiction* (London: Routledge 1988), p. 144.
24 David Peace in "A World of Dread and Fear", *KPunk*, http://k-punk.abstractdynamics.org/archives/006370.html, accessed 10 April 2010.
25 Hutcheon, 1988, pp. 113–14.
26 Ken Smith, *A Civil War without Guns: 20 Years On: The Lessons of the 1984–5 Miners' Strike* (London: Socialist Publications, 2004), p. 17.
27 Bakhtin, "Discourse in the Novel", 2004, p. 333.
28 Bakhtin, "Problems of Dostoevsky's Poetics", in Morris, 1994, p. 8.
29 M. M. Bakhtin, "The Problem of the Text", in Caryl Emerson and Michael Emerson (eds.), *Speech Genres and Other Late Essays*, trans. Vern W. McGee (Austin: University of Texas Press, 1986), p. 103.
30 David Peace in Stephanie Benson, "The Strange Language of David Peace", *Europolar*, 11 February 2009, http://www.europolar.eu/index.php?option=com_content&task=view&id=66&Itemid=30, accessed 30 September 2009.
31 This technique is notably employed in *GB84* to reveal the duplicitous machinations of political discourse during the coal dispute: 'Words in *her* ear; words that win wars. For the Prime Minister is winning *her* war; her many, many wars – *The IRA British Leyland. GCHQ. Cammell Laird. CND. The* Belgrano. *The GLC.*
She never rests. *Ever* [. . .] *These are* her *words; her words that win wars; her many, many wars.*' [336]
32 Ralph Winston Fox, *The Novel and the People* (London: Lawrence & Wishart, 1937), p. 128.
33 David Peace, "GB84 Interview", *BBC Online*, http://www.bbc.co.uk/dna/collective/A2436509, accessed 19 January 2005.
34 Hutcheon, 1988, p. 110.

35 Peace, 2004, p. 247. Peace goes on to interrogate the finality of 'Year Zero' in *Tokyo Year Zero*. John Kirk, *Twentieth-Century Writing and the British Working Class* (Cardiff: University of Wales Press, 2003), p. 13.

36 David Peace, "State of the Union Rights", *Independent*, http://www.independent.co.uk/arts-entertainment/books/features/david-peace-state-of-the-union-rights-572067.html, accessed 19 January 2005.

chapter six The Life of Brian

1 Opening quotation from Brian Clough in ITV, *Clough: The Documentary*, ITV One, first broadcast Wednesday, 25 March 2009, 10:35–11:50 p.m. David Peace, "44 Jours Interview", *Dawdle Up Country*, http://dawdleupcountry.blogspot.com/2008/05/david-peace-interview.html, accessed 20 January 2010. David Peace, "The Big Issue Event: Q&A with Paul Johnston", *Edinburgh Book Festival*, 22 August 2009.

Brian Clough enjoyed success as a footballer, appearing twice for England before his career was cut short by injury and he became a manager. When he began his first managerial position in October 1965 aged thirty, Clough was the youngest manager in the football league at Hartlepools United (Phil Rostron, *We Are The Damned United: The Real Story of Brian Clough at Leeds* [Edinburgh: Mainstream, 2009], p. 18). (The team were later renamed Hartlepool United.) In a managerial career that stretched across three decades, Brian Clough revived two ailing British football clubs, making Derby County first division championships in 1972, then repeating this success with Nottingham Forest in 1978 and surpassing this again by winning the European Cup in successive seasons in 1979 and 1980, a feat that remains unmatched by an English manager since. At the height of his career as a manager, Clough was one of the most easily recognized faces and voices in the UK. Between his time at Derby and Nottingham Forest, Clough accepted a job as manager of Leeds United. This seemed a strange appointment since Clough had been overtly critical of Leeds and their 'dirty' style of play for a long time. His accusation was well founded but also historical to the team. In 1919 Leeds United was formed when Leeds City FC was expelled from the football league for making illegal payments to players. Clough had also been critical of their former manager Don Revie, who left the club only to serve his country as England manager, a job Clough himself deeply coveted. Ex-Derby player Roy McFarland commented that in contemporary terms Clough's decision to take the Leeds job was 'Like Arsene Wenger taking over the job at Man U, it's that extreme [. . .] it's not extreme enough!' (Roy McFarland, in ITV, *Clough: The Documentary*, ITV One, first broadcast Wednesday, 25 March 2009, 10:35–11:50 p.m.).

Don Revie 'was awarded English Manager of the Year three times between 1969 and 1972, and in 1970 he was given the OBE. All told, Revie took his team to two First Division titles, one FA Cup, one League Cup, two Inter-Cities Fairs Cups, one Second Division title and one Charity Shield. They also made it to three more FA Cup Finals, one more Inter-Cities Fairs Cup final and one European Cup-Winners Final' (Rostron, 2009, p. 29).

Peace's Clough boasts of his progression from the roots of a working-class beginning on '*Clairville Common to Great Broughton. From a fitter and turner at ICI to centre-forward at Middlesbrough Football Club and then captain of Sunderland*' [52]. He tells players how he went on to score '251 goals in 274 league games', a feat that motivates the firm assertion that 'it'll always be a fucking record because there'll never be another one like me. Never. Ever' [58]. Clough lasted just forty-four days as manager of Leeds United.

2 David Peace, "Culture Clash", *BBC Online*, http://www.bbc.co.uk/leeds/content/articles/2006/08/17/words_david_peace_the_damned_united_feature.shtml, accessed 20 January 2010.

3 David Peace, "44 Days in 1974", *Guardian*, http://www.guardian.co.uk/books/2009/aug/01/damned-utd-david-peace, accessed 20 January 2010.

4 David Peace, "44 Days in 1974", *Guardian*, http://www.guardian.co.uk/books/2009/aug/01/damned-utd-david-peace, accessed 20 January 2010.

5 Ray Fell in Rostron, 2009, p. 142.

6 David Peace, "Guardian Book Club Interview with John Mullan", *Guardian*, http://www.guardian.co.uk/books/audio/2009/aug/07/book-club-podcast-david-peace-damned-united, accessed 20 January 2010.

7 David Peace in Matt Dickinson, "The Panned United is still a work of genius", *The Times*, http://www.timesonline.co.uk/tol/sport/columnists/matt_dickinson/article5835251.ece, accessed 20 January 2010.

8 David Peace in Kevin Eason, "Collision that Transformed Clough's Life", *The Times*, http://www.timesonline.co.uk/tol/sport/football/article5870472.ece, accessed 20 January 2010.

9 David Peace in Brian Donaldson, "Rising Son: David Peace Does Japan", *The List*, http://edinburghfestival.list.co.uk/article/18674-rising-son-david-peace-does-japan/, accessed 12 November 2009. Peace later complained, 'If I was to write a novel about the last days of Edgar Allan Poe nobody would bat an eyelid – in fact, I'd probably win a prize for it. But to write a book about a football manager, that is something you shouldn't do' (Peter Geoghegan, "Belfast Festival: David Peace", *Culture Northern Ireland*, http://www.culturenorthernireland.org/article.aspx?art_id=2835, accessed 20 January 2010). Peace now claims that, 'There are days I wish I'd never written the bleeding book,'

and that, as a result of the storm of controversy caused by its publication, 'I couldn't watch football for a year' (David Peace, "Profile: David Peace", *The Times*, http://entertainment.timesonline.co.uk/tol/arts_- and_entertainment/books/article5821830.ec, accessed 20 January 2010).

10 Brian Clough's son Simon waded into the debate, claiming that 'David Peace has done a hatchet job on my Dad and portrayed him as a raving lunatic at a time when I was ten years old. I know it's not true. It will be grossly unfair if people think there's a grain of truth in it' (Simon Clough in Matt Dickinson, "The Panned United is still a work of genius", *The Times*, http://www.timesonline.co.uk/tol/ sport/ columnists/matt_dickinson/article5835251.ece, accessed 20 January 2010).

11 David Peace in Matt Dickinson, "The Panned United is still a work of genius", *The Times*, http://www.timesonline.co. uk/tol/sport/ columnists/matt_dickinson/article5835251.ece, accessed 20 January 2010. Peace claims that when he began writing the novel 'Brian Clough was still alive and 80% of it was finished before he died' and has repeatedly assured reporters that the representations of his novel were not written with the intention of offending the Clough family (David Peace, "The Damned United Author Surprise Row", *BBC Online*, http://news. bbc.co.uk/1/hi/wales/8074187.stm, accessed 30 May 2009).

12 Actor Philip Glenister, who played detective Gene Hunt in *Life on Mars*, a retro BBC police detective series set in 1970s Manchester, claims that 'Before we started *Life on Mars*, I was researching what people looked like up North back then. I happened to be in a BBC shop, and there was this DVD of *Match of the Day* – the best of the 60s, 70s and 80s. I bought it, and the first disc I played was the 70s one. There was this great moment when they were interviewing Brian Clough: him behind his desk, and the interviewer saying, "What happens if one of your players disagrees with you?" He paused, and looked at this guy, and said, "Now look, young man – basically, they come to me, we talk about it for half an hour, and they realise I was right all along". That was the key: I thought, "That's Gene Hunt"' (Philip Glenister in John Harris, "When Men Were Men", *Guardian*, http://www.guardian.co.uk/media/2007/feb/13/genderissues.broadcas ting, accessed 20 January 2010).

13 R. W. Connell, *Which Way Is Up?* (Sydney: Allen & Unwin, 1983), p. 18.

14 David Peace, "44 Days in 1974", *Guardian*, http://www.guardian.co.uk /books/2009/aug/01/damned-utd-david-peace, accessed 20 January 2010.

15 The darkness offered by this narrative approach can be viewed as a deliberate reaction against the multiple narrators of *GB84* as part of

Peace's 'back to basics approach' with *The Damned United*. His use of a single narrator also bears influence from his first novel *1974* in which one narrator narrates all twelve days of the plot.

16   David Peace, 'Guardian Book Club Interview with John Mullan', *Guardian*, http://www.guardian.co.uk/books/audio/2009/aug/07/book-club-podcast-david-peace-damned-united, accessed 20 January 2010.

17   David Peace, "Guardian Book Club Interview with John Mullan", *Guardian*, http://www.guardian.co.uk/books/audio/2009/aug/07/book-club-podcast-david-peace-damned-united, accessed 20 January 2010.

18   Founded in 1888, The Football League is a competition involving football teams from across England and Wales. In 1992 the top twenty-two teams split from the League to form the Premier League. Since 1995 the League has been divided into three divisions – the Championship, League One and League Two.

19   In a podcast interview for his publishers Faber, Peace claims that he tries 'not to reflect, I just try to write, but in the course of doing interviews one of the things I've realised is that the books all deal with defeat' (David Peace, "Interview with David Peace", *Faber and Faber Online*, http://www.faber.co.uk/author/david-peace/, accessed 3 February 2010).

20   Watergate became the biggest political scandal in 1970s America. It originated in a break-in and attempted wire-tapping incident in the DNC (Democratic National Committee) Headquarters at the Watergate office complex in Washington DC. An FBI investigation linked the suspects to the President's re-election campaign and uncovered an interception system used by the President to record conversations. Nixon was reluctant to hand over the tapes made by this system, initially releasing only transcripts and then erasing sections of the tapes before the Supreme Court was forced to step in to make Nixon hand over all evidence to the investigating team. An analysis of the recordings implicated the President in attempts to cover up the break-in. Facing near-certain impeachment, Nixon resigned on 9 August 1974 and was later pardoned by his successor Gerald Ford. The incident shook faith in the office of president and led the public to question those in positions of leadership.

21   David Peace, "Talking Books: David Peace May 2003", *BBC Online*, http://www.bbc.co.uk/bradford/culture/words/david_peace_intv.shtml , accessed 19 May 2004.

22   Tetley's Bitter is a popular British ale brewed in Leeds.

23   David Robinson, "Interview: Author David Peace is riding high, so why does he plan to stop soon?", *The Scotsman*, http://thescotsman.scotsman.com/critique/Interview-Author-David-Peace-is.5509954.jp, accessed 20 January 2010.

24 Clough's second-person narrative notes that *'There was a magpie on your lawn when you left your house for the airport. There was also one on the tarmac as you got off the plane at Turin. Now one's just flown into the window of the hotel bar. But you don't believe in luck, superstitions or rituals – You believe in football; football, football, football'* [194]. After their fight Clough notices, *'The blood of a dead magpie running down the windows of the hotel bar – The blood of your best mate running down the knuckles of your hand – The first time you've spoken to anyone since your mam passed on'* [195].

25 Clough hears 'Syd [say] something like: *'Anything to do with peacocks is fatal . . .'* [73] and that *'Their scream forebodes rain and even death . . .'* [74]. He later 'says something that sounds like, *"So long as they were kept, the daughters of the house would have no suitors for their hands . . .'* [101] and 'something that sounds like: *"Yesterday, upon the stair, I met a man who wasn't there. He wasn't there again today. I wish that man would go away"'* [277]. Syd's snide comments function to reinforce an existing paranoia and doubt in the new manager and increasingly draw Clough's attention to the numerous bad omens surrounding his time at Leeds.

26 Pierre Bordieu, "Sport and Social Class", in C. Mukerji (ed.), *Rethinking Popular Culture: Contemporary Perspectives in Cultural Studies* (Berjley: University of California, 1991), p. 361.

27 Historically the real Brian Clough had 'always seen himself as against authority. Anyone in a position of power, from club chairmen to the FA, was there to bang heads with' (John Harris, "When Men Were Men", *Guardian*, http://www.guardian.co.uk/media/2007/feb/13/genderissues.broadcasting, accessed 20 January 2010).

28 Barney Ronay, "Anyone want to play on the left?", *Guardian*, http://www.guardian.co.uk/football/2007/apr/25/sport.comment1, accessed 20 January 2010.

29 Bordieu in Mukerji, 1991, p. 364.

30 The later half of the twentieth century witnessed a growth in the role and presence of the media in sport. Big business, celebrity, media and money came together at this turning point in forming modern football as we know it today. Celebrity commentators or 'pundits' became a regular feature of televised games and football managers rose to a position of greater authority, most notably represented by Alf Ramsey as the first England manager to be allowed to pick the national team. Due to the increased televising of games and post-match interviews, the manager also became a psychological warrior, providing not only effective guidance for his team, but also publicity and a public face for the club. Brian Clough was the first TV evangelist of football, emerging as a TV celebrity through his role as a pundit on London Weekend Television's *The Big Match*. Clough's on-screen presence was also

different – he stared into the camera, speaking directly to supporters at the expense of his fellow panellists. He also spoke the same language as the supporters, expressed their frustrations and even appeared on Calendar TV in a head-to-head confrontation with Don Revie on the same night he parted company from Leeds. For further discussion on sport and celebrity, see Garry Whannel, *Media Sport Stars: Masculinities and Moralities* (London: Taylor and Francis, 2001).

31 George Best was a well-known and much loved British footballer of the 1970s. He enjoyed success with Manchester United and represented Northern Ireland before becoming one of the first real celebrity footballers. However, his playboy lifestyle off the pitch led to alcoholism and media over-exposure, culminating in his death in 2005 at the age of fifty-nine.

32 David Peace, "44 Days in 1974", *Guardian*, http://www.guardian.co.uk/books/2009/aug/01/damned-utd-david-peace, accessed 20 January 2010.

33 David Peace, "44 Days in 1974", *Guardian*, http://www.guardian.co.uk/books/2009/aug/01/damned-utd-david-peace, accessed 20 January 2010.

34 David Peace in Jeff Dawson, "Filming The Strife Of Brian", *The Times*, http://entertainment.timesonline.co.uk/tol/arts_and_entertainment/film/article5853228.ece, accessed 20 January 2010.

chapter seven Occupation and Defeat in the *Tokyo Trilogy*

1 Opening quotation from David Peace, "Interview with David Peace", *Faber and Faber Online*, http://www.faber.co.uk/author/david-peace/, accessed 3 February 2010. This chapter will analyse the first two novels of the *Tokyo Trilogy* available at the time of writing – *Tokyo Year Zero* (London: Faber, 2007) and *Occupied City* (London: Faber, 2009). In this chapter the titles appear in shorthand references – *TYZ* (*Tokyo Year Zero*) and *OC* (*Occupied City*).

2 Peace claims that 'The title was actually inspired by Rossellini's film "Germany Year Zero," set among the ruins of Occupied Berlin. My next book, the second book in a trilogy, continues the homage, *Tokyo Occupied City* being inspired by Rossellini's "Roma Open City"' (David Peace, "Author Q&A", *Random House Academic Resources*, http://www.randomhouse.com/acmart/catalog/display.pperl?isbn=9780307263742&view=qa, accessed 10 February 2010). Both films form part of a trilogy that examines post-war Germany. The trilogy is notable for its realist approach and refusal to shy away from depicting the near-total destruction of the country. As a result, it is widely regarded as a useful social document of the time.

3 Richard Storry, *A History of Modern Japan* (London: Penguin, 1968), p. 227.

4 Storry, 1968, p. 237.

5 Storry, 1968, p. 237.

6 Conrad Totman, *A History of Japan* (Oxford: Blackwell, 2000), p. 442.

7 As Totman reflects, 'War crimes trials identified and punished thousands of those held accountable for the war and some of its excesses, with about 940 being executed. Purges removed another 220,000, mostly former military officers, from positions of authority in government, business, education, and the media, while thousands of other people resigned from responsible positions before being examined. The remnants of the military system were dissolved, equipment destroyed, and some six million military and civilian personnel repatriated from the former empire' (Totman, 2000, p. 444).

8 Storry, 1968, p. 253.

9 T. Morris-Suzuki, *Showa: An Inside History of Hirohito's Japan* (New York: St Martin's Press, 1985), p. 196.

10 Roman Cybriwsky, *Tokyo* (Chichester: John Wiley and Sons, 1998), p. 91.

11 Minami goes on to encounter another old man by the roadside whose watch keeps stopping dead. 'I lose track of the time,' he sighs. 'Because there's no end is there? They tell us that it's over, that we're at peace, but it doesn't feel like peace, doesn't feel like it's ended to me. What about you?' [*TYZ*, 306]. Even in the Kodaira case it is Mitsuzo's watch that eventually reveals the truth of the case and unites past crime with present justice.

12 Storry, 1968, pp. 245–6.

13 David Peace, "David Peace Interviewed by Jorge", Podcast No. 144, *The Bat Segundo Show*, http://www.edrants.com/segundo/bss-144-david-peace/, accessed 13 February 2010.

14 David Peace, "David Peace Interviewed by Jorge", Podcast No. 144, *The Bat Segundo Show*, http://www.edrants.com/segundo/bss-144-david-peace/, accessed 13 February 2010.

15 http://www.bbc.co.uk/bradford/content/articles/2008/06/02/david_peace_2008_feature.shtml, accessed 10 February 2010.

16 David Peace, "David Peace Interviewed by Jorge", Podcast No. 144, *The Bat Segundo Show*, http://www.edrants.com/segundo/bss-144-david-peace/, accessed 13 February 2010.

17 Minami is also involved in crime as a drug addict who is controlled by the local gang boss.

18 "In a Grove" was first published as a short story in Japanese monthly *Shincho* in 1922. Drawing on modernist searches for identity, the fractured nature of the self and the impossibility of objective truth, the story presents seven different accounts of the murder of a samurai in a woodland grove, all of which are offered from different people and perspectives and contradict one another. In the years since the publi-

cation of this story, the phrase 'in a grove' has become most importantly a modern Japanese idiom used to describe a situation where no certain conclusion can be drawn due to contradictory, insufficient or indecisive evidence.

19 The final chapter of *Occupied City* is a rewriting of the Noh drama *Sumidagawa* in which a woman looking for her young son Yoshida, who has been stolen by slave trader, meets a ferryboat man who takes her on a trip across the river to show her the mound that is her son's grave.

20 The medium explains to the writer that he is about to engage in '*a ghost-story-telling game popularized during the Edo period. By the mid-seventeenth century its form was established among samurai as a playful test of courage, but by the early nineteenth century it had become a widespread entertainment for commoners. The game begins with a group of people gathering at twilight in the pale-blue light of one hundred lit candles, each covered with a pale-blue paper shade. Each person in turn then tells a tale of supernatural horror and at the end of each tale one wick is extinguished. As the evening and the tales progress the room becomes dimmer and gloomier until, after the one hundredth tale has been told and the last candle blown out, the room is in complete darkness. At this moment it is believed that real ghouls or monsters will appear in the dark, conjured up by the terrifying tale-telling*' [*OC*, 2–3].

21 David Peace, "In Conversation with Kester Aspen", Waterstones Leeds Q&A to launch *Occupied City*, 13 August 2009.

22 Like the Shiinamachi bank massacre, the Author's Note that ends *Occupied City* is written in the Year of the Rat and outlines the fate of Hirasawa and the various campaigns to clear his name.

23 Unit 731 was a covert chemical and biological research unit of the Imperial Japanese Army accused of human experimentation during World War II. Located in the Pingfan district of Harbin in North West China, the unit became an infamous symbol of the covert practices of the Japanese army. In the post-war years General MacArthur controversially gave the scientists of Unit 731 immunity in exchange for the secrets of their wartime research. In *Occupied City*, the Teikoku Murderer's claim that 'The Emperor was our owner, Major Ishii was our boss' implicates the government and army in a wider 'Deathtopia of fleas and flies, of rats and men' [*OC*, 258].

24 David Peace in Manuella Baretta, "The Noir in David Peace's Shadow: A Conversation with David Peace", *Other Modernities*, Universita degli Studi di Milano, 6 (2008): 95–102, p. 96.

25 Storry, 1968, pp. 238–9.

26 Storry, 1968, p. 238; E. O. Reischauer, *The Japanese* (Cambridge: The Belknap Press of Harvard University, 1981), p. 105.

27 John Dower, *Embracing Defeat: Japan in the Wake of WWII* (London: W. W. Norton and Co., 2000), p. 211. John Dower uses this text to offer

an alternative view of events from the perspective of the people on the ground that bears many parallels to the approach and content of Peace's *Tokyo Trilogy*.

28 David Peace in Baretta, 2008, p. 97.

29 Totman, 2000, p. 443.

30 Dower, 1999, p. 23.

31 Takemae Eiji, *Inside GHQ* (New York: Continuum, 2002), p. 78.

32 Due to the waste of the new occupiers' bureaucracy [*TYZ*, 206], food is also shown going to waste while ordinary people starve.

33 However, for the rest of the population the occupation does not bring the benefits of reform to the ground. Minami confesses that 'I haggle. *To eat.* I barter. *To work.* I threaten. *To eat.* I bully. *To work*' [*TYZ*, 45].

34 Eiji, 2002, p. 165.

35 Eiji, 2002, p. 70. In *Tokyo Year Zero* Minami claims that 'Other women worked as geishas and prostitutes, barmaids and waitresses, frequent adulterers and sexual deviants, girls built of stronger stuff' [*TYZ*, 200].

36 David Peace in Cathi Unsworth, "David Peace: Rising Son", *YOURFlesh Magazine*, http://www.yourfleshmag.com/artman/publish /article_1145.shtml, accessed 10 February 2010.

37 Defending these representations, Peace asserts that he 'was raised in West Yorkshire which is not the most liberal place to be raised, then Japan and I've chosen to write about those places, if I was a woman I would be moving out of those places, this doesn't mean I'm a sexist or a misogynist' (David Peace, "David Peace Interviewed by Jorge", Podcast No. 144, *The Bat Segundo Show*, http://www.edrants.com/ segundo/bss-144-david-peace/, accessed 13 February 2010).

38 Peace in Baretta, 2008, p. 102.

39 David Peace in Cathi Unsworth, "David Peace: Rising Son", *YOURFlesh Magazine*, http://www.yourfleshmag.com/artman/ publish/article_1145.shtml, accessed 10 February 2010.

40 David Peace in Chris Verguson, "Profiles: West Yorkshire Confidential", *BBC Online*, http://www.bbc.co.uk/bradford/content/ articles/2008/06/02/david_peace_2008_feature.shtml, accessed 27 May 2009.

41 David Peace in Cathi Unsworth, "David Peace: Rising Son", *YOURFlesh Magazine*, http://www.yourfleshmag.com/artman/ publish /article_1145.shtml, accessed 10 February 2010.

42 David Peace, "David Peace Interview", *Peter Geoghegan's Blog*, 30 September 2009, http://www.peterkgeoghegan.com/2009/09/30/ david-peace, accessed 3 March 2010.

43 David Peace in Stephen Phelan, "The Past Master", *Sunday Herald*, http://www.sundayherald.com/arts/arts/display.var.2490831.0.0.php, accessed 10 February 2010.

Conclusion: His Dark Materials

1 David Peace, "Talking Books: David Peace May 2003", *BBC Online*, http://www.bbc.co.uk/bradford/culture/words/david_peace_intv.shtml , accessed 19 May 2004.

2 Steven Connor, *The English Novel In History: 1950–1995* (London: Routledge, 1996), p. 1.

3 David Peace, "David Peace plans to quit novels", *Channel 4 News Online*, http://www.channel4.com/news/articles/arts_entertainment/ books/david+peace+plans+to+quit+novels/3316987, accessed 10 April 2010.

4 Tony Grisoni in Gerard Gilbert, "Red Riding: Yorkshire Noir on TV", *Independent*, 4 March 2009, http://www.independent.co.uk/arts-entertainment/tv/features/red-riding-yorkshire-noir-on-tv-1636631.html, accessed 10 April 2010.

5 *Heartbeat* was a British police drama set in 1960s Yorkshire. Made and broadcast by ITV, it ran for over 370 episodes from 1992 to 2008. With stories centring on a small village in the North Riding of the Moors, the series offered a safer, rose-tinted perspective on the same place and time that Peace went on to re-present in his novels.

6 David Peace, "The Future of the Mystery Novel", *Media Bistro*, http://www.mediabistro.com/news/media_menu/listen_the_future_of _the_mystery_novel_151474.asp?c=rss, accessed 20 November 2009.

7 Andy Harries in LeftBank Pictures, *The Damned United Production Notes* (London: LeftBank Pictures, 2009), p. 8.

8 Andy Harries in David Cox, "The Damned United Should Have Never Been Made", *Guardian*, 30 March 2009, http://www.guardian.co.uk/film/filmblog/2009/mar/30/damned-united-brian-clough, accessed 10 April 2010.

9 John Fowles, "Notes On An Unfinished Novel", in Thomas MacCormack (ed.), *Afterwords: Novelists on their Novels* (New York: Harper, 1969), p. 138.

10 The Haut de la Garenne scandal was revealed in 2008 when the former children's home and youth hostel became the centre of an investigation into allegations of child abuse on the island of Jersey. Several past residents suggested that people on the island had known or suspected what was occurring at the children's home for many years but chose to ignore their suspicions. As a result of the investigation several former members of staff were convicted.

Michael Todd was Chief Constable of Greater Manchester Police from 2002 until 2008. He went missing on 11 March 2008 and rescue workers later discovered his body on Mount Snowdon in Wales. He had died from exposure, having been found wearing only the lightest of clothes. The reasons behind his death remain a mystery.

John Humble, otherwise known as 'Wearside Jack', spent the 1970s writing letters to newspapers purporting to be the Yorkshire Ripper as well as producing hoax Ripper tapes in his thick, Geordie accent. These false communications misled police, meaning that the real Ripper, Peter Sutcliffe, was able to carry on his killing spree for much longer. The Wearside Jack case was reopened in 2005 when police used DNA from the envelopes containing his letters to track down the suspect. Humble was brought to trial at Leeds Crown Court on 9 January 2006 and sentenced to eight years' imprisonment.

Reports of the prisoner abuse scandal at Abu Ghraib began to emerge in 2004. Accounts of prisoners being tortured, raped and sodomized by their Allied captors shocked the Western world. In response to this abuse several soldiers were court marshalled and imprisoned. The scandal challenged the image of the occupying army as a force intended to improve, rather than abuse, the occupied country and its people.

Early 2010 saw a series of strikes by public sector workers in the UK. The period was labelled by the press the 'Spring of Discontent' as an echo of Callaghan's own Shakespearean assessment of the impact of a series of public sector strikes during the winter of 1979 in the UK.

Jose Mourinho is a Portuguese football manager who, like Brian Clough, is famous for his ambition, controversy and outspoken relationship with the press.

11   Madeline McCann disappeared, assumed abducted, on 3 May 2007 from her parents' holiday apartment in Praia da Luz, Portugal. She remains missing to this day. Portuguese police came under criticism for their handling of the case, including their haphazard collection of forensic evidence and failures to investigate other known disappearances of children in the area.

Natascha Kampusch was abducted in Austria at the age of ten in 1998, but escaped from her captor in 2006. Her case fascinated the international media and raised issues regarding police cover-ups and child abuse.

Shannon Matthews disappeared on 19 February 2008 from her home in Dewsbury, West Yorkshire. The search for the missing nine-year-old was likened to the case of Madeline McCann until Shannon was found, in the house of a family friend, near to her home. In the wake of her rescue, it emerged that Shannon's parents, inspired by the case of Madeline McCann, had engineered her disappearance in an attempt to gain reward money and fame.

Bibliography

Ashwork, G. J. (ed.) 2005: *Sense of Plane: Sense of Time*. Aldershot: Ashgate.

Bakhtin, M. M., trans. Michael Holquist and Caryl Emerson, 2004: *The Dialogic Imagination: Four Essays*. Austin: University of Texas Press.

Baretta, Manuella, 2008: "The Noir in David Peace's Shadow: A Conversation with David Peace", *Other Modernities*, Universita degli Studi di Milano, 6, 95–102.

Barnes, Julian, 2005: *Arthur and George*. London: Jonathan Cape.

Barstow, Stan, 1973: *A Kind of Loving*. London: Corgi.

Beckett, Andy, 2004: "Political Gothic", *London Review of Books*, 26:18.

——, 2009: *When the Lights Went Out: What Really Happened to Britain in the Seventies*. London: Faber.

Benjamin, Walter, 1973: *Illuminations*. London: Fontana.

Benson, Stephanie, 2009: "The Strange Language of David Peace", *Europolar*, http://www.europolar.eu/index.php?option=com_content&task=view&id=66&Itemid=30, accessed 30 September 2009.

Bilton, Michael, 2006: *Wicked beyond Belief: The Hunt for the Yorkshire Ripper*. London: HarperCollins.

Blair, Tony, 2008: "Blair apologizes to Guildford Four family", *Guardian Unlimited*, http://www.guardian.co.uk/politics/2005/feb/09/ northernireland.devolution.

Booker, Christopher, 1980: *The Seventies: Portrait of a Decade*. London: Allen Lane.

Bradbury, Malcolm, 2001: *The Modern British Novel*. London: Penguin.

Bragg, Melvyn, 2008: "The Damned United". *The Southbank Show*, ITV One.

Braine, John, 1969: *Room at the Top*. London: Penguin.

Brannigan, John, 2003: *Orwell to the Present: Literature in England 1945–2000*. Basingstoke: Palgrave Macmillan.

Brierley, Walter, 1983: *Means-test Man*. London: Spokesman Books.

Bruce, David, 2009: "Killing Kit of the Ripper", *Yorkshire Evening Post*, 22 February 2003, http://www.yorkshireeveningpost.co.uk/news/KILLING-KIT-OF-THE-RIPPER.239646.jp.

Carruthers, Mary, 1990: *The Book of Memory: A Study of Memory in Medieval Culture*. Cambridge: Cambridge University Press.

Clark, Katerina and Holquist, Michael, 1984: *Mikhail Bakhtin*. London: Harvard University Press.

Connell, R. W., 1983: *Which Way is Up?* Sydney: Allen & Unwin.

Connor, Steven, 1996: *The English Novel in History: 1950–1995*. London: Routledge.

Cox, Barry (ed.), 1977: *The Fall of Scotland Yard*. London: Penguin Books.

Cox, David, 2009: "The Damned United Should Have Never Been Made". *Guardian*, 30 March 2009, http://www.guardian.co.uk/film/filmblog/2009/mar/30/damned-united-brian-clough, accessed 10 April 2010.

Currion, Paul, 2009: "Balls to the British Novel". *The Unforgiving Minute*, http://www.currion.net/tag/david-peace/, accessed 27 May 2009.

Cutter, Alex, 2009: "The Madhouse of the Skull". *Fluxeuropa*, http://www.fluxeuropa.com/jamesellroy-quartet.htm, accessed 27 May 2009.

Cybriwsky, Roman, 1998: *Tokyo*. Chichester: John Wiley and Sons.

Davenport-Hines, Richard, 2004: "Bulger, James Patrick (1990–1993)". *Oxford Dictionary of National Biography*. Oxford: Oxford University Press.

Davies, Tom, 1986: *Black Sunlight*. London: Futura.

Dawson, Jeff, 2009: "Filming the Strife of Brian". *The Times*, http://entertainment.timesonline.co.uk/tol/arts_and_entertainment/film/article5853228.ece, accessed 20 January 2010.

Derrida, Jacques, trans. Peggy Kamuf, 1994: *Spectres of Marx: The State of the Debt, the Work of Mourning, and the New International*. London: Routledge.

——, 1989: "The Ghost Dance: An Interview with Jacques Derrida". *Public*, 2 60–73.

Dickinson, Matt, 2009: "The Panned United is still a work of genius". *The Times*, http://www.timesonline.co.uk/tol/sport/columnists/matt_ dickinson/article5835251.ece, accessed 20 January 2010.

Donaldson, Brian, 2009: "Rising Son: David Peace Does Japan". *The List*, http://edinburghfestival.list.co.uk/article/18674-rising-son-david-peace-does-japan/, accessed 12 November 2009.

Dos Passos, John, 2000: *The 42nd Parallel*. London: Mariner Books.

——, 2000: *The Big Money*, London: Mariner.

——, John, 1996: *Nineteen Nineteen*. London: New American Library.

Dower, John, 2000: *Embracing Defeat: Japan in the Wake of WWII*. London: W.W. Norton and Co.

Eagleton, Terry, 2004: "At the Coal Face". *Guardian*, 6 March 2004.

Eason, Kevin, 2009: "Collision that Transformed Clough's Life". *The Times*, http://www.timesonline.co.uk/tol/sport/football/article5870472.ece, accessed 20 January 2010.

Eiji, Takemae, 2002: *Inside GHQ*. New York: Continuum.

Ellroy, James, 1998: *LA Confidential*. London: Arrow.

Ellroy, James, 1998: *The Big Nowhere*. London: Arrow.

——, 1998: *White Jazz*. London: Arrow.

——, 1993: *The Black Dahlia*. London: Arrow.

Emerson, Caryl and Emerson, Michael (eds.), trans. Vern W. McGee, 1986: *Speech Genres and Other Late Essays*. Austin: University of Texas Press.

Ferguson, Euan, 2004: "The Last English Civil War". *Observer*, 29 February 2004.

Fox, Ralph Winston, 1937: *The Novel and the People*. London: Lawrence & Wishart.

Freud, Sigmund, 2003: *The Uncanny*. London: Penguin.

Geoghegan, Peter, 2009: "Belfast Festival: David Peace". *Culture Northern Ireland*, http://www.culturenorthernireland.org/article.aspx?art_id= 2835, accessed 20 January 2010.

Gilbert, Gerard, 2009: "Red Riding: Yorkshire Noir on TV". *Independent*, 4 March 2009, http://www.independent.co.uk/arts-entertainment/tv/ features/red-riding-yorkshire-noir-on-tv-1636631.html, accessed 10 April 2010.

Gordon, Avery, 2008: *Ghostly Matters: Haunting and the Sociological Imagination*. London: University of Minnesota Press.

Granelli, Roger, 1997: *Dark Edge*. Bridgend: Poetry Wales Press.

Gregorits, Gene, 2008: "These Endless Fucking End Days: A Chat with David Peace by Gene Gregorits", http://gene-gregorits.com/ DAVID%20PEACE.html, accessed 12 December 2008.

Harris, John, 2009: "When Men Were Men". *Guardian*, http://www.guardian.co.uk/media/2007/feb/13/genderissues.broadcasti ng, accessed 20 January 2010.

Hart, Matthew, 2006: "An Interview with David Peace". *Contemporary Literature*, 47.4, 546–68.

Hickey, David, 2008: "Peace follows turbulent times". *Japan Times*, 6 July 2008, http://search.japantimes.co.jp/cgi-bin/fl20080706x1.html, accessed 13 July 2009.

Hines, Barry, 1973: *A Kestrel for a Knave*. London: Penguin.

Home Office, *Regina v R v McIlkenney (1991)* 93, Cr.App.R, 53–4.

Horsley, Lee, 1995: "Unpublished Interview with James Ellroy". 7 October 1995.

Hutcheon, Linda, 1988: *A Poetics of Postmodernism: History, Theory, Fiction*. London: Routledge.

ITV, *Clough: The Documentary*, ITV One, first broadcast Wednesday, 25 March 2009, 10:35 p.m.–11:50 p.m.

Judt, Tony, 2009: *Reappraisals: Reflections of the Forgotten Twentieth Century*. London: Vintage.

Kennick, William E., 1956: "The Language of Religion". *The Philosophical Review*, 65, 56–71.

Kimmelman, Michael, 1992: "Francis Bacon, Artist of the Macabre, Dies".

The New York Times, 13 April 1992, http://www.nytimes.com/ 1992/04/ 29/arts/francis-bacon-82-artist-of-the-macabre-dies.html?scp=2&sq= man%20who%20paints%20those%20awful%20pictures&st=cse, accessed 1 February 2010.

Kirk, John, 2003: *Twentieth-Century Writing and the British Working Class*. Cardiff: University of Wales Press.

Kpunk, "A World of Dread and Fear". *KPunk*, http://k-punk.abstractdynamics.org/archives/006370.html, accessed 10 April 2010.

Lacoue-Labarthe, Philippe, trans. C. Fynsk, 1989: *Typography: Mimesis, Philosophy, Politics*. Cambridge, MA: Harvard University Press.

LeftBank Pictures, 2009: *The Damned United Production Notes*. London: LeftBank Pictures.

Lyotard, Jean François, 1979: *The Postmodern Condition: A Report on Knowledge*. Manchester: Manchester University Press.

MacCormack, Thomas (ed.) 1969: *Afterwords: Novelists on their Novels*. New York: Harper.

Marquesse, Mike, 2004: "David Peace: State of the Union Rights". *Independent*, 5 March 2004.

Marx, Karl, 1964: *The Eighteenth Brumaire of Louis Bonaparte*. London: Progress.

McNamee, Eoin, 2004: "Hand-Held Narrative". *Guardian*, 11 April 2004.

Menke, Ludger, 2009: "Podcast No. 3: Interview mit David Peace", *KrimiBlod.De*, http://krimiblog.de/447/podcast-interview-mit-david-peace.html, accessed 15 January 2009.

Mighall, Robert, 2003: *A Geography of Victorian Gothic: Mapping History's Nightmares*. Oxford: Oxford University Press.

Morris, Pam (ed.), 1994: *The Bakhtin Reader: Selected Writings of Bakhtin, Medvedev and Voloshinov*. London: Arnold.

Morris-Suzuki, T., 1985: *Showa: An Inside History of Hirohito's Japan*. New York: St Martin's Press.

Morson, Gary Saul and Emerson, Caryl, 1990: *Mikhail Bakhtin: Creation of a Prosaics*. Stanford: Stanford University Press.

Morton, John, 2007: "The Criminally Underrated Novels of David Peace". *Guardian*, 9 August 2007, http://www.guardian.co.uk/books/booksblog/ 2007/aug/09/thecriminallyunderratednove, accessed 17 May 2009.

Mukerji, C. (ed.), 1991: *Rethinking Popular Culture: Contemporary Perspectives in Cultural Studies*. Berjley: University of California.

Newburn, T. 1999: "Understanding and Preventing Police Corruption: Lessons from the Literature". *Police Research Series*, Paper 110. London: Home Office.

O'Rourke, William, 1996: *Notts: A Striking Novel*. New York: Marlowe & Company.

Orwell, George, 1950: *Shooting an Elephant*. London: Secker and Warburg.

Osborne, John, 1978: *Look Back in Anger*. London: Faber.

Peace, David, 2010: "44 Jours Interview", *Dawdle Up Country*, http://dawdleupcountry.blogspot.com/2008/05/david-peace-interview.html, accessed 20 January 2010.

——, 2010: "David Peace plans to quit novels". *Channel 4 News Online*, http://www.channel4.com/news/articles/arts_entertainment/books/david+peace+plans+to+quit+novels/3316987, accessed 10 April 2010.

——, 2010: *Occupied City*. London: Faber.

——, 2009: "44 Days in 1974", *Guardian*, http://www.guardian.co.uk/books/2009/aug/01/damned-utd-david-peace, accessed 20 January 2010.

——, 2009: "Author Q&A". *Random House Academic Resources*, http://www.randomhouse.com/acmart/catalog/display.pperl?isbn=9780307263742&view=qa, accessed 10 February 2010.

——, 2009: "Book Munch Classic Interview: David Peace". *Bookmunch*, http://www.bookmunch.co.uk/view.php?id=1341, accessed 10 August 2009.

——, 2009: "Bradford and Yorkshire People: David Peace". *BBC Online*, http://www.bbc.co.uk/bradford/content/articles/2009/03/03/david_peace_2009_feature.shtml, accessed 10 August 2009.

——, 2009: "Culture Clash". *BBC Online*, http://www.bbc.co.uk/leeds/content/articles/2006/08/17/words_david_peace_the_damned_united_feature.shtml, accessed 20 January 2010.

——, 2009: "David Peace Interview". *Peter Geoghegan's Blog*, 30 September 2009, http://www.peterkgeoghegan.com/2009/09/30/david-peace, accessed 3 March 2010.

——, 2009: "David Peace Interviewed by Jorge", Podcast No. 144. *The Bat Segundo Show*, http://www.edrants.com/segundo/bss-144-david-peace/, accessed 13 February 2010.

——, 2009: "Guardian Book Club Interview with John Mullan". *Guardian*, http://www.guardian.co.uk/books/audio/2009/aug/07/book-club-podcast-david-peace-damned-united, accessed 20 January 2010.

——, 2009: "h2g2 BBC Author: David Peace". *BBC Online*, http://www.bbc.co.uk/dna/h2g2/A3126188, accessed 10 August 2009.

——, 2009: "Hero or Villain". *Independent on Sunday*, 8 March 2009.

——, 2009: "In Conversation with Kester Aspen". Waterstones Leeds Q&A to launch *Occupied City*, 13 August 2009.

——, 2009: "Interview with David Peace". *Faber and Faber Online*, http://www.faber.co.uk/author/david-peace/, accessed 3 February 2010.

——, 2009: "Peace Le Roman Tokyo année zéro payot-rivages". *Payot and Rivages*, http://www.payot-rivages.net/index.php?id=30&selection_auteur=Peace,+David, accessed 10 August 2009.

——, 2009: "Profile". *Telegraph*, http://www.telegraph.co.uk/culture/ tvandradio/4980191/David-Peace-author-of-Red-Riding-and-The-Damned-United-profile.html, accessed 10 August 2009.

——, 2009: "Profile: David Peace". *The Times*, http://entertainment.timesonline.co.uk/tol/arts_and_entertainment/books/article5821830.ec, accessed 20 January 2010.

——, 2009: "Q Hero: David Peace". *Q Magazine*, April 2009.

——, 2009: "Snapshot of the Time". *Yorkshire Post*, 4 March 2009, http://www.yorkshirepost.co.uk/features/Snapshot-of-time.5037932.jp, accessed 27 May 2009.

——, 2009: "The Big Issue Event: Q&A with Paul Johnston". *Edinburgh Book Festival*, 22 August 2009.

——, 2009: "The Damned United Author Surprise Row". *BBC Online*, http://news.bbc.co.uk/1/hi/wales/8074187.stm, accessed 30 May 2009.

——, 2009: "The Future of the Mystery Novel". *Media Bistro*, http://www.mediabistro.com/news/media_menu/listen_the_future_of_the_mystery_novel_151474.asp?c=rss, accessed 20 November 2009.

——, 2009: "West Yorkshire Noir?". *BBC Online*, http://www.bbc.co.uk/bradford/content/articles/2008/05/16/david_peace_feature.shtml?page=2, accessed 27 May 2009.

——, 2008: "Ready for War". *Stop Smiling Magazine*, http://www.stopsmilingonline.com/story_detail.php?i=707, accessed 2 December 2008.

——, 2008: "The Red Riding Quartet". *Crimetime*, http://www.crimetime.co.uk/features/davidpeace.php, accessed 10 April 2010.

——, 2008: *Tokyo Year Zero*. London: Faber.

——, 2007: *The Damned United*. London: Faber.

——, 2005: "State of the Union Rights". *Independent*, http://www.independent.co.uk/arts-entertainment/books/features/david-peace-state-of-the-union-rights-572067.html, accessed 19 January 2005.

——, 2004: "Crisp Sandwiches and Pickets". *New Statesman*, 3 January 2004.

——, 2004: *GB84*, London: Faber.

——, 2004: "GB84 Interview". *BBC Online*, http://www.bbc.co.uk/dna/collective/A2436509, accessed 19 January 2005.

——, 2003: "Talking Books: David Peace May 2003". *BBC Online*, http://www.bbc.co.uk/bradford/culture/words/david_peace_intv.shtml, accessed 19 May 2004.

——, 2002: *1983*. London: Serpent's Tail.

——, 2001: *1980*. London: Serpent's Tail.

——, 2000: *1977*. London: Serpent's Tail.

——, 1999: 1974. London: Seprent's Tail.

Phelan, Stephen, 2009: "The Past Master". *Sunday Herald*, http://www.sundayherald.com/arts/arts/display.var.2490831.0.0.php, accessed 10 February 2010.

Reischauer, E. O., 1981: *The Japanese*. Cambridge: The Belknap Press of Harvard University.

Robinson, David, 2009: "Interview: Author David Peace is riding high, so why does he plan to stop soon?". *Scotsman*, http://thescotsman/critique/Interview-Author-David-Peace-is.5509954.jp, accessed 20 January 2010.

Ronay, Barney, 2009: "Anyone want to play on the left?". *Guardian*, http://www.guardian.co.uk/football/2007/apr/25/sport.comment1, accessed 20 January 2010.

Rose, Jonathan (ed.), 1997: *Innocents: How Justice Failed Stefan Kiszko and Lesley Molseed*. London: Fourth Estate.

Rostron, Phil, 2009: *We Are The Damned United: The Real Story of Brian Clough at Leeds*. Edinburgh: Mainstream.

Royale E., 1998: *Regional Identities*. Manchester: Manchester University Press.

Samuel, Raphael, 1998: *Theatres of Memory: Vol II. Island Stories*. London: Verso.

Sharpe, Phil, 2004: "GB84: A Powerful Tribute to the Miners' Strike". *Socialist Future*, 20 April 2004, http://www.socialistfuture. org.uk/msf/articles/reviews/GB84.htm, accessed 29 April 2004.

Silet, Charles, L. P., 1995: "Mad Dog and Glory: A Conversation with James Ellroy". *The Armchair Detective*, 28 (Summer 1995) 236–44.

Sillitoe, Alan, 1960: *Saturday Night and Sunday Morning*. London: Pan Books.

Smith, Ken, 2004: *A Civil War without Guns: 20 Years On: The Lessons of the 1984–5 Miners' Strike*. London: Socialist Publications.

Sprinkler, M. (ed.), 2008: *Ghostly Demarcations: A Symposium on Jacques Derrida's Spectres of Marx*. London: Verso.

Soans, Catherine and Stevenson, Angus (eds.), 2005: *Oxford Dictionary of English*. Oxford: Oxford University Press.

Storey, David, 1968: *This Sporting Life*. London: Penguin.

Storry, Richard, 1968: *A History of Modern Japan*. London: Penguin.

Totman, Conrad, 2000: *A History of Japan*. Oxford: Blackwell.

Tressell, Robert, 2005: *The Ragged Trousered Philanthropists*. London: HarperPerennial.

Turner, Alwyn, 2008: *Crisis? What Crisis? Britain in the 1970s*. London: Aurum.

Unsworth, Cathi, 2009: "David Peace: Rising Son". *YOURFlesh Magazine*, http://www.yourfleshmag.com/artman/publish/article_1145.shtml, accessed 10 February 2010.

Upson, Nicola, 2001: "Hunting the Yorkshire Ripper". *New Statesman*, 20 August 2001, http://www.newstatesman.com/200108200036, accessed 10 April 2008.

Verguson, Chris, 2008: "Profiles: West Yorkshire Confidential". *BBC*

Online, http://www.bbc.co.uk/bradford/content/articles/2008/06/02-/david_peace_2008_feature.shtml, accessed 27 May 2009.

Wainwright, Martin, 2009: *True North.* London: Guardian.

Waites, Martyn, 2003: *Born Under Punches.* London: Pocket.

Whannel, Garry, 2001: *Media Sport Stars: Masculinities and Moralities.* London: Taylor and Francis.

Williams, Michael, 2004: "No Fucking End in Sight". *BBC Online,* 12 March 2004, http://www.bbc.co.uk/bradford/culture/words/david _peace_gb84.shtml, accessed 19 March 2004.

Williams, Raymond, 1989: *Loyalties.* London: Hogarth.

White, Hayden, 1978: *Tropics of Discourse: Essays in Cultural Criticism.* Baltimore: The Johns Hopkins University Press.

Wright, Roy, 2009: "Huddersfield Town fan David Peace is behind TV's darkest tale". *Huddersfield Daily Examiner,* 5 March 2009.

Wright, T., 2000: *The English Question.* London: Fabian Society, 2000.

Index

Fictional characters are identified by the gloss (fictional) after the name. Where surnames for characters have been used in the book, characters are filed under their surname. If surnames are not given, characters are filed under their first name.